CRUDE
AWAKENING

CRUDE
AWAKENING

Money, Mavericks, and Mayhem in Alaska

AMANDA COYNE AND
TONY HOPFINGER

NATION
BOOKS

New York
www.nationbooks.org

Copyright © 2011 by Amanda Coyne and Tony Hopfinger

Published by Nation Books,
A Member of the Perseus Books Group
116 East 16th Street, 8th Floor
New York, NY 10003

Nation Books is a co-publishing venture of the Nation Institute and the Perseus
Books Group.

Books published by Nation Books are available at special discounts for bulk
purchases in the United States by corporations, institutions, and other organizations.
For more information, please contact the Special Markets Department at the Perseus
Books Group, 2300 Chestnut Street, Suite 200, Philadelphia, PA 19103, or call
(800) 810-4145, ext. 5000, or e-mail special.markets@perseusbooks.com.

Designed by Brent Wilcox

Library of Congress Cataloging-in-Publication Data
Coyne, Amanda.
   Crude awakening : money, mavericks, and mayhem in Alaska / Amanda Coyne and
Tony Hopfinger.
      p.   cm.
   Includes bibliographical references and index.
   ISBN 978-1-56858-447-8 (hardcover : alk. paper) —
ISBN 978-1-56858-692-2 (e-book)   1. Alaska—Politics and government—1959–
2. Petroleum industry and trade—Alaska—History.   3. Petroleum industry and
trade—Political aspects—Alaska—History.   4. Petroleum industry and trade—
Corrupt practices—Alaska—History.   5. Political corruption—Alaska.   6. Political
culture—Alaska.   I. Hopfinger, Tony.   II. Title.
   F910.5.C69 2011
   979.8'05—dc23

                                                                    2011026213

10 9 8 7 6 5 4 3 2 1

For our fathers, John and Anton

There are strange things done in the midnight sun
By the men who moil for gold;
The Arctic trails have their secret tales
That would make your blood run cold...

—"The Cremation of Sam McGee,"
from *Songs of a Sourdough* by Robert W. Service, 1907

CONTENTS

Acknowledgments   ix
Prologue   xiii

PART I The Good Old Boys

1 They Built a Dream, and Others Drilled It   3
2 A Small Man and a Big Pipeline   17
3 Alaska, the Land of Oil and Money   33
4 Oil Patch People   49
5 Clinging to Guns and Religion in Wasilla   61
6 Bill and Ted's Excellent Adventure   79

PART II Pipe Dreams

7 If You Can't Beat the Good Ol' Boys, Become a
   Good Ol' Girl   99
8 Neverland Meets Lord of the Flies on Crack   111
9 Oinkers, Pit Bulls, and Frank   129
10 The Corrupt Bastards   147
11 Republican Death Picnic   165

PART III Breakup

12 Glittering Generalities and Pipe Dreams   179
13 Hopefully Slow Gas Will Begin to Pass . . . Quickly   195
14 Exxon, Don't Let the Door Hit You in the Stern   205
15 Crude Awakening   219
16 Breakup   237

Epilogue   253
Notes   263
Index   273

ACKNOWLEDGMENTS

When the phone rang on the morning of August 29, 2008, we were as surprised as the rest of the country that Arizona senator John McCain had picked Alaska governor Sarah Palin to be his running mate in the 2008 presidential election. As reporters in Alaska, we'd chronicled Palin's rise in state politics over the years, going back to her 2006 gubernatorial win. Shortly after Palin was elected governor, Amanda was contracted to write the first biography of the former Wasilla mayor. The publisher wanted a quick, glowing profile of Palin and why she appealed to Alaskans. But as the Palin administration unfolded and Amanda reviewed the governor's early years, Palin increasingly seemed like a fluke who got her fifteen minutes of fame thanks to a shakeup in the Alaska Republican Party and Alaskans' growing distrust of the oil companies—the lifeblood industry in the forty-ninth state. As governor, she embarked on a controversial—and popular—crusade to reform the state's dealings with the oil industry. We knew she possessed a special political charisma, but her success in Alaska seemed more the result of chance and circumstance than a calculated vision for her home state, her smarts, or her background. Amanda decided the Palin Cinderella story needed more time to unfold, and so she ended her contract for the biography project.

Another story was developing simultaneously. The state's relationship with oil had erupted into a corruption scandal. Some of Alaska's biggest names, including then-Senator Ted Stevens, had become caught up in a sweeping FBI probe into Bill Allen, the head of the state's largest oilfield services company, and his dealings with politicians. In March 2008 we first began drafting a proposal for this book, aiming to tell the story of how Alaska politics and oil became intertwined over more than forty years. Then, when McCain picked Palin six months later, we added what we knew about the governor and the impact of her policies on the state and its economy. The result, we hope, is a book charting Alaska through the lens of oil and politics, focusing on three larger-than-life characters: Ted Stevens, Bill Allen, and Sarah Palin. We recognize that we've just scratched the surface and there is much more to tell. And we understand that we've given short shrift to people and events that shaped Alaska. For that, we apologize. To the extent we've come close to telling the story we set out to write, we have many to thank.

We have often thought that others were more equipped to write this book than we were, including Hal Bernton, Craig Medred, and Michael Carey, veteran journalists who have shaped Alaska through decades of reporting and stories. Hal encouraged us to write this book back in 2008, helping us hone the theme and dive deeper into the corruption scandal, especially Bill Allen's alleged sexual crimes and the Justice Department's foibles in the case. Craig helped us carry that idea out through his masterful editing, his vibrant ideas, and his keen mind. We, like all Alaskans, are more than lucky to have Craig Medred by our side. Michael Carey, one of Alaska's great historians and writers, helped with checking our facts in the early years of Alaska, as well as the tone and narrative. We also relied on Michael's evolving sense of the state through his columns in the *Anchorage Daily News* over the decades.

Nobody in our professional careers has believed in us like Alice Rogoff. From the time we met in June 2009, she supported us in writing this book while also giving us the amazing opportunity to build *Alaska Dispatch*. We will forever be grateful for her trust, encouragement, optimism, and friendship, as well as her love of Alaska. We thank our agent Gail Ross, who took a big chance on signing up two relatively unknown writers. Our editor, Carl Bromley at Nation Books, took an even bigger chance by buying into the idea and giving us much needed encouragement and space to explore the themes of the book along the way.

Over the years our editors at *Bloomberg News* and *Newsweek* have helped us see the potential in Alaska news. We'd like to thank all the hardworking reporters at the *Anchorage Daily News,* who have kept those tribal fires lit. You've reminded us why newspapers—the first drafts of history—are so vital for a community.

Our colleagues at *Alaska Dispatch*—journalists who led the coverage on many of the events chronicled in the last chapters of this book— deserve huge credit for their understanding and patience as we finished the project. Publishing an online news site with a small staff is incredibly time-consuming, and the reporters and editors at times did double duty so we could write this book. We could not have completed this writing project without the support of our families, particularly our parents— John, Tony, Kathy, and Patricia. Each of you, in your own way, inspired us to write a better book than we would have otherwise.

And we're indebted to the many Alaskans who wrote the story of the state before us, and those who took the time to sit with us and help us understand what a beautiful state with a beautiful story we live in, and what's truly lost if we don't keep telling its story, each in our own way.

PROLOGUE

Late on the evening of May 7, 2006, Alaska state representative Pete Kott left the Capitol building and strolled a few blocks through downtown Juneau to the Baranof Hotel. He rode the elevator to the sixth floor and knocked on the door of Suite 604. Kott was anxious to tell his friends the good news.

A retired Air Force captain with a graduate degree in public administration, Kott had served as a Republican representative in the state House for fourteen years. Along the way, in addition to considerable legislative expertise, he'd acquired a drinking problem. After a couple of good gulps of wine, Kott, his eyes twinkling as he smiled, described to his friends—two executives and a consultant for Alaska's largest oil contractor, VECO Corporation—how his strategy to kill a bill that would raise state taxes on oil companies was coming together. Kott spent the next half-hour bragging about his performance earlier that day. He said he'd "outsmarted the fox" and delivered a "sucker punch."

"I use 'em and abuse 'em," Kott said. "Fuck 'em."

"That was like watching a maestro at work," one of the men in the room said of Kott's handiwork on the House floor.

"That's exactly right," said Rick Smith, a VECO vice president. "This guy's pretty good, right? Boy, I'll tell you what, it's every, every year, I mean, I've been with Pete and coming down to crunch time, he, he makes this shit happen."

Also present in Suite 604 was VECO founder Bill Allen. An oilman most of his life, Allen was a godfather character in Alaska's oil patch.

Politically connected, he was in Juneau in 2006 buying influence in the legislature to keep oil taxes favorable for his clients, "the three big boys," as he referred to them: Exxon Mobil, BP, and Conoco Phillips. Part of that effort involved laying the groundwork in the legislature for an upcoming bill that would lock in taxes for decades on the oil companies in exchange for their promise to build a 3,500-mile natural gas pipeline, estimated to be one of the most expensive private energy projects in U.S. history. The gas pipeline was to be Alaska's next boom. The state needed it more than ever now that its oil reserves were running dry. Allen needed the pipeline and lower taxes for his clients so that his oil-contracting firm would continue to prosper. Now 70, he wanted to sell the company. A pipeline project on the horizon would boost VECO's price tag. Allen had the ear of the Alaska oil executives. Some of them rooted him on, turning a blind eye to the bribery.

Allen booked Suite 604 for the 2006 legislative session. It was known as the "Animal House" among legislators, oil lobbyists, and the governor's top aides, who all routinely dropped in to visit Allen and his sidekick Rick Smith. They called themselves the "Corrupt Bastards Club" after a newspaper column that had accused them of corruption. And like many Republican lawmakers, Kott revered Allen, calling him "Uncle Bill."

"I had to get 'er done, so I [could] come back here and face this man right here," said Kott, pointing at Allen. "I had to cheat, steal, beg, borrow, and lie."

"I own your ass," Allen responded.[1]

It was such alcohol-laced conversations, many involving legislators in Alaska's rain-drenched capital, that lent tone, shape, and substance to the state's largest oil-fueled political scandal, an epic tale of greed and corruption that began a half century ago and continues to play out today. In late August 2006, the FBI secretly persuaded Allen to plead guilty to bribing a slew of state politicians, as well as admit to doing favors for Ted Stevens, the longest-serving U.S. Senate Republican in history. Agents revealed to Allen that they'd accumulated thousands of hours of wiretapped phone calls, along with video surveillance from Suite 604, which included footage of him handing hundred-dollar bills to politicians.

Allen, who allegedly had a penchant for teenage girls, confessed almost immediately when he was picked up, eventually detailing how he used his oil-contracting firm to renovate and expand Stevens's cabin. Allen confessed to paying more than $240,000 in phony consulting fees to the senator's son, Ben Stevens, who was president of the Alaska Senate. Allen helped fund extravagant fund-raisers for U.S. Representative Don Young, replete with a pig roast—a nod to Young's proudly prolific pork barrel spending on Alaska. And in 2006, when the state legislature had Alaska's future in its hands, Allen admitted to paying off Kott and other key lawmakers to swing crucial votes. At stake was not only whether to increase oil taxes, but whether to provide industry a host of incentives to jumpstart construction of a $40 billion natural gas pipeline—a project that could spark a construction boom the likes of which Alaskans hadn't seen since the 1970s.

The seeds of this tale were planted early in Alaska's short history as a state, sprouting when the oil industry took root forty years ago and the state's most prominent politician began his ascent. Senator Ted Stevens became nearly as powerful as Alaska's lifeblood industry, gaining a national reputation for securing tens of billions of dollars for his home state between 1968 and 2008—the year he lost reelection after being convicted in federal court for failing to document Allen's renovations to his home, as required of senators on their financial disclosures. Stevens's and Allen's careers paralleled the rise of the oil economy, and by the late 1990s they were good friends. They even owned a racehorse together. Stevens was at the height of his power then, holding the purse strings to the federal budget as chair of the Senate Appropriations Committee. Allen asked favors of Stevens, but he mostly helped the senator out of friendship, no doubt influenced to some extent by Stevens's frequently aired complaint that he'd sacrificed his Harvard law degree to serve the public.

Alaska had been a state for only nine years when oil workers struck the elephant field, Prudhoe Bay, in 1968. Before that, its economic future hinged on logging, mining, fishing, and military bases. But with a suddenly rich oil economy, Alaskans became comfortable and complacent, working for the oil companies at wages far greater than those in the lower forty-eight states, and numerous businesses, both old and new, profited from the industry. The state planned little for the future, beyond establishing an oil wealth savings account. By 2007 the Alaska Permanent Fund, started three decades earlier, swelled to $40 billion, a piggy bank to get the state by when the oil wells eventually ran dry. But few imagined that day. By the early 1980s, the Permanent Fund yielded annual dividends for every man, woman, and child. Maybe they didn't approve of their leaders' close ties to Bill Allen and Big Oil, but they appreciated getting that yearly oil dividend check. (Alaskans don't pay state income tax or sales tax.) They worried little what the rest of the country thought of Stevens's funneling home billions of federal dollars or the state's immense oil wealth.

Leading Alaskans into this trance was a group of old-guard politicians and businessmen who came of age when Alaska was still a territory. They understood the state's relationship with industry as a business deal: The people of the state owned the oil, and the companies bought leases and paid taxes to develop it. Keeping the crude flowing and the state prospering required a delicate dance of negotiating and hobnobbing with executives from Texas to London. As the years progressed, oil bred a crude culture of business and politics in Alaska, tainted with corruption and the mishandling of resources. Alaskans accepted this as part of doing business. If they turned a blind eye to what their leaders were up to, it was only because some of them didn't know that it could be done otherwise, and the ones who did were greedy and bloated themselves, living in a northern Neverland, far from the eyes of the rest of the country. The FBI and Justice Department were supposed to change that. But then, it seemed, the Alaska Neverland ethos got to them too. In the end, the feds stood accused of playing as dirty as the people they were investigating—and in some cases, dirtier.

It may well be that things happen in Alaska that wouldn't happen in states with long histories and established social networks—places where physical magnificence and an excess of natural beauty, set always in nature's extremes, don't overwhelm, don't usurp the senses, senses that otherwise might be used to create stable, well-run communities. Add oil to that mixture, a big, gushing elephant field that brought in billions of dollars so early in the state's history, and the voices of judicious and honest

Alaskans, of which there are many, were drowned out by other, louder voices. The ones who thought the oil and the money would last forever. The ones who wanted more of everything, and felt it was their God-given right to have it.

By the late summer of 2006, FBI agents finally had the evidence they needed to swarm the offices of the Alaska legislature in Anchorage, looking for clues of lawmakers taking bribes and favors from Bill Allen. Those raids would have ramifications that spilled far beyond Alaska's borders. They would tarnish the reputations of federal agents and prosecutors, the suicide of another, end the career of one of the most important men in the country, and spawn a new leader, a new *kind* of leader: the wife of a snowmobile racer, a mother of five, a caribou hunter and salmon slayer. Indeed, the timing, as would often be the case for her, was a gift for a former small-town mayor who had just defeated Governor Frank Murkowski in the GOP primary election a week earlier. Sarah Palin was a forty-two-year-old Republican who had been causing a ruckus within her party for the past two years. Out of the ashes of cronyism and corruption, she was born.

The FBI raids seemed to confirm for many Alaskans that Palin—a self-described reformist advocating government transparency—was the real deal, pure and courageous for standing up to those "corrupt bastards" in her party. In contrast to those good old boys, Palin seemed squeaky clean. By then, Palin had divided the Alaska Republican Party, winning over a group of conservative Alaskans who, in retrospect, might have been the first tea partiers of America, and riding on their backs all the way to the governor's mansion in late 2006.

For a brief moment under her tenure, Alaskans largely came together and were reminded of the idealism around which the state had been formed in the first place. It was an idealism borne out of a philosophy of collective ownership of the state's oil, which funded nearly 90 percent of state government through taxes, royalties, and fees paid by the oil companies. Some in the past had tried to wrench Alaska away from its corporate dependency, but the fight had proved too difficult. But then Palin swept into office, promising to bring Alaskans back to the days when they loved and respected their state and each other. To bring Alaska back to its constitution, penned in a time, before the oil boom, when the dream was pure and Alaska-size.

"I will unambiguously, steadfastly, and doggedly guard the interests of this great state as a mother naturally guards her own," Palin told Alaskans. "Like a nanook defending her cub."

And she did—until she didn't anymore.

If Alaska had been an abstraction to you before Sarah Palin's rise to fame, you've probably by now seen at least a little of this state—the soaring mountains, the dangerous, choppy seas, the vast stretches of untouched land—but you might not have heard much about Alaska's relationship to oil. Through reality TV, you've seen quirky people in quirky towns talking to the camera about their quirky lives, and you might have thought, "How charming; I must visit."

It is charming. About 710,000 people, a few more than the population of Washington, D.C., are flung out across an area more than twice the size of Texas. And although its larger cities have many of the amenities of the Lower 48, it's also its own country, holding to its own values—where perceptions of class are far less entrenched than in the rest of the nation. It simply doesn't matter what clothes you wear, what kind of car you drive, how big your house is, where you did or didn't go to school. Alaska has its version of royalty but no blue bloods. In fact, if blue blood is sensed, and the bearers of it are not kicked out, they are made to feel extremely uncomfortable. In old-time Alaska, if you behaved badly enough, you were given what was called a "blue ticket," a ride on the first steamer south to the West Coast. The blue ticket had nothing to do with blue blood, but surely some recipients were East Coasters, carrying with them their East Coast attitudes and their East Coast values, which simply don't transfer.

Idyllic mountains, glaciers, choppy seas foaming with salmon: a place that encourages you to be yourself—the real self, the self without entrapments. It is its own country, and being governor of Alaska is like being president of your own country.

But Alaska can also be ingrained and ingrown, and incestuously corrupt. And perhaps more insidious, petty and small-minded, particularly if you were born and raised here and don't have a window to the world outside—an understanding of how other states evolved and flourished, from modest ambition and hard work, through the necessary stages of maturation. But Alaska skipped much of that, jumping the line. Nine years after statehood, wildcatters found oil at Prudhoe Bay, and the boom was on, the newfound, easy, and oil-drenched prosperity spawning, among other things, an Alaskan kind of wild ambition, built on the belief you can do anything and you can be anything as long as you have the skills that Alaska requires: the ability to endure the midnight sun and winter darkness, to fend for yourself during the booms and busts, to know how to use tarps and duct tape creatively, as well as how to stay warm, handle a shotgun, and deal with big oil companies to keep it all going. And beyond that, why shouldn't this translate elsewhere, as some Alaskans who haven't spent much time outside the state believe? If you can be anything you want to be in Alaska, why not in the rest of the country?

In the early hours of August 29, 2008, when the networks began announcing that Republican presidential candidate John McCain had chosen as his running mate a young, attractive woman, Alaskans were no less shocked than the rest of the country. We'd known the McCain camp considered Governor Sarah Palin, then 44, earlier in 2008, but we thought her hopes were all but dashed by midsummer. Her ratings, once the highest of any governor in the nation, were dipping in the weeks before McCain made his surprise pick. Her combative relationship with fellow Republicans and the lifeblood oil industry of Alaska had started to take a toll. Meanwhile, Palin was enmeshed in the biggest political scandal of her career, dubbed "Troopergate," a tawdry family feud that'd spilled over into her administration and spawned a state investigation. Troopergate threatened to soil Palin's two-year Cinderella story. Then, just as the walls were closing in, McCain, who still saw stardom in Palin, plucked her from the wilderness, her timing, as always, impeccable.

Some of Palin's more forward thinking Alaskan supporters recognized that a few successes in the forty-ninth state don't translate easily into the credentials usually thought necessary for being president. But many thought otherwise. After all, in Alaska, Bill Allen, who grew up as a migrant fruit picker, could become a political kingmaker. In Alaska, that same person could rub shoulders with leaders of some of the most powerful companies in the world. In Alaska, that person could befriend one of the most powerful men in the country, Senator Ted Stevens. In Alaska, a small-town mayor who went to five colleges and couldn't name what she read could charm a whole state, become governor, and extract billions of dollars from oil companies, and then just quit her job, without seemingly a second thought.

And why not, when you're in a state that's so much about a state of mind? Always in the process of becoming, not yet arriving. A state in a state of adolescence, still very much finding its way.

This book is an attempt to capture that state of mind, as well as trace the political and economic forces that have acted on the fifty-two-year-old state of Alaska, as it continues the struggle to shape its identity. It's the story of the rise and fall of Ted Stevens and Bill Allen, two of the biggest characters in a state full of big characters. They helped make Alaska and, each in his own way, helped pave the way for Sarah Palin to come into and then exit the country. It's the story of Alaska coming of age, all of its big hopes and dreams paid for by oil, a finite resource.

PART I

THE GOOD OLD BOYS

CHAPTER 1

They Built a Dream,
and Others Drilled It

Soon oil would rule Alaska. Soon the sheen of oil would spread through this frontier so widely that without it, Alaska's future would become unimaginable. Crude would make everything that was about to happen to Alaska possible: wealth and corruption, growth and environmental degradation, soaring hopes and fading dreams. Alaska's best known leaders—Sarah Palin and Ted Stevens—were born out of oil, as was the lesser known Bill Allen, who was nonetheless as influential as any leader in Alaska. Eventually Alaska's oil would spread throughout the country, helping to fuel America, to supply energy to a growing populace. And it would help energize an emerging party led by a small-town Alaska mayor, who had an Alaska-size confidence in her ability to lead America.

All of this would have been unimaginable back in the winter of 1955–1956. Oil wasn't much on the minds of the delegates who met in the student union at the University of Alaska in Fairbanks to pen a constitution for a state that did not yet exist. Alaska was still a U.S. territory managed by the federal government. Many residents sought self-determination—statehood—and had embarked on a peaceful and popular uprising against the federal government to take control of the vast hinterland they called home. Drafting a state constitution was a first step toward realizing the dream; the U.S. Congress and the president would have final say on whether Alaska became a state. But that would come later. First, Alaskans, most of them anyway, wanted to prove to the

3

rest of the country they were reasonable and capable enough to write their own founding rules of the land. And so the territory chose fifty-five representatives to ponder and debate how Alaska, as a state, would be formed and structured. The delegates came from the far corners of a land that stretches 1,400 miles from top to bottom, 2,400 miles from one side to the other—an area almost a fifth the size of the lower forty-eight states—so big that if Alaska is superimposed on a map of the continental United States, it stretches from the Canadian border to the Gulf of Mexico, from the Atlantic to the Pacific.

At the time of the constitutional convention, about 208,000 people called Alaska home. Delegates hailed from the urban centers of Anchorage, Juneau, and Fairbanks, as well as the small towns and villages, places with names like Kotzebue, Ketchikan, and Homer. They carried with them the smell of asphalt and pine, wood smoke, whale blubber and seal oil, of the hard, barren north and of soggy rain forests and little cabins in the middle of a vast wilderness. Some came out of that Alaska wilderness and traveled long distances by boat to reach the territory's few roads, where they then could jump in cars and trucks to make the last leg of the journey. Some carpooled. One delegate hitchhiked. They were businesspeople, lawyers, miners, fishermen and homemakers, and eccentric sourdoughs. Among the fifty-five were six women and one Alaska Native, the mayor of the Tlingit village of Klawock in southeastern Alaska.

The delegates huddled for seventy-five days in what is now called Constitution Hall at the University of Alaska in Fairbanks to realize a dream akin to creating a new country: a new state, free to elect its own officials, free to manage its resources—fish, minerals, wildlife, and oil—and free to organize and live by its own rules. This constitution would be based on the people's needs and on other constitutions that had come before it. Most of the drafters were Democrats. A few were Republicans. Politics, though, was put aside for the sake of the larger purpose. Many still say this represented Alaska's finest hour, before the big oil strike.

At the time, a few believed that vast oil reserves would be found someday and somewhere in the 586,412 square miles that made up the territory, or off its 6,640 miles of coastline, much of which, both on-shore and off, still hadn't been explored. There had been sightings of black stuff, including up north in the Arctic, where early explorers took note of how it created sparkling rainbow sheens on lakes. They found tarry mud that trapped caribou in their tracks, and met resident Eskimos who burned scraps of the oil-soaked tundra for fuel. Many of these reports came from a vast area, flat as the moon, called the North Slope, a misnomer if ever there was one. Back before oil was discovered and big machines marched across the tundra, nothing diverted the eye from the flatness save the herds of thousands of caribou that migrated across parts of the North Slope. Today the oil workers up there like to say with a straight face that there's a woman behind every tree, and then laugh when you look around. In the summer, a line of clouds in the distance can lead you to believe that the person who designed this swath of barren landscape had humanity enough to put a city within reach. And then you look again and curse the designer for being a trickster. In the winter, this is a frozen apocalypse. Even if there was oil, who would be crazy enough to try to get it out?

At the time of the constitutional convention, Alaskans were more concerned about fishing and minerals, controlled by alleged robber barons and Outside corporations (yes, "Outside," with a capital "O"—that's how Alaskans refer to anybody who doesn't live in their state), and a federal government proving increasingly incompetent in managing the huge territory and its rich resources. Having little say in how territorial lands were divided and developed, Alaskans wanted to take control of the resources in the territory that were comprised of more than 98 percent federal land. As it was, if oil was found, or for that matter, gold or other minerals, the feds had control of the development, including land leasing and royalties.

The drafters of the state constitution called for managing resources in the interests of the people. They had a particular concern for fish traps, of all things. Alaskans depended on fishing to keep their state afloat, and a battle had been brewing for years over canneries and fishing companies wreaking havoc on what was supposed to be a sustainable industry. Commercial fishing was big business for Alaska, and Outside canneries had deployed the traps, jeopardizing the prized salmon fishery. Fish traps would be banned.

For all of the optimism and hope, though, many Alaskans saw a different path to independence. Some wanted to secede from the United States and form their own country. (Later they would form their own party—the Alaska Independence Party—the party Todd Palin once belonged to and Sarah Palin respected.) But the real fight came nationally. A coalition of Democrats and Republicans couldn't see Alaska's potential, and thought that the state would forever be a ward of the federal government, with a small population unable to pay its share of taxes in exchange for the huge influx of federal dollars that would be needed to develop and sustain Alaska. Partisan politics too played into the debate. Alaska's lone territorial delegate to Congress, Bob Bartlett, was a Democrat. So was its territorial governor, Ernest Gruening. The Republicans had a weak majority in Congress, a majority they might lose if Alaska became a state. Another group, southern Dixiecrats, didn't like the idea, either. Alaska Democrats, they thought, were the wrong kind of Democrats— the kind who supported civil rights.

Corporations that made fortunes from Alaska's minerals and fisheries were also nervous about the call to make Alaska a state. At the constitutional convention, there was a steady cry over how Outside businesses had no interest in Alaska's future, how they couldn't be trusted as good corporate neighbors, and how Alaska as a state would inevitably face conflict over managing resources that would require private enterprise to develop. Alaska, as a state with only a couple hundred thousand people, would need to raise tax revenue, and an obvious way was leasing and taxing the development of minerals or oil or timber on state land. But generating interest in such development would demand negotiations with the very companies that extracted the resources and policy decisions from a citizen-elected legislature. As some developing countries have learned, a government's short-term desire to make money can lead to the destruction of resources, with nothing left to show for it. At the convention, Bob Bartlett, the territorial delegate to Congress, warned of not only exploitation but a corporate lockup of Alaska's riches, foreshadowing the state's future in many ways:

Two very real dangers are present. The first, and most obvious, danger is that of exploitation under the thin disguise of development. The taking of Alaska's mineral resources without leaving some reasonable return for the support of Alaska governmental services . . . The second danger is that outside interests, determined to stifle any development in Alaska which might compete with their activities elsewhere, will attempt to acquire great areas of Alaska's public lands in order *not* to develop them until such time as, in their omnipotence and the pursuance of their own interests, they see fit.[1]

Alaskans' efforts so strongly resembled creating a new country that the number of delegates chosen for the Alaska constitutional gathering mimicked the fifty-five-member Philadelphia Constitutional Convention of 1787. A world away from Philadelphia, Alaskans could have met in the breathtaking territorial capital of Juneau, a town hugging the steep mountains and rain forests in the Alaska panhandle. Or they could have convened in Anchorage, a town in the south-central part of the territory that was still finding its purpose but at least had a few decent restaurants. Instead, they chose cold, isolated Fairbanks, in order to avoid the distraction of the lobbyists and politicians in Juneau and Anchorage. And they thought that a university set the appropriate tone.[2] They certainly didn't choose Fairbanks for the town's physical appeal or weather.

Fairbanks rises amid the hills and domes in the heart of Alaska, which Alaskans call the "Interior." Rugged individuals who relocate to Fairbanks develop a "nostalgia that knows no cure," as Thomas Arthur Rickard wrote in *Through the Yukon and Alaska*, "forever yearning for the boundless horizon, the untainted oxygen, and the perfect emancipation of life on the far outposts of empire."[3] On the far outposts indeed; even today for many Alaskans, Fairbanks holds its own mystique. In the short summer, temperatures can cook past 90 degrees. The town is a northern Alice in Wonderland, with huge vegetables and flowers that bloom in neon colors. Everything is alive under the nearly unsetting subarctic sun, and the town goes dizzy and crazy. But Fairbanks really comes into itself in the winter, when it gets so cold that the very air freezes, blanketing the city in ice fog. Metal on metal groans and tires freeze flat against the ground. The sun is only an idea, appearing on the horizon just long enough to remind residents that it's keeping company with others in some distant warm place before winking and leaving the landscape to the spirits of a shivering darkness. When the constitutional convention opened, the temperature was 16 below, a warm winter day. Just before midnight one evening, the chair of the convention interrupted a heated floor debate to say that "the temperature is now about 40-below, and if the delegates have their cars out there, they probably should start them in order that they will start."[4]

This clearly was not Philadelphia. The town of Fairbanks had never attracted many civic and aesthetically minded folks. The early settlers of Fairbanks, and to a certain extent the rest of Alaska, cared little about churches and community centers and well maintained yards. The European artisans who carved faces into rock, who made the bricks and lovingly put them into the mortar, the ones who carved mottos into the marble of Midwestern courthouses, tended to stay far away from Alaska, or they quickly succumbed to the realities of near Arctic construction. Generally people settle for utility over beauty.

Nonetheless, the constitution that came out of this town was beautiful. Learning from what other states had done wrong, Alaska hoped to have the best government of any state in the country. And perhaps the biggest idea this constitution incorporated, the biggest, most audacious idea of all, came right out of a philosophy that had at the time captured the imaginations of many in the rest of the world: collective ownership. The framers of the constitution wrote that when the territory became a state and Alaska got more than 100 million acres that had been in federal hands, the natural resources on it and under it would belong to all Alaskans. Not to those who happened to have lucked out on a plot of land. Not to those who bought up acreage on speculation. Not to oil scouts or gold prospectors or fishing moguls. No. In Alaska the state would own and manage much of the resource wealth, and elected leaders would ensure that the wealth went to benefit the people, spawning a socialistic streak that would run through the fabric of the state.

On February 6, 1956, more than 1,000 people showed up in Fairbanks to watch the constitutional delegates sign the final draft of their 14,400-word document and to hear one of the final resolutions read aloud. It was entitled "You Are Alaska's Children" and it went like this:[5]

> We bequeath to you a state that will be glorious in her achievements, a homeland filled with opportunities for living, a land where you can worship and pray, a country where ambitions will be bright and real, an Alaska that will grow with you as you grow. We trust you; you are our future. We ask you to take tomorrow and dream; we know that you will see visions we do not see. We are certain that in capturing today for you, you can plan and build. Take our constitution and study it, work with it in your classrooms, understand its meaning and the facts within it. Help others to love and appreciate it.

After the constitution was written and voters approved it, the state sent emissaries to Washington, D.C. A *New York Times* article said some of the more fervent statehood supporters threatened to start another party if Congress didn't support their cause. They'd call it the "Tea Party" and they would "stage the equivalent of the 'Boston Tea Party,' to dramatize Alaska's plight." The party never emerged, but the battle over statehood rippled through the Beltway in the late 1950s. One of the men leading the charge on behalf of Alaskans was Ted Stevens.[6]

In 2006 on a cold December afternoon in Fairbanks, just down the street from where the constitution was drafted fifty years earlier, one of Alaska's children would take the oath of office to become the first female and the youngest governor ever to swear to uphold the Alaska constitution. She had done what the founders beseeched Alaskans to do. Governor Sarah Palin promised to represent a new era, with a new generation taking the reins of a state that had lost much of its earlier dream and vision. The events leading up to Palin's inauguration confirmed, in many ways, the fears of those idealistic souls who had made Alaska a state. From political corruption to oil-fueled spending sprees to a culture openly dependent on the federal government, Alaskans in 2006 had found themselves at a crossroads. The charismatic Palin sensed an opportunity to hark back to a time when Alaska believed it could champion its own destiny and wrestle control from the corporations and the federal government. Nearly 5,000 Alaskans gathered to watch Palin be sworn in. Two former governors, Republican Wally Hickel and Democrat Bill Sheffield, were there. Outgoing governor Frank Murkowski skipped the events. By then, his name had been sullied by political blunders and a corruption scandal, including allegations that he'd sold out Alaska to Big Oil. Four surviving delegates of the Alaska constitutional convention—Seaborn Buckalew, Jack Coghill, Vic Fischer, and George Sundborg—were there; with them was Katie Hurley, who'd served as chief clerk of the convention. She was from Wasilla and knew more about Palin than the other dignitaries did, but she nonetheless applauded with them.

Palin had spent much of her gubernatorial campaign in 2006 talking about Alaska's constitution, about how the resources belonged to all the people and how she was going to make sure that Alaskans got "our fair share" of the wealth—mostly the oil and natural gas under lease by multinational oil companies, which, as Bartlett had warned, were developing it as they saw fit.

"It's eerily prophetic," Palin told the crowd. "Today we stand on the threshold of a new frontier, and these pioneers still speak to us from the past."[7]

At the time Palin styled her hair in a schoolmarmish bun; her makeup was light, her suits off the rack. What the crowd saw was a humble, attractive Alaska servant. They roared, "Sarah! Sarah! Sarah!" How could they not love this bright, fresh face? The woman who promised to bring Alaskans back to the days when they loved and respected their state and each other. To bring Alaska back to that constitution, penned in a time, before oil, when the dream was pure and Alaska-size. Alaskans didn't know much about Palin, except that when she smiled, she seemed to smile at everyone, no matter their politics, background, or occupation. Her smile lit up Alaska. She promised a bold new way, one that would try to wrestle power back from the oil companies and "good old boy" politicians that had come before her. And it worked, for a while.

There on the podium with her was five-year-old Piper, her youngest child, princess for the day, wearing a tiara. And there were Bristol and Track and Willow and her husband, Todd. "I will unambiguously, steadfastly and doggedly guard the interests of this great state as a mother naturally guards her own," Palin said. "Like a nanook defending her cub."

Alaska had begun a radical transformation even before statehood, though hardly anyone noticed at the time. In 1957, during the heat of the statehood battle, an oil find—not a huge one but sizable enough—was made on Alaska's Kenai Peninsula not far from Anchorage. Additional exploration over the next few years revealed more oil and natural gas in the area, as well as offshore beneath the muddy waters of Cook Inlet. Oil wasn't the only reason the territory became a state, but for those who doubted whether Alaska had a fighting chance of supporting itself, the oil discoveries of the late 1950s showed the new state had promise. On July 7, 1958, after years of congressional wrangling, President Dwight Eisenhower signed the Alaska Statehood Act, and the Last Frontier officially joined the Union six months later. The new state took ownership of 104 million acres—an area larger than California—that had been managed by the feds. Among the tracts the state picked up were large swaths of the North Slope, some 2 million potentially oil-rich acres between the Beaufort Sea and the Brooks Range, including an area called Prudhoe Bay. It was here, nine years later, that Alaska's future would be found.

In late 1967, a crew of frustrated wildcatters was about to give up looking for oil at Prudhoe Bay. They were drilling for the Atlantic Richfield Company—ARCO, as it was called—and Humble Oil, now Exxon. Other wells sunk on the North Slope had turned up dry, and this was their "last shot," as Bob Anderson, chairman of ARCO at the time, said.[8] It was 45 below on the day the drill bit broke the frozen ground and continued down through the permafrost. Deep into the cold earth went the drilling pipe, slowing when it encountered each new layer of rock. Sometimes a geologist would halt the operation and sample the rock and debris that rose out of the hole. At about 1,000 feet, large pieces of wood, about 42,000 years old, began to come up—tamarack, it was later revealed.[9] At 3,300 feet, geologists began getting excited. The rocks were showing traces of crude when examined under fluorescent lights but weren't porous enough to hold large amounts of oil. The drilling continued deeper toward the scent of oil.

At 5,335 feet, an ARCO geologist later wrote, the mood began to feel like a "hot streak at the craps or blackjack tables at Las Vegas."[10] The drillers crossed into siltstone, a good sign. Then, at 8,000 feet, a stream of natural gas erupted out of the hole "with a roar that was something like the rumble of a jet plane overhead that you could not only hear but feel through your feet." Finally down further, there was oil, flowing heavy and thick. A second well showed much the same. It was an elephant field.

Prudhoe Bay turned out to hold more than 13 billion barrels of recoverable oil, making it the biggest oil find in North America and the eighteenth-largest discovery in the world. Almost overnight, oil made Alaska the Saudi Arabia of the north—America's oil province. And it would undergo a boom the likes of which America hadn't seen since the Klondike gold rush. What a decade ago had been a territory of a couple hundred thousand people was now on the verge of a new beginning, and soon the state would lease more tracts at Prudhoe Bay as the oil companies that already had a foothold on the North Slope were frantically scrambling to size up the reservoir before they invested in more acreage.

Soon the slope was overrun with drilling rigs and steel, trucks and pipes, bulldozers and fuel tanks, tents and teams of excited, eager men. Thousands of pounds of machinery, supplies, and cargo containers came north by flotilla. The scene around the Fairbanks airport resembled a "wartime staging area," a reporter wrote.[11] British Petroleum chartered five Hercules C-130s—the forty-foot cargo planes big enough to swallow tractors and trucks—costing $250,000 each a month to operate. It took 250 to 300 trips by the Hercules to supply a drilling outfit.[12]

The companies guarded what they found on the North Slope like military secrets. Security guards and fences popped up. Dogs prowled the area. Fortunes were at stake, and the state was filled with stories of intrigue and espionage, of oilmen bribing janitors to dig through the trash of other companies in search of geological notes that might provide an edge on where the crude was hiding under Prudhoe Bay. Planes went on scouting missions. Women, it was said, were hired to seduce men in the know. Oil executives from competing companies, it was rumored, dressed like roustabouts and infiltrated worksites. Alaska had turned into the setting for a spy novel.[13]

In September 1969, the state held the biggest oil lease sale in its short history. It was a monumental event that unequivocally consummated Alaska's marriage to Big Oil. The sale happened in Anchorage, a town still in the making when the oilmen arrived en masse. The largest-ever recorded earthquake in North America had crumpled Anchorage and other parts of the state only five years earlier. The city was still rebuilding, and now felt the oil boom knocking at its door. The oilmen from Texas, Oklahoma, and other states arrived in Anchorage on private jets to bid for leases on the slope. They were greeted by a security detail of twelve Alaska state troopers, three fire marshals, and a handful of cops.[14] They rented out entire floors of the few hotels in town. During the day, they huddled over notes and graphs, making final preparations on how much they would bid and on what tracts of land. At night they saddled up to the bar at the Petroleum Club, which opened in the 1950s in downtown Anchorage, straining their necks to listen in on the conversations of their peers around them.

On bid day, September 10, 1969, doors to the Sydney Laurence Theatre in downtown Anchorage opened at 7:00 AM. Hundreds of people rushed in, some to deposit their bids, others to grab a front row seat. Soon all 700 seats were taken. Alaska didn't have fancy houses. Cans of KLIM powdered milk and freezers packed with salmon and moose were common in households, and many in the state still lacked running water. The fashions were dated. There were no opera houses. But what Alaskans did have was a bard. Larry Allan Beck had started reciting Robert Service poems when he was a four-year-old living in Oregon, where he made twenty-five cents a day performing for loggers. He began his career in Alaska in 1967. He dropped out of law school to recite Service and his own poems in a thick, faux Scottish brogue, channeling the voice of old mining prospectors to tourists and civic groups all across the state. Soon he took his Alaska vaudevillian act on the road and traveled across America. In part because of his success, and in part because he was the most optimistic man most had ever met, Alaska's governor in 1971 ordained him, "Alaska's ambassador of goodwill." The last time someone asked, he said that he probably recited "The Cremation of Sam McGee" 10,000 times.[15]

But the question was put to him during his later years, when he was tired and broke. On the day of the big oil lease sale in 1969, he was young and fresh, and excited to be dressed as an old sourdough gold prospector. This was his most important audience to date, and he wrote his own poem to recite to the oilmen:

> *From the Brooks Range to the ocean*
> *With its capes and coves and isles*
> *There is mighty little motion*
> *Only miles and miles and miles*[16]

That was about to change. Soon there would be lots of motion, and oil executives salivated at the thought. They were the wild men of industry. They smoked, they drank, they had rough hands, and they swore. But they were well traveled. They flew to distant lands to seduce developing governments into allowing them to develop oil fields. They knew what was required in such situations. They clapped politely for the bard. They stood and took off their hats when the first chords struck, announcing the beginning of the Alaska state song, just as they did, no doubt, during rituals in Middle Eastern countries or during ceremonies in African nations that involved feathers and drums, during a dance where men wear skirts and where the oilmen were expected to shimmy along with them.

> *Eight stars of gold on a field of blue,*
> *Alaska's flag, may it mean to you,*
> *The blue of the sea, the evening sky,*
> *The mountain lakes and the flowers nearby,*
> *The gold of the early sourdough's dreams,*
> *The precious gold of the hills and streams,*
> *The brilliant stars in the northern sky,*

The "Bear," the "Dipper," and shining high,
The great North Star with its steady light,
O'er land and sea a beacon bright,
Alaska's flag to Alaskans dear,
The simple flag of a last frontier.[17]

It wasn't until after 10:30 AM that Alaska's commissioner overseeing natural resources began to call out the bids, sparking collective gasps from the audience. British Petroleum, partnering with Gulf Oil, bid $97 million on six parcels; Phillips Petroleum bid more than $72 million for just one tract, or $28,233 per acre, the highest per acre in U.S. history. Another consortium of five companies plunked down $270 million for tracts.[18] The Alaska state budget for 1969 was around $100 million. But on that early fall day, the oilmen spent more than $900 million on leases—the equivalent of about $5.5 billion today. Thomas E. Kelly, Alaska's commissioner of natural resources, declared bids that day set a world record for a competitive oil lease sale.[19] The stage was set now for a new era in Alaska politics, for the state's leaders now had money in their pockets to spend—or save—or invest. Those decisions would unfold in the coming years, though everybody knew the significance of what had just occurred in that Anchorage theater.

The next day, an editorial in the *Anchorage Daily News* channeled Bob Bartlett's wisdom of fourteen years earlier, reminding Alaskans that with great wealth comes great responsibility: "Whether it will turn out to be not 'Alaska's Biggest Day since Statehood' but rather her 'Greatest Day,' will depend on how the state meets the challenge of overnight affluence." Will the state "dissipate this bonanza" in runaway spending, or "keep its cool" and develop a "prudent long-term program?"[20]

Oil was very much on the minds of the thousands who came to watch Palin take her oath of office, a half century after those pioneers met at Constitution Hall. In 2006 much was at stake in Alaska. The oil fields were drying up. Political parties were fractured. The corruption was now public, thanks to a massive FBI investigation. Palin promised another future, another boom. She promised clean government and a fresh start.

16 CRUDE AWAKENING

She bubbled with frontier enthusiasm. "At the start of the convention," Palin said, harking back to those heady days when the constitution was being drafted, "delegate Bob Bartlett saw two distinct futures for Alaska: One of wise resource development leading to wealth and industry. One of servitude, stemming from loss of control over our resources, that leads to despair."

"America is looking for answers," Palin continued. "She's looking for a new direction. The world is looking for a light. That light can come from America's great North Star, it can come from Alaska."[21]

Alaskans had no idea what Palin meant. They had no idea that she was practicing on them, and no idea that when she was done practicing, she would leave them for a bigger political stage. They had no inkling that she would leave Alaska fractured and confused, without a clear future, wondering where that light went.

CHAPTER 2

A Small Man and
a Big Pipeline

Alaska, especially in its early years, was a state where you could leave your mark, literally ensuring yourself a place in the history books. If you weren't an oilman, cannery owner, gold mine operator, or bottom-feeder—occupations that could make a man rich in Alaska—you still could pursue the priceless commodity of power, even (or especially) if you rose from humble beginnings, as Ted Stevens did. He held his Senate seat on his own for forty years, making him the longest-serving Senate Republican in U.S. history. Alaskans called him "Uncle Ted." Tenacious and witty, hardheaded but sentimental, Stevens possessed an endearing quality that was remarkably nonpolitical when he finally became U.S. senator. He was genuinely driven to help his fellow Alaskans. Oil may have been the cordwood that ignited Alaska's economy, but Stevens was the man who tended to the fire and helped it grow. He was better known among longtime Alaskans for what he did—not what he stood for, even though his extraordinary career later was tainted by helping friends. If Stevens was doing good for the state, that was all that mattered. Alaskans overwhelmingly supported this adage, or least paid homage to it, for if you were not on his side, you risked falling out of favor with Uncle Ted. And for some, that could mean losing a career, missing a lucrative contract, or being sent back to Outside.

Theodore Fulton Stevens was born in Indianapolis during the roaring 1920s. He was six years old when the good times came to an abrupt halt on October 29, 1929. Things got bad for his family. His father lost his eyesight during the Depression. His parents divorced. He and his father and three siblings moved from Chicago back to his hometown, Indianapolis, to live with his paternal grandparents, where he helped support his blind father and a mentally challenged cousin by hawking newspapers on the street.[1]

When his grandfather died, he was sent to live with his aunt and uncle in sunny Southern California. In Manhattan Beach Stevens was able to relax, with the help of a happy-go-lucky uncle, Walter, whom Stevens adored. His uncle had become an inventor after fighting in World War I. According to Stevens, he invented the waffle iron and the sandwich toaster but didn't fill out the proper patent paperwork. He ended up not only losing his patents but having to pay a fine for criminal patent infringement. "Or something like that," Stevens told a friend later. Walter lost a million dollars, Stevens said, right around the time of the 1929 crash. He then decided to move to California. "He moved to the beach and said, 'Hell with it, I'm going to enjoy life.'" And he taught his young nephew to enjoy life too.[2] Stevens bought a 1931 Pontiac convertible and a surfboard. He and his best friend, Russell Green—who bought the famous Simi Winery in Healdsburg, California, in the 1970s—spent the last years of Stevens's childhood running through the sand and riding the waves.[3] Until 2008, when he left his job under a cloud of suspicion, the surfboard stood in Ted Stevens's Senate office in Washington.

During World War II, Stevens flew transport planes to support military aviation legend Claire Lee Chennault's Flying Tigers and Chinese forces fighting the Japanese. He wanted to fly fighter planes in combat but never got the chance because someone in his graduating class booed the "goddamn" colonel who gave the graduation speech.[4] Still, he earned the Air Medal and Distinguished Flying Cross. He loved aviation and continued flying throughout his life. He'd go on to ensure that Alaska, which depended on planes to connect the more than 220 villages, cities, and towns in what is still a mostly roadless state, had airstrips and runway lights and the latest aviation technology. After the war, Stevens earned a political science degree from UCLA and a law degree from Harvard law school. Then he moved to Washington, D.C., to work for a law firm, where he was assigned as legal counsel to Alaska's only coal mine, which at the time was trying to land a supply contract with the military.[5] He volunteered to work for Dwight D. Eisenhower's presidential campaign. And when Ike won in 1952, the first Republican to occupy the White House in twenty years since Herbert Hoover, Ted Stevens hoped he would land a job in the U.S. Department of Interior. But the job fell through. His legal work for the Alaska coal mine company, however, presented a new direction for the young lawyer. Mine owner Emil Usibelli's attorney hired Stevens into his Fairbanks firm.[6] A newlywed, Stevens took it, later saying that he and his wife, Ann, were "two kids with no money"—he needed a job and Alaska was an adventure. It was also a place to leave a mark, which he didn't waste any time doing.[7]

In 1953 Stevens borrowed $600, and he and Ann headed up the bumpy Alaska Highway in their overloaded Buick. Even though he would make his way back to Washington, where he would eventually become third in line to the presidency, he never left Alaska. Within six months of arriving in Alaska, he was appointed as U.S. Attorney in Fairbanks, much to the dismay of the legal community, which viewed him as a carpetbagger. A diminutive man, Stevens crushed crime throughout the town. Legend had it that he went with the Fairbanks police on gambling and prostitution busts, crashing down doors, armed with a revolver. He had a ferocious temper and soon had a mission: to help Alaskans realize statehood. Just weeks after the constitutional convention, a friend of his helped him land a job where he had hoped to work before coming to Alaska—the U.S. Department of Interior, an influential agency that oversaw much of the natural resource development of the nation. As the agency's legislative counsel, he worked under newly appointed Interior secretary Fred Seaton.

Both men shared a dream of seeing Alaska become a state, and Stevens was given free rein to lobby for Alaska's goal at the federal level, earning the moniker "Mr. Alaska." Part of that effort involved lobbying congressmen and senators, even though there were rules against his doing so as an employee of the Interior Department. Stevens and his staff studied the lawmakers and created a punch card for each, listing, as Stevens recalled, whether "they were Rotarians or Kiwanians or Catholics or

Baptists, and veterans or loggers—the whole thing." Then they tracked down Alaskans with the same religious affiliations or interests and brought them to Washington to talk to the lawmakers. They also planted editorials in newspapers to turn up "the heat" on those senators who were on the fence.[8]

Party identification in Alaska had little, if anything, to do with national affairs. While the Vietnam War waged, while students protested, while the civil rights movement marched, while cities burned, Alaska was mostly interested in what was going on within its own borders. And in Alaska by the early 1960s the glow of statehood had started to dim and the real business of acting like a state was at hand. Republicans charged that the Democrats, who were in power in Alaska, were holding back development. Alaska still only had one major highway, and the state relied on the federal government for its bread and butter. Democratic leaders in the state legislature spent their time fighting over power. In the majority for so long, they had become complacent. But that was nothing compared to what was going on with the state's U.S. senators, former territorial governor Ernest Gruening and former territorial representative Bob Bartlett. Once the best of friends, they began to grow distant by the 1960s.[9]

Gruening, appointed by President Franklin Roosevelt as Alaska's territorial governor in 1939, came to the state with lofty goals befitting someone with a lofty background. Born in New York City to a noted physician, Gruening was raised in the city and went to private schools before earning a medical degree from Harvard University. Instead of practicing medicine, though, he went into journalism—which, unlike medicine, he had a passion for—and eventually rose to editor of *The Nation,* where he enlisted such writers as H. L. Mencken, Sherwood Anderson, and Theodore Dreiser.

He went on to edit the *New York Post* and write a widely acclaimed book, *Mexico and Its Heritage,* which landed him a role in fashioning the New Deal policy on Latin America. When his father died, he came into a modest fortune. Gruening was well traveled and spoke fluent French, German, and Spanish.[10] He knew how to wear a suit and tie. He rode horses and played tennis and read poetry. This was the man President Roosevelt sent north to endear himself to Alaskans, to a state full, as one early pioneer described it, of "miners, sourdoughs, cheechacos [sic], gamblers, Indians, Negroes, Japanese, dogs, prostitutes, music, drinking!"[11]

Strangely enough, Gruening did win over Alaskans. He grew to love the state, and like so many before and later, he gave everything to it. He wasn't a warm man but he became respected. He did so with the help of the affable, nearsighted Bob Bartlett. Bartlett was from Fairbanks—the quintessential Alaska town. And Bartlett, the gold miner turned journalist turned secretary of Alaska (a position that paid well but carried few responsibilities), was quintessentially Alaskan and taught the staid, erudite Gruening how to talk to Alaskans. Working in Juneau at the time Gruening arrived, Bartlett jumped in when Gruening asked him if he wanted a bigger hand in shaping the territory.[12]

Their relationship grew into something like father and son while Gruening was territorial governor and Bartlett was his second. But when Bartlett left to be Alaska's territorial delegate to Congress, he realized that he didn't need Gruening anymore. By the 1960s, when both were U.S. senators from Alaska, they were pretty much done with each other. Bartlett felt Gruening was condescending toward him, treated him like a minor, took credit for the hard negotiating that Bartlett himself had done and for his skills at getting media attention. Bartlett didn't much like Gruening's arrogance. "His Honor," he began to refer to Gruening in letters to friends. "His Worship."[13] That Gruening was Harvard educated, had a way with words, could deliver a speech in both French and German, held his head in a certain way when he spoke, had a sense of superiority, and all the rest began to drive Bartlett crazy.

He also began to resent Gruening's vigor. Even though seventeen years Bartlett's senior, Gruening was in excellent shape and liked to show off by jumping into the Arctic Ocean when visiting Barrow, say, while the cameras clicked away. Bartlett, on the other hand, was smoking himself to death, and it showed. His hair was going gray. His eyes had hollowed. He had suffered heart attacks, had diabetes, and was in constant pain. He tried to hide his health problems, but people began to hear about his frequent trips to the hospital. All anyone had to do was to look at him to know that he was sick. It might not be fair to say that Alaska Republicans were rubbing their hands in glee—they liked Bartlett—but they desperately wanted either his or Gruening's Senate seat, and they began to prepare for it. Ted Stevens led the way.

Ted Stevens had long aspired to be a U.S. senator. Not because he wanted to change the world. He wasn't an idealist. He didn't have much to say about international affairs, about the war in Vietnam or about the cold war with the Soviet Union, or even about those young people with flowers in their hair. But he did desperately care about developing Alaska. He also cared about politics. He wasn't in it for the prestige. He was in it for the game, the fight, and he saw in Alaska a place where he could play it well.

After his stint in the Interior Department, he moved to Anchorage and set up a law firm, and then ran hard against Gruening in 1962. He played dirty against Gruening, saying in a speech that Gruening might not "live through" his term and accusing him of using his office for monetary gain.[14] He also called him, ironically enough, "a cantankerous old man." Stevens said that Gruening's "appetite for personal publicity" had "omitted his own colleague, Alaska's senior Senator Bob Bartlett."[15] It was all true, but the public felt safer with Gruening than with the relatively unknown Stevens. Still, Stevens collected 41 percent of the vote, proving that Gruening was vulnerable. Running as a Republican moderate in 1964, Stevens then won a seat as a state representative. Stevens, a member of Alaska's delegation to the Republican National Convention, urged the party to distance itself from the kind of anti–federal government, pro–state's rights "extremism" represented by Barry Goldwater. Alaska needed the federal government's largess, Stevens argued. The more conservative Republicans in the state deplored the move. Still, when Republicans roared into the Alaska House in Juneau in 1966, Stevens was elected House majority leader by his fellow Republicans.[16]

Stevens ran again for Gruening's seat in 1968 but lost in the primary to well funded Elmer Rasmuson, owner of Alaska's largest bank. It was a bitter race that left Stevens devastated, according to friend and law partner Jack Roderick. "He was so low. I had never seen him so low," Roderick recalled. "He just couldn't be consoled. He thought his career in politics was over. He was even talking about opening up an electronic shop. I said, 'Ted, what do you know about electronics?' He just stared out the window. That's when I knew that he would never be a good business man. That his life was in politics.'"

Stevens did play the part of a good Republican, though, and campaigned for Rasmuson. It didn't help. The handsome, energetic Mike Gravel had toppled eighty-one-year-old Gruening in the Democratic primary and was now roaming through Alaska's bush. (Yes, the same Gravel who ran for the 2008 presidential nomination when he was in his late seventies. The one who ran those quixotic, avant-garde campaign ads, staring into a camera intensely for nearly two minutes before turning around, tossing a rock in a nearby body of water, and walking off camera. Another ad called "Fired" showed him starting a fire. Both of them turned into YouTube sensations. Gravel said that before McCain picked Palin, he was the most famous Alaskan. And perhaps that's true.) Then in his thirties, Gravel looked like a movie star and played the part well in his last campaign commercial, a twenty-minute biopic of the kind Alaskans hadn't seen before. And it worked. With a little help from Bartlett, Gravel beat Rasmuson.

On December 11, 1968, before undergoing surgery, Bob Bartlett sent a memo to his staff saying that if he died on the operating table, "I have a strong feeling, although no definite knowledge, that the governor of Alaska would not appoint a successor of my political faith," as recounted by Alaska writer and historian Donald Craig Mitchell.[17] Bartlett died later that day. His obituary in the *Anchorage Daily Times* read: "The people of this state who loved him are known for their individualism, divisiveness, sectionalism, arrogance, and clannishness . . . On 10 different occasions the stubborn, unmanageable, belligerent, and politically erratic populace of Alaska handed him the crown with election returns as much as 81 percent in his favor."[18]

These would be big shoes to fill. Ted Stevens thought he would be the one to fill them. The decision was in the hands of Governor Wally Hickel, a Republican who liked to say that he came to the territory after

World War II with thirty-seven cents in his pocket. Hickel was a self-made businessman and politician from blue-collar roots who was dyslexic and didn't read well. After an earthquake destroyed much of Anchorage in 1964, Hickel led the charge to rebuild the city. He began construction on the Hotel Captain Cook, the most upscale of Alaskan hotels at the time and, some would say, today as well. Alaskans adored their governor because he was one of them. Energetic, charismatic, and ambitious, his eyes set on the future, dedicated to growing Alaska in a big way. Through the decades, there wasn't a problem anywhere for which he couldn't find an Alaska-size solution. A drought in California? Alaska's got lots of water. Let's build a giant hose to the Lower 48. No way to get to Russia from the United States? Let's build a tunnel across the fifty-three-mile-wide Bering Strait. As governor in the 1960s, Hickel ordered, without public hearings or official permits, an ice road built from Fairbanks to the North Slope oil fields, in order, he said, to open up Prudhoe Bay to oil exploration. "I drove (the tractor) the first six or seven miles myself," Hickel bragged. "I got off and I told Jim, I said, 'Don't you shut this thing off until you get to Prudhoe Bay?'"[19] Jim and the gang didn't. They bulldozed through the sensitive tundra, right through the permafrost, for hundreds of miles to Prudhoe Bay. Then summer came, and the Hickel highway turned into a ditch. Then it began to freeze again, and as land that's been damaged in Alaska tends to do, it rebelled—heaving and buckling as frost formed, making the road unusable. The scar from that highway remains visible to this day, but until he died, Hickel claimed that the road was worth it. "That road changed Alaska," he later said. "It opened up the minds, the hearts and hopes of Alaska."[20]

In late 1968 a young, energetic Wally Hickel was about to leap into national politics. President Richard Nixon had appointed Hickel secretary of the Interior. Before heading to Washington, D.C., though, Hickel had to choose a replacement for Bartlett. The law had read that in the case of a death of a senator, the governor, who was in charge of naming a replacement, had to choose from the same party as the outgoing senator. But when the Republicans, led largely by Stevens, swept the state legislature in 1966, they got to work changing the law of succession. They knew that either Gruening or Bartlett would be gone sooner or later. And the Republicans were going to make sure that at least one Senate seat belonged to them. In 1967 Stevens, then the majority leader of the Alaska House, along with his fellow Republicans in the Alaska legislature, rammed through a bill that called for the governor to appoint either a Republican or Democrat to the U.S. Senate should a seat become vacant.[21]

Hickel had a bench of Republicans to choose from during the last three weeks of 1968, but it was Stevens who stuck out, the scrappy state legislator and former Interior Department lawyer. The one who knew about politics. As Hickel recalled in a 2008 interview, "I wanted a young guy who could be back in Washington for the next 20 or 30 years so we could gain some seniority to get things done up here. And that's what he did for us."

Less than a year after Ted Stevens joined the Senate, three big oil companies—Atlantic Richfield, British Petroleum, and Humble Oil (Exxon)—teamed up to order $100 million worth of four-foot diameter steel pipe from Japan because no American steel companies could make the kind of pipe in mass quantity needed to build the Alaska oil pipeline. They needed to get the oil from the North Slope oil fields in the Arctic to an ice-free seaport in southern Alaska, where oil tanker ships would transport their loads to refineries on the West Coast and beyond. From sea level at Prudhoe Bay, the 800-mile-long oil pipeline would climb 4,700 feet to cross the formidable Alaska Brooks mountain range. Then it would cross thirty-four major rivers and streams and climb through more mountains, before descending quickly to the southern Alaska harbor town of Valdez, nestled on the shores of Prince William Sound, where the tankers awaited. The project would end up costing more than $8 billion—about $30 billion today. Undertaking what was the most expensive private project in U.S. history threw up challenges even before the pipe segments arrived in Alaska.

One problem rose above all: the pipeline would run across lands claimed by Alaska Natives. In the late 1960s, about 17 percent of residents were Alaska Native, including Inupiat, Yupik, Athabaskan, and Aleut. Most lived in villages lacking roads to the outside world, not to

mention electricity and running water. A developing country in the country of Alaska, villages sprinkled across the hinterland. The bush represented
then, as today, a special corner of America—cultures rooted in hunting
and fishing that make visitors feel as if they are stepping back in time.
The story of conquest in Alaska, which began with the Russians in the
late 1700s, is not much different from what transpired in the Lower 48.
Disease and epidemics paved the way for missionaries, teachers, government officials, and resource developers, who in turn left their own scars on
Native cultures—ordering Alaska's indigenous people to stop dancing like
"devils," slapping their hands for speaking their languages, devastating
the populations of whales, sea otters, and other animals that the people depended on. Still, in the mid-twentieth century Alaska Natives continued
to live on large swaths of their ancestral lands that were as much a part of
their identity as their culture and livelihood. Ted Stevens respected this
throughout his life, playing a pivotal role in trying to preserve a way of life
that was in danger of slipping away.

Although Alaska was granted more than 100 million acres of federal
land when it became a state in 1959, Native people had never reached a
settlement with the federal government on who really owned the land
they lived on. Now, a decade late, the state had selected a chunk of its 100
million acres, oil had been discovered, and a big pipeline was about to
slice through the entire state—and it would pass through the ancestral
lands of many First Alaskans.

The Native lands claim was not new to Ted Stevens. As a federal attorney in Fairbanks, he had traveled throughout Alaska's rural communities. Later, when he went to the Interior Department, he began
advocating for a land settlement. Stevens had seen the abject poverty
across Alaska. No lights, no toilets, no running water. No way to get in
and out of the villages. He fell in love with Alaska Native culture, but he
also saw the Native land settlement as a pragmatic issue that needed to be
solved. Also, Stevens knew that if he could leave his mark on a land
claims settlement liked by Alaska Natives, he would gain a foothold in
the rural part of the state, which often voted Democrat.[22]

The issue was thorny and jaded by the politics of the day. Some white
Alaskans (especially Stevens's fellow Republicans), motivated by greed

and racism, feared a generous land settlement. But Stevens believed that if Alaska Natives were granted land for their use, there would be that much less land in the hands of the federal government. Resentment of federal bureaucracy was a throwback to the issues that drove the territory to statehood. Stevens would make a career out of ridiculing the federal government and those from Outside for not understanding the "unique challenges" of developing and running a state in the north. As for the specific land claims settlement, Stevens and others envisioned something more than a federal reservation system for Alaska Natives. Corporations owned by Alaska Native people themselves should be given the land and a cash settlement they could use to launch new companies, developments, and investments. In time, Stevens predicted, these new corporations would develop their land and natural resources and bring yet more development to Alaska. This kept the land out of federal hands and would give Native people the opportunity to become self-sustaining—not wards of the Bureau of Indian Affairs, as had happened with some Indian reservations in the Lower 48.[23]

Stevens was instrumental in pushing for passage of the Alaska Native Claims Settlement Act, along with the oil companies, which wanted a speedy end to what could have delayed the pipeline construction even more. In December 1971, President Richard Nixon signed it into law, creating the largest land claims settlement in U.S. history. Along with 44 million acres, the settlement act provided nearly $1 billion to establish corporations owned by the various tribes and twelve geographically defined Native regions of Alaska—a social experiment that is still playing out today. With the passage of land claims legislation, environmental suits remained the final barrier to construction. The Wilderness Society, the Environmental Defense Fund, and others opposed the pipeline slicing through one of the last great wildernesses in America, arguing that there hadn't been a thorough environmental review of the project. Stevens fought for a bill to classify the project a national security priority—not a hard sell in the politically charged atmosphere caused by the Arab oil embargo of 1973—and thus render moot suits filed as delaying tactics. And finally, in one of history's rare U.S. senatorial deadlocks, he was instrumental in persuading Vice President Spiro Agnew, presiding as president of the Senate, to break a tie vote, thus authorizing pipeline construction to proceed. He did all of this, and so much more, with grit and determination. In his early years as a senator, he twisted arms and screamed and threatened. In this way his reputation was made, and his fate in Alaska was sealed. His wife Ann, by all accounts an extraordinarily nice, even-tempered woman, made him read self-help books to try to control his temper. They worked, to some degree.[24]

There wasn't an Alaskan who wasn't touched by the pipeline boom in some way. What had been a peaceful, quiet state dotted with mountains, glaciers, and vast expanses of tundra inhabited by military men, free-spirited businessmen, Alaska Natives, long-haired cabin dwellers, everyone searching for that last little bit of freedom, turned into an oil-fueled cash machine. Newcomers flooded the state hoping to make big bucks building the pipeline. They came from Oklahoma and Texas and brought with them their southern drawls and barbecues. They came from California seeking adventure. They brought their hard, East Coast edge to Alaska, and their Midwestern work ethic. Heeding advertisements and articles promising more than a thousand dollars a week for unskilled workers, and much more than that for those who knew how to use a blowtorch or a hammer, they arrived in trucks and vans and station wagons driven up the Alaska Highway. Some drove big Winnebagos filled with bigger dreams.

While a little radio station in Nome informed listeners about a successful whale hunt or a blizzard on the horizon, the radios on the Alaska Highway blared "Like a Rhinestone Cowboy" and invited listeners to do the hustle. They sang along with The Captain and Tennille; Earth, Wind, and Fire; and the Eagles. They saw eagles—birds of prey that had been all but wiped out in the Lower 48—soaring in the skies. They saw moose and caribou and bears, and miles and miles of untouched land. Tires blew along the bumpy, dusty highway. Radiators steamed. Windshields shattered. Shocks were trashed. But still they came. In the rest of the country, the news was that Saigon was surrendering. One war was over and another was beginning. Protests and pot were on the way out. Disco and cocaine were coming in. Watergate conspirators John Mitchell, H. R.

Haldeman, and John Ehrlichman were hauled into court to end the long Watergate saga. They were found guilty and sentenced to prison. Unemployment exceeded nearly 8 percent. The median U.S. household income was $11,800. Alaska was hiring and paying bundles. It was a "black gold" rush. Young American men headed off to the Last Frontier to make more money than they ever imagined.

Eight oil companies formed a consortium to tackle the enormous construction project. Taking its name from the Aleutian word for Alaska, which means "the great land," the Alyeska Pipeline Service Company began building segments of the pipeline simultaneously all along the route, with the help of more than 28,000 workers. At the time construction was proposed, Alaska had around 300,000 people; there were more people living in Toledo, Ohio. By the end of the 1970s the population had grown to 400,000.

Some of these newcomers plopped down in Anchorage, which was not on the pipeline route but was where the oil company executives put up shop. They donned suits and ties and worked in oil company offices. Some bought large swatches of real estate and opened up bars and strip clubs for the pipeline workers on break. Oil money helped finance Alaska's first malls and spawned whole neighborhoods of cheap tract housing almost overnight. Some people bought cabins on spruce-filled lots with views of mountains and glaciers. Some boomers went to the Matanuska Valley, about forty-five minutes north of Anchorage, and settled in a dot of a town called Wasilla along the newly built George Parks Highway, which continued north for a few hundred miles to Fairbanks, construction central.

In summer, workers struggled against clouds of ravenous mosquitoes, beneath a sun that stayed a big ball in the sky even at midnight. In the winter, in the dim, eerie light of noon, there were whiteouts, frostbitten toes, and temperatures so cold that engines had to run twenty-four hours a day to keep from freezing. Across the wilderness were thirty-one work camps, each housing from 200 to more than 3,000.[25] The beige trailers clustered together to form compounds. Some had movie theaters, and small transmitters set up in each camp allowed the workers to watch TV in the privacy of their rooms. One of the fanciest facilities was BP's at

Prudhoe Bay, a permanent camp for workers on the oil field. It had a state-of-the-art gym, as well as solarium with two live birch trees imported at a price of $40,000—the only trees for miles and miles. Muzak floated through the corridors. The large living areas were dressed in sleek black leather and chrome. The BP Hilton, as it was called, even had a heated pool. From the outside, it looked like a space station or an Antarctic research outpost.[26] Inside the BP Hilton, and other camps dotting the tundra, workers played cards, sneaked tokes, fought with each other, and feasted like kings on gourmet dishes prepared by skilled chefs. And then they went back to work—seven days a week, twelve or more hours a day.

Construction unions, headed by Teamster Union leader Jesse Carr, took control of most of the pipeline workers and, for a while, pretty much the whole state. Carr made sure the workers got nice digs and good food while they welded the sections of steel pipe, dug through the permafrost, drove the trucks from one camp to the next, mopped the makeshift floors and scrubbed the outhouses, charted courses and cracked eggs, and always at the end of a rotation raked in the cash. Some became obese and lazy while Carr stashed the cash in trust accounts and bought himself fancy cars and property in California. He and his union held powerful sway over state politicians. Bored, overworked, and overpaid, the workers stuffed their pockets full of dough and went looking for fun when they left the camps on break. Invariably, they descended on Alaska's cities. Fairbanks took the brunt of it. Cars jammed the roads. Prostitutes strutted among them in downtown Fairbanks, trying to solicit business. Cocaine was in high demand. The phone system ran out of numbers. Store shelves were perpetually empty. Housing was nearly impossible to find, and the shelters were overflowing with people sleeping on the floor.[27]

As far back as early 1900s, prostitution in Alaska, particularly in Fairbanks, was well tolerated. Prostitutes were often known to the community by their first and last names. But the pipeline boom was something new. Pimps wearing broad-brimmed leather hats spent their days in Fairbanks cafés, keeping close eyes on their girls, "up from Seattle and San Francisco, who turn tricks for $100."[28] Eskimo girls began to walk the streets.

In 1975 the rate for murder, rape, and robbery in Fairbanks jumped 12 percent in the first quarter of the year alone. Fairbanks cops earned on average $1,620 a month. Security on the pipeline paid about $1,000 a week.[29] All over the state people abandoned their jobs to join pipeline and drilling crews. Carpenters, salesmen, clerks, reporters, mechanics, and bus drivers left their communities, and many of those towns floundered in their absence. All of it—the crime, the greed, the living for the moment, not to mention the fact that Texas barbecue began to be served at potlucks all over the state—had turned Alaskans against each other. Who are we? they wondered. Wasn't there a dream about how this state was going to be developed? Wasn't that dream alive just a few short years ago?

Jump now to late July 1977. There's a party in Valdez, the terminus of the new trans-Alaska oil pipeline. This town had been a sedate place known for its cascading waterfalls, jagged peaks, deep winter snows, silver salmon, and commercial fishermen. The pipeline boom had overrun Valdez, propelling its population from 1,000 to 10,000. And now it was about to begin another new chapter. At its deepwater port, oil tankers were now ready to begin transporting the North Slope's crude south through Prince William Sound, out into the Gulf of Alaska, and on to refineries thousands of miles away. And so this party in the summer of '77 was to welcome the first barrels of oil oozing their way down the 800-mile pipeline.

It was a beautiful day, and women lined up on stages wore tight T-shirts sprayed with cooking oil to commemorate the oil's arrival and Alaska's new future.[30] Alyeska Pipeline Service, the consortium that built the pipeline, gave away free beer, and when it ran out, Valdez bars pitched in with more. People danced in the streets, vomited on the streets, and promised to keep in touch, now that the construction was done. Many of them were going to pack up and go home, go back to the United States. Many planned to leave this foreign land with its numbing winters, its never-setting sun, its lonely stretches of forsaken land—a place that the smarter people knew was going to live high when oil prices were high and a lot of it was rushing down the pipeline. Everyone knew that the oil was going to run out someday. It had to. But that was tomorrow.

In 1978, a year after the pipeline pumped its first barrel of oil, Ted Stevens and his wife Ann were returning to Anchorage when a crosswind slammed their plane into the runway. She died that day. Stevens, who was injured in the crash, was one of only two survivors. Rumor has it that when he awoke in the hospital room, his first words were, "Am I still senator?"[31] The day after the crash, he was dictating letters from his hospital bed. He told his assistant then that the brain contained several "boxes" and that some information that's too painful to process gets shoved into one of those boxes until we are ready to deal with it.[32] He might not have dealt with it then, but over the years, friends say he grew despondent and bitter over Ann's death. But still he fought from his D.C. perch, watching as Alaska oil production peaked at 2.1 million barrels a day, providing the nation with 20 percent of its domestic oil production, and Alaska with more than 85 percent of its state income. He watched as prices tumbled and production began to decline. Slowly at first, then rapidly. He did all he could to prop up his beloved state by steering staggering amounts of federal money to Alaska, and it worked for a while. But it couldn't last forever, and he knew it.

Into the new millennium, the Alaska Republican Party, some state lawmakers and bureaucrats, and Alaska's congressional delegation—the latter so powerful it became known as the "Alaska mafia" in certain Beltway circles—overzealously planned for another boom with another pipeline, this one carrying natural gas from the Arctic oil fields. It was all going to work out. Alaska's future would be secured for at least another couple of decades, they told Alaskans. The state's leaders were going to make sure of that. Then they got sloppy, and Sarah Palin came along.

CHAPTER 3

Alaska, the Land of Oil and Money

Juneau is arguably the most picturesque of all of the nation's state capitals, and the only one not connected by road to civilization. It's a little Alaska, a little Seattle, a little Switzerland, all in one. You can take a ferry to Juneau or you can fly. If you choose the latter, it's best to fly to Juneau at night, so that you don't have to see the mountains looming in front of the plane. The city is squeezed in along a narrow passage between the Coast Range and Douglas Island. Waterfalls cascade across the steep, forested flanks of the surrounding slopes, which serve as sentries or prison walls, depending on the time of year. In the summer, the sun shines on the tourists, on the quaint San Francisco–inspired houses terraced into the mountains, on the blue glaciers, on the eagles soaring, on the whales breaching, on the salmon spawning, on those happy people roaming the streets and wading along the shore in their rubber boots. Indeed, in the summer when the sun is shining, you'd be hard-pressed to find a happier, more beautiful town than Juneau, Alaska's Shangri-la.

But that's in the summer. In winter the terrain and the darkness close in. The mountains suck in all the air. The sky turns a metallic gray and spits ice. The steep sidewalks glaze over and are impossible to walk on. The one main road in the town demands studded tires, and even if you can drive, you can't go anywhere. Driving to the edge of the city and back again only reminds you that there's no way out. Booze helps. It also helps that getting to one of the many Juneau bars is easy from Alaska's Capitol building. In the 1970s and 1980s, one of the favorites was the Red Dog Saloon. Alaskans have always yearned some for the cowboy culture, with the horses and the hats and the big open sky. Alaska has only the big open sky, in parts of the state, on certain days. But bars will always try to cater to a fantasy. The Red Dog Saloon put in swinging doors, covered the floor in sawdust, hung rifles and antlers on the walls, and set up a piano with honky-tonk pouring out of it, thanks to the keyboarding skills of an Alaska Native.[1] And of course the bar had bourbon that was served to politicians by the barrel far from the eyes of constituents. Much of Alaska's policy was shaped in bars like the Red Dog Saloon, where politicians also decided how to spend the money. All that money.

Perched up the hill from the bars and not far from the Capitol is the governor's mansion. From 1974 amid the pipeline boom and to 1982, when oil prices soared beyond anybody's imagination, a man resembling Moses watched from the hill as a crude mix of oil and politics unfolded below. He was Jay Hammond, a charismatic politician who called himself a Republican, because that's what tough guys out of the military were back in the day. But he was an Eisenhower conservative—and at heart a conservationist. Early on he was an advocate for trying to sustain a viable fishing industry in Alaska. At that time, the pre–drill baby drill time, that was okay in most circles. It was even respected, except among ardent pro-business Republicans, who never did like Hammond. They disliked his distrust of big industry, including the oil companies.

Hammond, who'd served as a pilot with the Marine Black Sheep squadron (which inspired the *Baa Baa Black Sheep* television show in the 1970s) in the South Pacific during World War II, had bought an airplane and flew into the country in the 1950s. He got a job with the federal government to shoot wolves from airplanes. Wolves at the time were considered varmints in Alaska, and the government paid guys like Hammond and other pilot-hunters to eradicate them. Hammond's wolf hunting didn't last long. He fell in love with Alaska and grew soft on the wolves. He married an Alaska Native woman and settled into a cabin along the shores of Lake Clark, an idyllic body of water nestled in the Aleutian Mountains. He got involved in local politics and ran for state office, reluctantly. On his way to winning the governor's seat in 1974, he called himself the "bush rat governor." It stuck.

In his gubernatorial reelection bid in 1978, Hammond faced a Republican challenger who touted himself as a big idea man set on developing Alaska. Wally Hickel, the Republican governor who in 1968 appointed Ted Stevens to the U.S. Senate and who cut a path through the tundra to Prudhoe Bay, called his opponent "zero growth Hammond." Two visions for Alaska stood in opposition to each other, represented by two men commensurate with the energy to fit this huge state: the two faces of Republican politics in the 1970s.

Hickel was known for saying things like, "You can't just let nature run wild," and "A tree looking at a tree really doesn't do anything," and "They used to roll out the red carpet for the doers. Now they roll out the criticism, the restrictions, the bad press. Developer has become a dirty word." Hickel was an enigma in many ways. On the one hand, he understood that the north must be settled, and he wanted it done with roads and bridges and dams and railroads. He wanted big projects and he wanted those big projects yesterday. But he wasn't an industry stooge. Far from it. President Nixon appointed him Interior secretary, and Hickel then ordered a halt to all offshore drilling following the 1969 Santa Barbara oil spill, which was the largest offshore platform spill in U.S. waters until the 2010 Deepwater Horizon spill in the Gulf of Mexico. To say that he shut it down is a tame way to describe it. What he is reputed to have told oil executives when he arrived in California after a good look at the situation was "Shut these fucking rigs down."[2] He also signed an order adding all eight species of great whales to the endangered species list. All of this made him a darling of the fledgling national environmental movement. To add to it, he became a hero to the peaceniks when Nixon fired him over his vocal opposition to expanding the Vietnam War into Cambodia.

Jay Hammond also had a way with words, which he expressed often in rhyme. "Hammondese," some called it. He said things like "Heaven help us should we not remain aware that 'environment' is not an obscene, four-letter word. It has eleven letters, just as does the word 'development'"; and "Two types of people are attracted to Alaska: one sees new ground to plow up, the other to preserve the wilderness." A rough-and-tumble fisherman and hunting guide with a gleam in his eye, Hammond carried a salt of the earth bravado at a time when greed and living for today reigned. Handsome, bearded, and grizzled, he often dressed in a flannel and a beret. He was admired by Sarah Palin's teacher father, Chuck Heath. The bush rat governor was the only politician Heath admitted to following before his daughter got involved in politics. Mostly, Heath said, "because he hunted and fished."

In the 1970s, a progressive streak still cut through Alaska, although it was losing ground to oil industry conservatives. Hammond straddled the political divide, showing concern for the overnight development sweeping the frontier and the threat it posed to the environment and cities, while also recognizing that oil was finite. Flush with cash, he championed looking for new economies to bridge the day the oil fields went into decline. People likened him to a big bear. The state had an idea of what kind of politician it should have, and Hammond fit the bill, though barely for a second term.

In 1978, a year after oil began flowing through the trans-Alaska oil pipeline, Hammond squeaked out a bitter GOP primary victory against Hickel, winning by only ninety-eight votes. He went on to win the general election. If Hammond learned anything, it was that time was short and he needed to leave a legacy. He also needed an idea, and so he pointed the way to something very different. What he came up with was new in form, but very much in keeping with Alaska's constitutional ideals of resources belonging to the people and collective ownership.

Alaska was no stranger to big dreams and big projects, even before Big Oil arrived, and was an easy target for those in the Lower 48 who wanted to make a quick buck or experiment on Alaska, or a little of both. Pro-business Alaskans, the crowd that would later dislike Hammond, advocated for projects like building a manmade harbor above the Arctic Circle, thirty miles from the Arctic village of Point Hope, one of the oldest Inupiat Eskimo communities in Alaska. In the late 1950s, they were delighted when the U.S. Atomic Energy Commission announced that it was planning to explode four thermonuclear bombs (with the destructive power of 160 Hiroshima bombs) to do so. It was viewed as a symbol of Alaska coming into its own. "We think the holding of a huge nuclear blast in Alaska would be a fitting overture to the new era which is opening for our state," wrote the *Fairbanks Daily News-Miner* in an editorial.[3] Then Alaska Natives and environmentalists got wind of the project. They said no and convinced the rest of Alaskans in their right minds to say no. Eventually the project was disbanded and the guys who had planned it packed up their briefcases and headed home. One of those involved, Edward Teller, the father of the hydrogen bomb, took with him an honorary degree from the University of Alaska.

The Rampart dam was another big idea. It would stop the flow of the majestic Yukon River in Rampart Canyon, about 100 miles from Fairbanks. Running 2,300 miles, the Yukon would be stopped with a concrete span 530 feet high and nearly a mile long. The dam would create an 11,000-square-mile manmade lake, a reservoir about the size of Lake Erie. More than a half dozen Native villages would disappear under several hundred feet of water, displacing more than 1,200 people. A massive amount of moose and bird habitat would be lost, and no one knew what it would do to the fabled Yukon salmon. The dam would produce electricity to supply up to 5 million households, even if there were fewer than 250,000 people in all of Alaska. Dreamers dreamed big in the north. Companies were ready to build the dam until opponents—among them future U.S. congressman Don Young—demanded a price tag on the project. The cost? More than $8 billion in today's dollars and three decades to build. The men with the plans for Rampart packed their suitcases and went back to their simpler lives in the Lower 48.

More big projects materialized in the wake of the North Slope oil discovery and amid the go-go decades of the 1970s and 1980s. In Anchorage, civic leaders were convinced their city, population 115,000, would double in size in the near future. Where was Anchorage going to house all these people? A call was put out for help. Ideas were needed, and a company out of Tulsa, Oklahoma, heeded the call with plans for an $800 million, climate-controlled suburb dubbed "Seward's Success."[4] A series of interconnected domed, heated malls leading to houses were envisioned. At more than 600,000 square feet, the dome city would initially have space for 5,000 people. It would be unlike anything in the world. No coats or boots or even cars would be needed. Ever. Seward's Success was to be built across the Cook Inlet from Anchorage. The problem? No bridges. But the company out of Tulsa had a solution for that too. First, build a high-speed aerial tramway of the kind you see at ski resorts, with each carriage capable of carrying 100 people. As more people moved to Seward's Success, a monorail was to be built. Anchorage boosters mooned over it. But it never advanced much beyond a promotional brochure. The population failed to double, and the company men went back to Tulsa, where malls needed to be built.

Failed or not, covered cities stayed on the minds of Alaskans. One man—Mike Gravel, Ted Stevens's counterpart in the U.S. Senate—got an idea. Denali National Park and Preserve, a cold, dark place with few winter tourists, could use a facelift. Would tourists come if they could be warm? Gravel's vision, eventually called "Denali City," was four square miles of Teflon dome, beneath which would be built a cozy universe of hotels, condos, theaters, tennis courts, and ice rinks.[5] He lobbied the state legislature for $500,000 to conduct studies of the project, promising later federal funds. The studies took him and his self-appointed design firm to London, San Francisco, Stuttgart, and Hawaii.[6] The project was actually taken seriously by some and might have stood a chance if Gravel had won reelection in 1980.

Given the size of past Alaska dreams, and given that Alaska was rich beyond its wildest dreams, Jay Hammond's ideas seemed practical: build businesses that sustain themselves and last through the ups and downs of oil prices. One of the big ideas at the time was to establish a vibrant dairy and barley business in the subarctic, supplying residents with fresh beef and dairy produced in Alaska. A report, issued at Hammond's request by University of Alaska agricultural professors, predicted the state could create a farming industry like that of the Midwest. Eventually, the report said, there would be so much production that exports could possibly rival oil and gas in the state's economy. "It is in fact possible that Alaska will be the prime agricultural state in the not so distant future," Hammond pronounced.[7]

And so the state held a lottery to give away land for those who wanted to develop dairy farms, 14,000 acres deep in the heart of muddy, alder-packed, bear-infested moose country. Investors needed only about 25 percent collateral to qualify for up to $2.4 million in credit to build and run farms with fifty cows.[8] Nobody really checked on the collateral, and nobody checked at all as to whether or not the farmers had any actual experience in farming.[9]

Because the cows needed something to eat, the state started a lottery to sell off another 70,000 acres of the Interior, on which barley would be grown. The plan looked great on paper. Only a few legislators were skeptical. One of them was Vic Fischer, a delegate to the constitutional convention.[10] His concerns were brushed aside. He was, after all, a no-growth Democrat. Was a little dairy and grain operation too much to ask for? Lots of other states had government-sponsored farming initiatives and some of them did well. Some states even found that farming was so important to their economies they could enter the export business. If those other states could, why couldn't Alaska? Fresh barley from Alaska? It had a certain ring to it. Who could resist it? Wouldn't the Japanese love it? The Koreans? Amid the dreaming, though, nobody got around to asking them what they thought.

In the beginning it didn't matter. Land was sold cheap. Chainsaws roared. Trees were felled, grain was planted, and the state bought nearly a million dollars' worth of railroad grain cars, twenty of them painted bright blue and emblazoned with the words "Alaska Agriculture Serving Alaska and the World." Then it began building an $8.5 million grain terminal in Seward, a town named after the secretary of state who championed the purchase of Alaska from Russia, surrounded by mountains about a two-hour drive from Anchorage. Valdez, the town with the deep-water port and the terminus of the trans-Alaska oil pipeline, was envious. So it built an even bigger and better grain terminal that ended up costing the city upward of $30 million.[11]

As it turned out, Alaska cows require a different kind of handling than those in the Midwest. You have to keep them warm, and that costs a lot. The subarctic soil was too muddy for cows. The grain to feed them was another problem. Barley didn't really grow well in Alaska. There was the short growing season to start with. Then came a series of events out of the Old Testament—a drought, a grasshopper infestation, and finally bison stomping through the fields—stomping on Hammond's dream. It might not have mattered much anyway. The barley that did grow was puny. The dairy cows went hungry. There were already a few small dairy farmers in Palmer, a town near Anchorage, who sold their milk to a state-subsidized creamery, and they were struggling. Milk imported from the West Coast was cheaper than Alaska milk. When things got bad for the Matanuska Maid Dairy, it began to buy cream from Seattle to mix in with its own Alaska milk to lower the price at the store. Something had to be done. And so the state took over the creamery. Millions of dollars later, the state owned Matanuska Maid Dairy and a handful of emaciated, disease-ridden cows. Eventually all the farms failed. The federal government began paying the farmers in Alaska's Interior, primarily in the area around the scrappy outpost of Delta Junction, *not* to farm. The railroad grain cars sat idle and lonely. All told, the state invested more than $100 million in 1982 dollars in Alaska agriculture and, as of 2011, Alaska still imported about 95 percent of its food.[12]

Cows and barley weren't the only investments Alaska's leaders embarked on when the state was suddenly flush with oil tax revenue in the late 1970s and early 1980s. There were new schools. Roads. Community centers. A hydroelectric project that was scrapped after $350 million in studies. A $3 billion petrochemical plant in Valdez that never got built and ended up costing the state about $60 million.[13] A multimillion-dollar fund to provide grants and loans to companies that would "identify new products, markets and technologies for renewable resource industries."[14] More than $1.7 billion in energy projects, all pretty much failures. There was a scheme to turn fish scraps into protein. A fox farm and a dog-powered washing machine. A $14 million brewery. All failures. But it wasn't all Jay Hammond's doing. Many of the boondoggles were the result of an out-of-control state legislature with too much money to spend and no idea of saving for the future.

Wars and revolutions in the Middle East aren't good for the rest of the country's pocketbook. But for Alaska, such uprisings bulge state coffers with oil tax revenue. All of this was largely thanks to the Iranian Revolution, followed by the Iran-Iraq War, which propelled oil prices to record highs shortly after crude began flowing down the trans-Alaska pipeline. State revenue ballooned from $765 million in the late 1970s to more than $4 billion in the early 1980s. Lawmakers could do nearly anything they wanted with the money. Bringing home the bacon to your people—those who decided whether to reelect you—was good politics. But it wasn't all misspent. Even in the mid-1980s, Alaska was still underdeveloped, with large areas of the state lacking infrastructure: proper school facilities, roads, plumbing, libraries, community centers, and so on. Many lawmakers were trying their best to give their constituents the basics, some semblance of civilization in one of the most untamed corners of the country—a northern tabula rasa money pit. But oil is a finite resource. Some level-headed politicians who remembered this tried to encourage saving for the future—the day the oil wells ran dry.

Because the state was giving away so much to so many so fast and losing so badly, its citizens and legislators began to complain. Why should their hard-earned money go to funding these projects? Why, if the state was generating billions and billions of dollars in tax revenue from the sale of the people's oil, should they pay income tax? Governor Jay Hammond was against repealing the state income tax. Without it, he reasoned, a major restraint on government was lost—Alaskans wouldn't have skin in the game on how the state's money was spent. "Once repealed, we'll never get it back until we've raided all other revenue sources, and/or traumatically cut even crucial state programs."[15] But Hammond didn't have enough political clout to justify vetoing a bill that set out to abolish the income tax. And so in 1980 the Alaska legislature gave the people what they wanted—no more income taxes. For Hammond, it would be one of his major regrets, something he still talked about up until his death in 2005. As he predicted, the income tax never came back. And from then on, Alaska was the only state in the country without a state sales tax or income tax. One stroke of the pen and Alaska became almost totally dependent on oil tax revenue for its existence. From the early 1980s to today, Alaskans would, in a sense, become addicted to oil.

One other bold new idea was born amid the oil boom—a socialistic policy, some argue, that resulted in paying an annual dividend to every man, woman, and child who called themselves Alaskan. The Alaska Permanent Fund was another huge experiment under Governor Jay Hammond's watch in a state full of wild ideas and big experiments. In 1976 Hammond led the charge to get voter and legislative approval for a constitutional amendment to pump at least 25 percent, minus taxes, of oil royalties into an income-generating fund, a sort of rainy day account for when the oil ran out. The idea was to take some of that tax revenue when the oil was still flowing and preserve it for the future. The Alaska Permanent Fund would grow over time through investments in stocks, bonds, and real estate around the world. And by enlisting Alaskans to decide when and if the fund should be spent, residents would have a stake in the young state's future.

Hammond and lawmakers later took things up a notch—why not give Alaskans a dividend from the fund? Then they truly would be invested in protecting the state's piggy bank from the Alaska legislature's reckless spending sprees. Besides, what better way to endear oneself to average Alaskans than cutting them an annual check—a portion of which came from the state's biggest and most powerful industry? And so that is how that legendary tale of Alaska paying its residents to live in the forbidding fortyninth state came to be. In 1982, the first year of the Alaska Permanent Fund dividend program, every Alaskan, man, woman, and child, received a $1,000 dividend. The dividends fluctuated based on the markets and the economy, and as the years went by, many Alaskans came to depend on that annual check to pay for groceries and college tuition, snowmobiles and refrigerators, Hawaii getaways and plasma televisions. Like their state leaders, Alaskans had a hard time saving for the future, perhaps why the state often ranked among the highest in the country per capita for credit card debt. (During Sarah Palin's tenure as governor, the Permanent Fund swelled to $40.4 billion, generating the following year a $2,069 dividend to more than 600,000 Alaskans. Along with that they got a onetime, Palin-sponsored $1,200 payout to offset high energy costs.)

Jay Hammond didn't get all he wanted out of the Permanent Fund, but the program did become the envy of oil-producing nations. Some in Alaska lambasted Hammond's plan, calling it a socialistic giveaway, arguing the money would be better spent building Alaska's infrastructure. Former governor Wally Hickel, for one, said, "There would be no Permanent Fund without Prudhoe Bay. But with a Permanent Fund mentality, you would have no Prudhoe Bay." "The Permanent Fund," he added, "won't give you a permanent economy."[16] And Hammond responded to critics, "Socialism is government taking *from* a wealthy few to provide what government thinks is best for all. The Permanent Fund dividends do just the opposite. They take from money which, by constitutional mandate, belongs to *all* and allows each individual to determine how to spend some of his or her share. What could be more capitalistic?"[17]

From 1978 until oil prices crashed in 1986, Alaska spent more than $30 billion. In the 1980s and 1990s, it wasn't unusual to see a bumper sticker in Alaska that read, "God, please give us another boom. We promise not to piss this one away." But at least Alaska had the Permanent Fund.

Now Alaskans were not only free of state taxes but actually got paid to live in the Last Frontier. The oil companies watched nervously. How likely would it be that, when Alaskans needed more money for state government, they'd support dipping into their piggy bank when they were addicted to those annual dividends? Who would Alaskans turn to when oil prices inevitably dropped, tax revenues shrank, and the wells began to run dry? The oil industry knew that for the state to keep government afloat, Alaska leaders would always come back to the trough that fed them, inevitably looking to raise taxes to compensate for their incompetence and immaturity. All of this came at a time when Alaska was on its biggest spending spree yet.

The oil companies—Atlantic Richfield, British Petroleum, Exxon, and others—took note of the events unfolding in this Arctic oil province, just as they might when there is unrest in Libya or Nigeria or Venezuela. Alaska might seem peaceful in comparison to such places, but it does have a democratically elected legislature. And for the oil industry, sometimes the latter is more difficult to deal with than a populist dictator.

As the legislature decided how to spend the oil money, the issue of how much the state would tax the oil companies always loomed in the background. Money flowed from oil production into the Alaska treasury mainly in three ways: an oil income tax, royalties paid to the state as landowner, and a severance tax—sometimes called a production or profits tax—paid because an irreplaceable public resource, oil, was being "severed" from the ground permanently. Royalties and the severance tax were by far the big sources of money. Alaska first designed an oil tax policy before the Prudhoe Bay discovery, when Alaska was a relatively small oil player. After this elephant oil field became a household name, lawmakers were at a loss. These were citizen legislators: fisherman and lumberjacks, teachers and miners, carpenters and dog mushers—not a tax expert among them. Because there was no other model, because there was no other place quite like Alaska at the time—with its Arctic climate and its state-owned lands, its monstrous oil fields—the state brought in experts of all stripes to consult on revisions to the oil tax code. But when the legislators didn't like what they heard, or when the oil companies told certain lawmakers not to like what they heard, they would dismiss the experts as from Outside and then hire another round of experts. Much to the dismay of the oil companies, which wondered when the hikes would end, this dance yielded increases in oil taxes— which were low from the start because Alaska didn't have good advisers when it was a smaller oil province—in 1973 and 1975, before the oil even came down the pipeline. Then again in 1977 and 1978.[18] When would this civil unrest end, the oil companies wondered? Industry had bet tens of billions of dollars on the North Slope oil and the risky pipeline and marine terminal project with the hope of earning huge profits. Every new tax hike chipped away at their margins and cast more uncertainty on their investment.

But then, as now, each company knew how much it really cost to produce the oil and how much that profit margin was. What Alaskans did know was that industry didn't like pay to taxes, just as they themselves didn't like to pay taxes. More taxes, the companies argued, could mean less investment—fewer new wells, less exploration, and perhaps less production altogether. The industry had other places to spend its money besides Alaska, where the logistics, harsh environment, and cost of doing business, they argued, added up to slimmer margins. A long-term and favorable tax policy was one way to ensure the companies stuck around. Still, the firms were raking it in, and some state leaders every so often tested the waters by proposing to tweak the tax structure. How much tweaking industry would tolerate was the great unknown.

Descending on Juneau year after year were oil executives and lobbyists, offering presentations that puzzled even the best analysts in the world. They always said pretty much the same thing: "We're willing to pay our fair share, but no more." And they warned that if they got squeezed too hard, if the state got too greedy, they'd pull out from Alaska. There was one major problem with this. Because not all of the companies announced how much profit they were making in Alaska, or how much it cost to develop the oil or exactly how much it cost to transport the oil, lawmakers had no idea what constituted squeezing too hard. The state asked for the information. The oil companies refused to provide it, or the information they did offer was inadequate.

Part of the issue revolved around where the oil was produced. The companies were dealing with oil on state land in a place where the constitution dictated resources are owned by the people and must be developed in their interests. In contrast, private land owners are easier to deal with. You give them a number for some acreage. Perhaps they'll want to know what you paid the other guy for the other plot down the road, but they generally don't require an opening of the books. They say yes or they say no, and you walk away or you don't. Dictatorships, oligarchies, theocracies, even communist countries, can be easier to deal with than Alaska. Oil executives can wheel and deal with them, all behind closed doors. They grease palms and they make promises. But in Alaska, with those state lands, there was no closed door, and the companies argued they'd lose their competitive advantage if other companies knew how much they were making in Alaska. There was another reason for not being more transparent. If Alaskans knew how much they were actually making off their oil, taxes might have been much higher. As it was, they could deduct the costs for producing the oil from their tax bill. And because the companies producing most of the oil also had control of transporting, refining, and selling it, they could inflate the production costs and make it up down the line, as numerous lawsuits would later prove.

And why shouldn't they? Wasn't the state already collecting billions in tax revenue, a state that, by the early 1980s, had rescinded its personal income tax, paid its residents a dividend from a fund that had been seeded with oil money, and still had cash left over to go on wild spending sprees? Alaskans might own the crude in the ground, but it was the oil companies that were doing the hard work of getting it out and taking the risks. They warned Alaskans not to bite the hand that feeds them, and one good way to do that was, and still is, is to keep things vague. "Classified information," a string of them testifying in Juneau would say. "Competitive advantage" they would say. "Use your judgment," they would say. Over and over, they would say the same thing, in front of any number of hearings on oil and gas taxes in any given year in Juneau. Styles may differ: wide ties versus skinny ties, handlebar mustaches versus small patches, beehives versus shags. Cocaine might be the drug of choice, or booze, or exercise.

Outside, the sky might be spitting ice or the sun might be shining on Alaska's Shangri-la. Inside, in the state Capitol, legislators would be yawning and stretching, bleary eyed, tired of charts and graphs and numbers that they didn't understand. Some would be thinking of lunch or dinner, others of the millions of dollars that might come into the state, money that could be spent developing a self-sustaining economy, others of the millions the state might lose. Thinking Alaskans own the resource. Thinking Alaskans don't deserve the resource. Dreaming of hunting season. Dreaming of moose shoulder or whale blubber dipped in seal oil. Mentally climbing the next peak or wetting a line in a favorite fishing hole or crimson salmon flesh on the grill. Wishing that someone would just tell them what to do. How to vote. How to explain the vote. The right way to vote.

It didn't matter what was going on in the rest of the country, what was being fought and won or lost Outside. Alaska is its own country. Its war always took place in the Capitol. Always, the presentation concluded with some version of this, as it did in this hearing in 1968:

Oil Industry guy: "We know that costs are high in Alaska. Take a cost, figuring whatever taxes are involved, and as a result of your location from market and these high costs, anything additional put on as a burden, cannot help but reduce the activity somewhere in the state, so that it becomes, in my estimation, the judgment factor on your part."[19]

Chuck Logsdon tried to use his best judgment. He had earned a Ph.D. in agricultural economics from the University of Washington and was eager to return home and help the state grow. In 1979 he began working for the state's petroleum revenue division as a low-level economist. Ten months later, his boss killed his wife and then himself. At age 30, Logsdon found himself up against some of the world's most powerful companies. He barged in. "Fools rush in where angels fear to tread," is how he describes it now. He couldn't get exact numbers on oil company profits and production costs then, and by the time he retired twenty-five years later, he still couldn't get those figures. "They're tricky devils," he said of the oil companies, with a hint of admiration in his voice.[20]

In 1981, pro-industry lawmakers led a legislative coup that ensured anti-tax Republican control, which in short order gave the industry a $150 million tax break and changed the way the taxes were calculated. It was nice for industry to have a legislature predisposed to giving oil companies tax breaks. It was so nice, in fact, that the industry began to get increasingly active in politics. As long as Hammond and his ilk were around, industry couldn't count on Republicans for blind support and couldn't count on Democrats for anything. The industry also began to understand that the suits and ties, the charts and the graphs, and even the money given to politicians sometimes proved counterproductive. Alaskans, after all, have always been suspicious of Outsiders. What the oil companies needed was a real presence in Alaska, not just in the hallways of the Capitol but among the business community and politicians who supported industry. Somebody who had a stake in the state and lived there permanently.

Enter Bill Allen.

Bill Allen—gruff, foulmouthed, and calculating one minute. Chivalrous and vulnerable the next. Looking for a country, chasing a dream, chasing oil. A political powerhouse who later landed in federal prison. Armed with a grade school education, some welding skills, a dream of building something big, Allen shaped the state in profound ways. The founder of VECO Corporation, an oilfield services company based in Anchorage, Allen endeared himself to his oil baron customers. Some say Big Oil enlisted him to do their bidding to keep Alaska "open for business," to keep taxes low and regulators off the backs of industry. Others claim it was Allen himself who took up the cause of lobbying on their behalf, if for no other reason than to give him that extra edge to land multimillion-dollar contracts from the biggest industry players.

Either way, by the 1990s, many Republicans who considered running for state office would seek his blessing, backed, of course, by generous campaign donations from Allen and his employees. Sarah Palin visited Bill Allen's house when she decided to make her first run for state office. Allen helped her in another way later when she ran for governor, after he got careless and Palin had turned on him and the rest of the Alaskan GOP establishment. Allen's demise would ripple across Alaska politics in the late 2000s, with FBI raids and embarrassing trials, lifting Palin up, and ultimately destroying the career and reputation of Allen's good friend, Ted Stevens.

CHAPTER 4

Oil Patch People

There's a picture of Bill Allen as a boy, rail thin, his pants held up by a belt wrapped twice around his waist. He was about eight years old. Years later his older sister, Addie Chancellor, showed it to a federal judge as she begged him to have mercy on her brother, who pleaded guilty to corrupting Alaska politics. She wrote a letter to go along with the picture: "The part of this picture that is interesting to me is that this marks the end of Bill's childhood."[1] Not that he'd had much of a childhood before then.

Bill Allen was born in 1937 on the high plains of the southern New Mexico desert into the kind of grinding poverty that dulls the eyes of children, lines the faces of young women, and makes men burn with rage. His parents were migrants raising nine children amid dust and despair. Allen was the second oldest. He spent his first years living in a tent along the Rio Grande River, where it cuts through Socorro, New Mexico, about an hour's drive north of Truth Or Consequences. A town of tumbleweed, wind, and dust, Socorro was once a promising mining and mill town. But even before the Great Depression hit, the ore was running out and businesses were shutting their doors. Everyone was poor, but Allen and his siblings were dirt poor, the "ragamuffins" at school, as they later recalled. They lived in crumbling adobe houses with dirt floors and no electricity or running water. Around the time somebody photographed the eight-year-old Allen, the family picked up and moved to Oregon. "We were short on food and clothing. Neither Bill or I went back to school; we started working in the fields immediately," Addie said. "When we got to Oregon, it didn't take long for Bill, Mom, and I to realize that working and taking care of the family was up to us. That was true then and it's true today."[2]

The family eventually migrated back to New Mexico, this time to the north end of the state, near the Four Corners. They lived in the town of Aztec, close to Farmington, where some of Allen's family members ended up settling. "Gas and oil patch folks," is how Allen's niece described the family. In the early days, there was no foreshadowing of the oil and gas patch. The area was first settled by pioneers looking for land to farm. They rejoiced when they happened on the Four Corners, an area of "luxuriant alfalfa and grains and thousands of trees bending with luscious fruit."[3] Pioneers rejoiced when they saw how the rivers ran through the otherwise parched land. In the 1950s, natural gas was discovered, and the alfalfa and pumpkin and peach fields were razed. In their stead grew pipes and pumps, drilling rigs and other pieces of metal from which gas flared, fire rising out of the desert like a Baptist's bad dream. With the discovery of natural gas came a new breed of people to the town—the Texans and the Okies—just as Alaska would experience a decade later. Engineers and geologists, drillers and surveyors, pipe fitters and roughnecks flooded the town. Oil patch people.

In 1952 Bill Allen, now fifteen, headed south to Gallup, New Mexico, and got a job with El Paso Natural Gas, a growing company that was fueling the boom in the western United States. Working twelve hours a day, seven days a week, he would recall later he thought he'd "died and gone to heaven."[4] He started out as a pipe fitter, soon rising to the ranks of welder—a good-paying job in the oil fields. His job took him to Texas and Oklahoma, and his sister Addie, who now was working for a telephone company, saved enough money for a down payment on a small two-bedroom house for their mother and siblings. They had money to buy clothes and food for their brothers and sisters. Bill made sure of that.

But that's as far as it seemed to go, even after he had become wealthy during his decades in the oil industry. On a hot day in early August 2009, a writer stood with Allen's niece outside her mother's home, where Allen's other sister Peggy also lived. It was a bruised trailer in a neighborhood of other bruised trailers, assessed at just over $30,000. A horse munched on grass in the backyard. Allen's niece didn't want to talk about her family or uncle, who was on his way to prison after pleading guilty to corrupting Alaska politicians. Her mother, she said, was dying, and it was all too much for her. "Look around you," she said. "It's the oil and gas patch. That's all you need to know about us, and all you need to know about my uncle."

That might have been true if Alaska hadn't happened. It might have ended there for Bill Allen if he had followed the narrative arc that life seemed to have drawn for him. He might have pocketed some of the money he made and settled in Farmington, in a neighborhood like his sister's. Next to the other oil and gas patch families. In a trailer, perhaps, with a widescreen TV and a view of the cactus and red canyons out his front window; drinking beer on the weekends, catching a rodeo maybe. But circumstances called him to the far north just as Alaska was about to go through its own oil boom. It was 1968 and Prudhoe Bay, the nation's largest oil field, had just been discovered. Allen thought he and his wife would be in Alaska for less than a year, but as he recalled in 1989 to a *Seattle Times* reporter, "I got up here and saw opportunity. . . . You could do anything you were big enough to do."[5]

Bill Allen got a job with an oilfield contractor in the newly producing off-shore reserves discovered over the previous eleven years in Cook Inlet, a muddy body of water with strong tides, where you can still see the glowing oil platforms from the hillside neighborhoods of Anchorage. He was often assigned to Atlantic Richfield's King Salmon platform. ARCO was the same player leading the charge on the North Slope and would become the biggest oil producer in the state. Smaller than some of the other oil companies, ARCO would become a household name in Alaska. Although ARCO was based in Southern California, Alaskans liked it better than other Outside companies, such as London-based British Petroleum, with its executives who drank tea, took "holiday," and regarded Alaskans as jolly good unshaven eccentrics. ARCO was the big player here, and Allen's knowledge of welding and pipefitting, along with his leadership skills, impressed his supervisors so much that, according to former ARCO Alaska president Harold Heinze, they set him up in his own business and

kept him in business. Backed by assurances from ARCO that the contracts would keep coming, he and another oil worker founded the VECO
Corporation.[6]

All through the 1970s, as Sarah Palin's father was teaching her to hunt
and Ted Stevens was establishing himself as Alaska's senator for life, Bill
Allen was establishing himself as Alaska's homegrown oil tycoon. His
business with ARCO had proved so lucrative that he began to expand
beyond the state's borders. In 1973, now divorced, he joined a venture
with a Norwegian firm that did platform work in the North Sea, where
an oil boom was under way. At about this time, he and his partner on the
Norway venture were investigated for giving kickbacks to Phillips Petroleum officials. His partner admitted to a Phillips investigator that he gave
watches and boots to officials with authority over contracts. A security
chief for Phillips suspected that Allen also received kickbacks but couldn't
prove it.[7] Alaskans had no inkling of that side of Bill Allen—the tendency
to cut corners, to get sloppy—until years later, when an *Anchorage Daily
News* reporter dug into Allen's background, highlighting the oilman's rise
and increasingly questionable dealings in politics. That reporter, Richard
Mauer, continued to chronicle Allen's rise and fall over the next twenty-
five years, but Alaskans didn't pay it much stock until Allen was finally
indicted for corrupting Alaska's political process. The business community and political elite had turned a blind eye. The truth was that many
influential Alaskans didn't really know Bill Allen. He generally stayed
away from the media glare. He would show up at functions, sometimes
with a beautiful woman on his arm, but most people assumed that that's
what you got when you got rich. They acted surprised years later about
his desire for young women—girls, in some cases, based on allegations
that consumed local and federal authorities over the years. What they
did know of Allen was that he seemed well respected by Big Oil; he was
a barometer of how the industry felt about future oil development and
state tax policies. Pleasing Bill Allen meant pleasing the oil companies.
And some Alaska politicians took the bait.

As the 1970s turned into the 1980s, Allen was enmeshed in a string of
ventures in Alaska and abroad. There was a venture to modify offshore oil
rig platforms in a Houston shipyard, another to develop a giant hovercraft

to service Arctic oil fields, and there was a joint venture with an Alaska Native corporation. Although he gained valuable insight into the oil business, the fast growth took a toll on VECO. By 1982, it was broke and filing for federal bankruptcy protection. In many ways, this was an amazing failure. Allen's company had collapsed at a time of record-high oil prices, when business was extraordinarily good in the oil patch, in a state that still had plenty of oil fields to develop and maintain. Even more surprising, perhaps, is that Allen's clients—especially Atlantic Richfield—stood by him. In fact, it was these companies VECO had to thank when the company emerged from bankruptcy. ARCO and other oil companies stepped up contracting with VECO, and by 1983 it was earning more than $90 million in annual revenue.[8] "I'm one of those who argued that if [Allen] needs body parts to stay alive, we'll find the body parts," recalled Harold Heinze in a 2011 interview, who was president of ARCO at the time.

VECO was pulling in more and more contracts off the North Slope, in part because it was a nonunion shop. Contract labor agreements were expiring and oil companies were opting to go with a nonunion player. The unions, once so powerful, had lost much of their clout. Bill Allen, on the other hand, might have run his company into the ground, but he'd been a loyal soldier over the years. "He's always stuck by the industry, and he deserves our support," an oil company executive told a local business magazine in 1987.[9]

Allen wanted to be their man on the ground; it was good business to please his clients, mostly ARCO (which eventually became Conoco Phillips), BP, and Exxon—the "three big boys," Allen called them. "My sense is that Bill is one of those people who looked to build an identity for himself," Heinze recalled. "He clearly comes to the recognition that hard work isn't going to cut it by itself. So he figures out that politics is probably it. Bill makes a conscious choice that politics was part of his portfolio. Nobody goes to him and says, 'You should do this.' It's more like, 'I did this! I did this! Love me more. Give me more pats on the head.'" More contracts, more money, more power.

Allen worked the political system in two ways: campaign contributions and lobbying. In each instance, he ran afoul of regulators and eventually the U.S. Justice Department. In his early political forays in the 1980s, he enlisted a man named Ed Dankworth to do his work in the Alaska legislature. A towering Texan with the requisite cowboy hat and lizard skin boots, Dankworth had commanded the Alaska state troopers and served in the legislature, including on the powerful Alaska Senate Finance Committee, which oversaw oil tax policy. By the time Allen hired Dankworth, however, his reputation was tarnished. In 1982, during his last year as a state senator, Dankworth and a partner hatched a plan to pay $900,000 for an old work camp from the pipeline days and sell it to the state for more than $3 million. From the Senate Finance Committee, he slipped an appropriation into the budget to purchase the "surplus property." Dankworth was criminally charged with breaking conflict of interest laws, but he caught a break.[10] As a lawmaker, he was protected under legislative immunity, a court ruled. Despite the cloud hanging over him, Dankworth the lobbyist proved extremely reliable, one of those guys Allen valued for "getting 'er done." "Allen wanted me to lobby in Juneau for one reason: so that if the oil companies had any trouble in Juneau, he could tell them, 'No problem; I will call down there and take care of things,'" he once told Alaska writer Michael Carey.[11] There are twenty senators in the Alaska legislature. Dankworth's efforts would earn him the title "twenty-first senator."

In 1983, with the help of Dankworth, VECO launched a program that amounted to straw campaign contributions to political candidates whom Allen deemed supportive of industry-friendly tax policies and regulations—or would be after they got his donations. Dankworth said he "talked to the oil companies" about the scheme, and "they had no objections to it."[12] Under state law, VECO as a corporation could not contribute more than $1,000 to any one political candidate. So Allen asked his employees to each contribute $100—the lowest contribution that didn't have to be reported—and then funneled the money from their paychecks to candidates. Dankworth pulled the strings, deciding which lawmakers got the contributions. What he was working on at the time was a coup of sorts in the Alaska Senate leadership, allegedly promising campaign contributions for senators who followed his plan.[13] In all, VECO employees and executives donated $100,000, making it the largest political donor in the 1984 elections. When state campaign regulators wised up to VECO's secret program, the company was fined $72,000 for the unreported and illegal contributions. Even after VECO appealed and the fine was reduced to $28,000, it was the largest fine in state history. And from then on, everyone knew who to go to for money.[14]

In the mid-1980s, Saudi Arabia turned on the hose, followed by other OPEC countries. America was glutted with cheap oil and oil prices plummeted. President Ronald Reagan stripped the solar panels off the roof of the White House. Alternative energy was yesterday's crackpot idea. Americans once again filled their gas tanks with gusto. It was bad news for Alaskans, especially those in Anchorage, the largest city in the state. Between 1980 and to 1985, Anchorage had been one of the fastest-growing cities in the country, swelling from 174,000 to 248,000, a 40 percent increase. Developers tripped over each other responding to the need for housing, eateries, bars. Strip malls and movie theaters sprang up like fireweed, $1 billion in new construction in 1983 alone. What had been sleepy swampland one week turned into rows of tract houses the next. Sleek office buildings and hotels, ice skating rinks, a sports arena, and a convention center. By the time of the crash in 1986, when oil prices dropped from $27 a barrel to less than $10 a barrel, the state had backed more than $6 billion in home mortgages. More than $1 billion of them would end up in default. The banking industry didn't do any better. More than a dozen failed during the crash. Real estate and property were auctioned off on the courthouse steps to bottom-feeders. Thousands lost their jobs. In 1987, 14,000 houses sat empty. About 20,000 Anchoragites left the state, many for good.[15] In Juneau there were budget crunches, and some lawmakers even suggested it was time to talk about reinstituting the personal income tax. Others thought the state should raise oil taxes, while another faction thought the key was to cut taxes to encourage the industry to keep drilling, to keep exploring for the next big oil field. In 1981 the Alaska legislature had promised an oil industry tax cut of about $150 million annually starting in 1987. But with the state economy still in the dumps, some lawmakers and the governor,

Democrat Steve Cowper, argued against following through on the state's commitment. Alaskans were hurting, they argued, and there was no way the state could afford the tax break during such dire times. There were also lawmakers who wanted to raise taxes even higher. The oil industry was dealing with civil unrest again in Alaska, the people rising up, the leaders pounding their chests. Oil company executives rolled up their sleeves and warned legislators to not mess with taxes. Harold Heinze, the ARCO president, was dismayed that lawmakers were ready to change the rules and renege on the promised tax cuts, let alone those who were talking about other increases. "It's like raising the high bar as I run toward it," he told a reporter in 1987.[16]

The companies spent thousands of dollars on television and newspaper ads to persuade the public—and the legislature—that "a stable tax climate" was of utmost importance to the development of new fields.[17] Meantime, Bill Allen and his proxy, Ed Dankworth, were there in the late 1980s to work their magic. Dankworth had key legislators on a short leash, checking in daily with them on where the conversation was headed, what was being proposed, and by whom. You can imagine the lobbyist meeting with lawmakers in smoky bars or hotel rooms or even suburban homes, discussing state oil tax policy behind closed doors, perhaps exchanging promises for key votes. At least, that's how Allen and his cohorts rolled in the mid-2000s during another legendary oil tax battle that would catapult Sarah Palin into the governor's mansion. The fight was on in 1987, and Dankworth and his loyal soldier-lawmakers actively pushed back on any urge to jack up oil taxes. Among them was state senate president Jan Faiks, one of the lawmakers benefiting greatly from VECO campaign donations. She called attempts to suspend the looming tax break "immoral." "What is our most important industry?" she told an *Anchorage Daily News* reporter in 1987.[18] "The oil industry, which produces all the income, or the government industry, which spends all the income?"

In the end, the bill died. The oil industry got its tax cuts. But talk of tinkering with Alaska's tax policy wasn't over. The next year, in 1988, the battle resumed and grew more heated. The state was forecasting a budget shortfall of $425 million. Allen, Dankworth, Heinze, and other oil executives got back to work, as did Faiks and GOP legislators sympathetic to the industry that had helped get them elected. They prevailed again.

And then in 1989 something happened, something big in the still young and impressionable state, a place where events still leave fingerprints. On the morning of March 24, 1989, Alaskans watched as the *Exxon Valdez* oil tanker sat idle, a gash in its hull leaking crude across the pristine waters of Prince William Sound. Many Alaskans would never awaken from the nightmare that was about to unfold—the environmental damage, the demise of the commercial fisheries. Exxon would become a dirty word in Alaska. And yet, as these things go, there was a silver lining for those who worried about the state's recession. By August 1989, Alaska had nearly 12,000 more jobs than the same month a year earlier. In all, some 15,000 workers would clean up the mess that Joe Hazelwood, the drunken captain of the *Exxon Valdez,* had made when the tanker slammed into Bligh reef. The town of Valdez, not far from where the tanker ran aground, once again exploded with activity. Food prices and rents soared. The bars were packed every night. Crime was again a problem. Unemployment plummeted throughout 1989. Wages across the state rose to keep people from leaving their jobs and heading down to the beach to scrub rocks and pick up dead birds. Floating hotels were built to house cleanup crews. Nearly 10 million pounds of groceries had to be transported in: 280,000 chickens, 24 tankers of milk, nearly 1,000 cows, and 500 pigs.[19] Thousands of masks, boots, gloves, and yellow rain suits were supplied to the workers.

Billions of dollars poured into Alaska as Exxon contracted with VECO to oversee the cleanup. Bill Allen would become a very rich man, not from developing oil but from mopping it up. From supplying fishermen-turned-cleanup workers with containment booms and food and nets to hiring thousands of subcontractors; from running the logistics of an operation that resembled a war zone to disposing the thousands of bird and fish carcasses littering the beaches. By September 1989, VECO had spent more than $460 million of Exxon's money on the cleanup. The disaster had turned into a boom, and there were plenty of thankful Alaskans, including Rick Eggleston, the owner of a welding supply shop in Fairbanks who had sold more than $2 million in shipping supplies to VECO. "I've already said that if Hazelwood runs for governor, and my guys don't vote for him, I'm going to fire every one of them," Eggleston told a reporter in 1989. "He's done more for us than any governor we've ever had. Too bad it had to happen from such a bad situation."[20]

Captain Joe Hazelwood did one more thing for Alaskans. Amid the oil spill, lawmakers were now in their third straight year debating whether to discontinue the 1987 oil tax break. Allen again deployed Ed Dankworth to the halls of the Capitol. The "twenty-first senator," though, didn't have much to work with. Oil was still lapping the beaches and the *Exxon Valdez* spill remained an international news event as legislators met in Juneau.

Lawmakers, even those Dankworth considered to be in industry's corner, were infuriated over the oil spill. Even if they didn't agree philosophically with the tax cut, their constituents wanted retribution. How could lawmakers not slash the tax credit on an industry that had proven so irresponsible that it would allow a drunken crew to pilot an oil tanker vessel through one of the most majestic spots in North America? Dankworth did his best to talk them out of it. "I just hope nobody wants to use the tax structure as a means of assessing a fine on the oil industry," Dankworth quipped.[21]

On the day the Senate met to vote on ending the tax credits—now potentially worth more than $200 million annually to the state, thanks to increasing oil prices—it appeared it would come down to two votes, one being Republican John Binkley's. If Binkley voted in favor of ending the credits, the other lawmaker had indicated he would do the same. Binkley had been on the fence and his fellow Republicans worried he'd cave, especially if he spoke to Governor Steve Cowper—a Democrat and the chief proponent of the measure. A few of them tried to keep him from talking to the governor. But as they were escorting him through the halls of the Capitol, Binkley told them he needed to step into his office. He said he'd be right back. Then he proceeded to flee down a fire escape. Minutes later he made his way through the fire escape door into Governor Cowper's office. They talked it over and Binkley told the governor he could count on him. Binkley, took his seat in the Senate, and voted to end the oil tax credit.[22] For long-standing supporters, it was the day

Alaska took its fate into its own hands. An aide to the governor likened it to having a baby. There was champagne and cigars, tears and hugs. It was estimated that repealing the oil tax credit would over time generate the equivalent in 2011 of $3.5 billion in tax state tax revenue. "We're smoking on Big Oil," one legislator proclaimed.

And still the oil lapped at the shoreline. Bill Allen and his oil executive friends might have lost the tax battle, but *Exxon Valdez* had rewarded him. Allen was now the most powerful businessman in Alaska. In November 1989, the fifty-two-year-old took some of that oil spill money and bought the *Anchorage Times,* a pro-development newspaper that historically wielded influence in the state. Allen blew through $40 million on the *Times,* folding the paper after only three years, having lost a war with the *Anchorage Daily News.* Still, he didn't lose his voice. Under a joint-operating agreement, the *Anchorage Daily News* agreed to allow the *Anchorage Times* to live on in a section on its editorial page. Until 2007, when he pleaded guilty to bribing Alaska politicians, Allen funded a staff of conservative writers, offering up a daily dose of columns in the state's largest newspaper that routinely promoted the oil industry and the Republican Party.

Bill Allen and Dankworth split about this time, but that didn't stop Allen's rise. He became an *éminence grise* in Alaska, even after he hit his head in a motorcycle accident in 2001, affecting his speech. Politicians continued to depend on him for their campaigns. The oil industry still relied on him as their voice on the ground. He even became influential in national politics, co-chairing the Alaska Finance Committee for the Bush-Cheney 2000 election campaign, while the state's congressional delegation counted on him for campaign fund-raisers and favors. Years later, Dankworth mused with Michael Carey, telling the Alaska writer that Allen's downfall was thinking that lobbying was all about buying people off. "He was just an old welder with no education," Dankworth said.[23]

And finally, there is one last event that happened in the wake of the spill. Larry Allan Beck—Alaska's beloved bard and goodwill ambassador, the one who performed for the oil executives on that fateful day of the big Prudhoe Bay oil lease sale three decades earlier—was now twice divorced, broke, and despondent. His was one of the best-known faces in Alaska, one of the most optimistic men anybody had ever met, with energy to spare. He had a television show in the early 1980s in which his wife would act the part of Mother Goose while he was Old Sourdough. He bought an advertising agency and made lots of money, but it all just sifted through his fingers. In the winter of 1989, he performed in 100 shows all across the Lower 48—clocking in about 20,000 miles. He recited his version of "The Cremation of Sam McGee" for probably the 10,000th time, in that Scottish brogue:

There are strange things done 'neath the midnight sun / By the men who moil for gold. / The arctic trails have their secret tales / That would make your blood run cold.

When the bard finished his tour, he visited his family in Oregon, where he checked himself into a hospital psychiatric ward. Beck talked the nurse, Vern, into letting him go outside on the roof to have a cigarette. Vern ran after him as he took a flying leap off the rooftop.[24]

Three days later, he was dead. Boom and bust.

CHAPTER 5

Clinging to Guns and Religion in Wasilla

Alaska, normally immune to zeitgeists unless they have to do with oil, was dragged into the late 1980s and 1990s culture war, as it related to oil and the pipeline. White missionaries and teachers have been in Alaska since the Russian Orthodox Church landed in the late 1700s, trying to "civilize" and save Alaska Native people and the rural villages. But before the pipeline non-Native Alaska was filled with mostly secular people who wanted to be left alone, were suspicious of clubs and fads, and had no interest in a pluralistic society. Many called themselves Republicans, not because it was the party of God but of guns, which they truly did cling to, mostly to save themselves from bears and wolves and the occasional ne'er-do-well trying to steal somebody's gold claim or woman. Alaska was a place for many to escape from God and churchgoing, and all the ensuing entrapments—fancy duds and potlucks in sterile basements, soup kitchens, and sing-alongs. Women joked that they came to Alaska to avoid wearing hats on Sunday.

The pipeline and 1970s left the debris of Oklahomans and Texans, the Dixiecrats whom Nixon had so assiduously courted and Reagan continued to court by campaigning in the South for states' rights. Pat Robertson, the television evangelist who ran for president in 1988, saw a constituency in Alaska. His people came up and worked hard at organizing the state, registering voters, urging them to run for school board and city council and then beyond.

"We need you to hang in there," Robertson said to Alaska supporters in a statewide conference call in 1988. "We're not just talking about
1988. We want to see a conservative Republican majority elected in the
state legislature, and then, in each state, we want to see conservative
congressional delegations. The same with the Senate. And by 1992,
we'll come back again and be in a position to take the whole thing."[1] A
majority of the state's delegates at the 1988 Republican National Convention voted for Robertson. And when he lost, they returned to Alaska
and continued to push for changes in the state Republican Party, with
ARCO employees joining forces with GOP state delegates.[2] They successfully advocated for tweaking Republican primary voting rules, ensuring that only low-tax, anti-abortion candidates had any chance of
succeeding.

It didn't work all across Alaska. But it did take root in the smaller
towns of south-central Alaska, like Kenai and Soldotna, as well as parts
of the Matanuska Susitna Valley, a broad swath of rural land about the
size of West Virginia, a forty-minute drive north of Anchorage. The Mat-
Su Valley, it's called, or just the Valley, or just Mat-Su. It can be the
most beautiful spot on earth as the Talkeetna Mountains in the wild,
cold distance capture the last glow of the setting sun. The southern
peaks of the looming, saw-toothed Chugach Mountains often greet
Alaska State Fair goers with the first hint of winter dusting their peaks.
You can see what drew people here and why they stayed. You can see
the vast open area where a person can follow his or her own dream;
you can see the pioneer under a huge sky swirling with northern lights.
You can hear the wolves howling in the distance and smell the cold and
the burning spruce. You can feel freedom. But as you drive around the
jumble of the Valley, with all those unmarked back roads, you can also
feel alienation—lost and alone, twirling in a land without boundaries
and rules.

Sarah Palin stepped into the political ring in 1992, winning a seat
on Wasilla's city council. It was the same year a group composed of
twenty churches, along with anti-abortion activists, fought to unseat
the board of directors at Valley Hospital in Wasilla—the only hospital
in the Mat-Su—in hopes that a new board would ban abortions. One

of the most active churches in the battle was the Assembly of God, Palin's church.

Wasilla, the largest city in the Valley, was the center of the Christian Right in Alaska. A growing town outside a major city, Wasilla offered wide-open spaces and few regulations, a community that was still forming, still in the making. A place where you could build a shack or a palace, and nobody would treat you differently for it, a community with little history to weigh it down with local mores and conventions. Still is much the same today. If you want to move to a place where you can spend your mornings speaking in tongues, your afternoons hunting moose, and your evenings in one of the many watering holes, come to Wasilla.

Wasilla officially became a town in 1917 due to its proximity to gold mining and location along the Alaska Railroad. By the late 1920s, it had all but died. It was saved, just barely, when in the 1930s the federal government started handing out tracts of land, part of a New Deal agriculture program, dubbed the Matanuska Valley Colony experiment, set up by President Franklin Roosevelt. Farmers came from all over the Midwest to set up the cooperative. They were given a plot to clear, a new life, and a view to die for. But the land in Wasilla wasn't as good as the land in the neighboring settlement, Palmer, just a few miles down the road. Although the program had attracted enough residents to keep the town going, it was Palmer where most of them settled.

Both cities have the same breathtaking view of the mountains, but they couldn't be more different. The Midwesterners arrived in Palmer bringing a cooperative spirit, which is still reflected in the neat blocks, the picket fences, the quaint downtown, with pedestrian crosswalks and where people wave as you pass. Wasilla does not have a quaint downtown. Wasilla has strip malls and bars that stay open until 5:00 AM. It has pawn shops and gun shops and a sense of disorder and chaos. Palmer is the seat of the Mat-Su borough government. Wasilla always had a virulent antigovernment strain running through it. Palmer and its city government thrived and grew. But in Wasilla one woman, Mary Carter, served as the city's justice of the peace, coroner, probate judge, district recorder, notary public, territorial tax agent, and postmistress until 1960. That was all the government the town wanted or needed.

Then came the 1970s, when a new highway sliced through the town, carrying workers and supplies north for construction of the trans-Alaska pipeline. When the pipeline was completed, some of those workers decided to stay in Alaska, and began scouting for cheap land. It was still a sleepy community; gravel pits were big business. Most residents worked in Anchorage, but some small businesses began to crop up: gun stores, a few bars and restaurants, and a grocery store that opened in 1977. But no real industry, no real way to support the community.

Such was Wasilla when Chuck and Sally Heath moved to the town in 1970. They lived in a small house close to the elementary school (later converted into city hall) that their daughter Sarah attended. In 2007, seven months after their daughter became governor, Chuck and Sally sat down in their cedar-shingled house with a writer and recalled how they'd been drawn by Wasilla's wild openness. It was a place where you could step out into the backyard, gun in hand, and land yourself a tasty moose dinner.[3] This was when Sarah Palin's approval ratings were among the highest of any governor in the country and before Alaskans began questioning whether she deserved them.

The Heaths' house was decked out in all things Alaska—horns and hides, skulls and nets, photographs of Chuck posing with his kills on hunting trips. And more pictures of hunts the Heaths took the four children on. Sitting around the dining table, interrupted occasionally by neighbors stopping by to chat and a constantly ringing phone, Chuck talked about how he met Sally in Columbia Basin College in Washington State. She had help from home, but he put himself through college working in a kitchen, driving a school bus, and toiling as a janitor. He wasn't there for the academics, he said. He was there to play football. They went to a movie on their first date, which he paid for with a sock full of pennies. She avoided him at first because she thought he drank too much. (When Sally said this, Chuck shook his head in mock exasperation.) After Sally finished school, she moved back to her hometown, Spokane, Washington, and Chuck got a job teaching and coaching football in Sandpoint. Located on the shores of

Lake Pend Oreille in northern Idaho, Sandpoint is a much prettier town than Wasilla, and it attracts many of the same kinds of hunting and fishing folks, as well as conservative Christians and anti-government types. About a year later, they ran into each other when Chuck was in Spokane for shoulder surgery.

A few years later, he was driving up the Alaska Highway and Sally was flying up with three small children, including newborn Sarah. It was 1964, and the family first settled in Skagway, a small coastal town in southeastern Alaska. He taught school and bartended, and they both drove a taxi. Idyllic years in gorgeous Skagway. The surf and the wind, years of tides and shellfish, of climbing mountains and braving storms. A true adventure. But there wasn't much to shoot for there, and Chuck wanted to achieve. They eventually settled about forty-five minutes north of Anchorage in Wasilla, a place where a man could feed his family from the backyard hunting. "We had everything we wanted," Chuck said. "Hares and grouse and moose. For five years in a row, I shot a moose in the same corner of the field in the backyard. On the sixth year there was a house there."

It was the beginning of the pipeline boom and Wasilla began to transform into what it has become: transient and on the gritty side. But that didn't seem to bother the Heaths. They hadn't come to Alaska for square blocks and tidy yards, or at least Chuck hadn't. He's a tell-it-like-it-is guy. He laughs easily and his voice carries. He's sinewy. His eyes twinkle with mischief. But Chuck also pushed the kids hard, he admitted. Sarah, perhaps the hardest, because she was the one "I couldn't make do things." They ran together in the mornings and Chuck was her coach in high school track. He rooted on "Sarah Barracuda" when she helped the Wasilla Warriors win the state girls basketball championship in 1982. He was always urging her to work harder, run faster, climb higher. "She takes after her father," Sally said. "All of [the children], though, tried to live up to Dad's standards. I'm too easygoing. I don't see that in any of the kids, and certainly not Sarah."

When you talk to Sally, you can see her living a different life. Not necessarily better, but different. Sally is soft. Her voice has a tremble in it. She made delicious salmon dip and chocolate chip cookies for an interviewer, which she offered with maternal generosity. But she held her cards closely, and she did so even before her daughter was famous.

In an earlier interview in 2006, while her daughter was running for governor, Sally was vague about her recollections of Sarah.[4] Who were her daughter's heroes? What was she like as a kid? Did she do well in college? To nearly every question, Sally answered, "I don't know. I'd really like to know that answer to that question." It's probably safer to assume that Sally was leery of the media, rather than she didn't know her daughter. Neither was she one to talk about feelings. Ask her what she did that day and she'd tell you all the details. Ask how she felt about what she did that day and her face closed. Ask her about her religious experience, the one that changed her life, and she got fidgety. Sitting around the dining table in 2007, Chuck rolled his eyes. ("We're praying for him," Sally said with tease in her voice.) If there is a why, Sally wasn't telling. But she was clear that it did happen: "The Experience." "To know where you've been and know where you're going. That's a nice thing," Sally said. She stopped attending the Catholic church and started going to a church where the parishioners waved their hands in the air and spoke in tongues. She and her kids were baptized by Wasilla Assembly of God Pastor Paul Reilly at Big Lake. Sarah would have been about ten years old then. That would have been in 1974.

Chuck wanted to get back to what was most important to him: his daughter. "Did you hear that they're talking about her as vice president?"

"Oh, Chuck," Sally said. "She won't . . . "

"I asked her about that," said Chuck. "We just laughed. I said, 'We need you here.' I told her, 'We need you here in Alaska.' She just laughed. I don't know what she was thinking about. She didn't show her hand on that. Same thing as maybe being senator, running for Senate. She wants to finish her job here. I know that, especially because she loves it."

The Heaths didn't pay much attention to politics. Before his daughter jumped into the fray, the only politician Chuck actively supported was Governor Jay Hammond, mostly because he was a hunter and fisherman. But the Heaths surely knew about Wasilla's first mayor, the flamboyant booster Charles Bumpus, who routinely made headlines in the local newspaper, the *Frontiersman*. Prior to being mayor, Bumpus had been forced to resign from the Wasilla city council in 1983 when he was sent to prison for tax fraud, allegedly having sheltered business dealings in a Belize corporation. When Bumpus beat the rap on appeal, he turned into a town hero and was "drafted" to run in Wasilla's first mayoral election in 1985. Once elected, to get the attention of Anchorage residents down the road who tended to view Wasilla as a backwater, he lobbied for Wasilla's own time zone. "Wasilla Standard Time" would fall a half hour ahead of the rest of the state, so that Wasilla residents could be the first to fishing holes and store sales, his ordinance stated. He also threatened to tinker with Wasilla's weather equipment to make it a few degrees warmer to appeal to visitors. He played the jazz saxophone, the clarinet, worked as a real estate developer, and was a libertarian. Bumpus was also a pragmatist and understood that for Wasilla to grow, it needed basic city services. He went so far as to put a sales tax on the ballot, so that Wasilla could afford its own policemen. He died in 1987 from a heart attack when he was forty-two years old, never seeing the sales tax pass.

This was a city at the time whose public works director resigned in the 1980s over water fluoridation, or, as he put it, "forced mass medication." This was place where you talked taxes, zoning, planning at your own peril. That same decade, a planner for the Mat-Su borough wanted to reshape a comprehensive plan that would, in part, set up standards for building and development. He was from Oregon and was a fan of walkable neighborhoods and town centers. He was fired when he tried to establish zoning rules. Adding insult to injury, his effigy was burned in a parking lot.[5]

It had always been this way, but with a twist. In perhaps the best history of Wasilla, city resident Louise Potter chronicled the town in the 1950s and early 1960s. Potter wrote about the trash piled up in yards; how the houses were crammed together in whatever way people wished; how chickens and pigs went wherever they wanted to go; how there was nothing to keep someone from "building next to a nice residence a cow barn or a commercial garage." All of this, she wrote, left some to view Wasilla as a "raw, course, crude and horrible place!" But even with the junk, there had been a sense of community, at least before the pipeline years. People banded together to try to make a more satisfying place to live. "In view of the almost total lack of local government organization here down through the years, as well as the presence here of so many genuinely rugged individuals, it is interesting to find a village and an area in certain ways so community minded," Potter concluded.[6]

The new Wasilla—the one that evolved after the oil discovery, the one that now clung to not only guns but God too, didn't like city planners or fluoride in the water. It was suspicious of the whole "community-minded" thing and didn't like taxes. Wasilla voters finally approved a sales tax in 1992 after a huge battle, as John Stein, Wasilla's mayor at the time, recalled. He worked tirelessly to get it passed so the city could hire a police force. And now he dreamed even bigger.

Stein was an easygoing guy generally respected by the community. He'd been mayor since 1987—Wasilla's second. Although he had a graduate degree in public administration, he didn't put on airs. He wanted to take Wasilla from chaos into something that resembled a real town. He envisioned harnessing that old, pre-pipeline sense of community, which to him involved having a police force, creating parks, building a walkable downtown, and so on.[7]

After the sales tax was passed, Mayor Stein hired Irl Stambaugh, a twenty-two-year veteran of the Anchorage police department, as Wasilla's first police chief. Standing 6 foot 2 and weighing 240 pounds, Stambaugh was a towering man but soft-spoken and articulate. He had a way of setting people at ease. In his first year, Stambaugh and the eight officers he hired made 206 DWI arrests, dealt with nearly 6,000 cases, and recovered over $1 million of stolen property.[8] The city was growing, and the sales tax provided more funds to the library and the city's small museum. Stein worked to get the city a new playground, and a horde of volunteers turned out to build it. A theater group relocated to Wasilla with the city's support. He thought he might even get some junk ordinances on the books to clean up some of the mess, and perhaps even a master development plan. He wanted the bars to close at 2:00 AM instead of 5:00 AM, and he wanted to keep guns out of bars and city buildings.

But there was a group in Wasilla that didn't much like the way Stein was leading the city. He'd always respected the libertarian strain in

Wasilla, but he began to see something different taking root in his city: the libertarian meets the Christian. Before the 1990s, he saw rough-and-tumble Wasilla as perhaps not the most aesthetically pleasing place to live, but a town in which people were generally accepting of one another's religions and lifestyles.

Stein would have placed Sarah Palin in that camp. In fact, he endorsed her for city council, a race she won as Stein's "handpicked" candidate. And during her time on the city council, he thought they did pretty well together. They had an amicable relationship and would even pass each other notes during an exercise class they took together.

It was around this same time that Alaska politics took a bizarre turn. Wally Hickel, the former Republican governor whom President Nixon hired and fired as his Interior secretary, roared back to the governor's mansion. Since the 1970s, he had run and lost three times, but in 1990 he found a way in. Arliss Sturgulewski was the candidate on the Republican ticket. Hickel, always skeptical of the oil companies' hold on Alaska politics, thought she was too much on their side. The same was true, he said, for the Democratic candidate, Tony Knowles, the former two-term mayor of Anchorage. So forty-eight days before the election, he decided to run as an Alaska Independence Party (AIP) candidate—a third party ticket—after the original candidate bowed out to make room for him. The GOP was furious with Hickel. He even got a threatening call from John Sununu, President George H. W. Bush's chief of staff, screaming at him, threatening to derail Hickel's development plans for Alaska. "John," Hickel yelled back, "when I'm elected, you'll see what tough is all about."[9]

He declined campaign contributions from oil industry executives, who threw their support to Sturgulewski, yet Hickel did the seemingly impossible, beating his Republican and Democrat opponents in the general election. And in the process, he lent some respectability to the AIP. Sarah Palin's husband, Todd, belonged to the AIP from 1995 to 2002. Some members supported Sarah in her mayoral races in Wasilla, and she videotaped an address for the AIP's annual convention in 2008.

Although the AIP didn't become an official party until the mid-1970s, the late Joe Vogler, the colorful founder of the party, said its roots stemmed from a 1911 protest in Cordova, a small fishing town on Prince William Sound. It was called the Cordova Coal Party. Vogler once said, "Like the Boston Tea Party, the folks down there threw some coal into the bay to signify their unhappiness with federal control over coal mining." Statehood drew more followers, and when the party was formed by Vogler, secession from the United States was its major goal.[10] As Vogler often said, Alaska was nothing more than a colony of America. It could do better on its own. "In the federal government are the biggest liars in the United States, and I hate them with passion. They think they own this country," Vogler told John McPhee in the late 1970s when the author was writing *Coming into the Country.* "Our goal is ultimate independence by peaceful means under a minimal government fully responsive to the people. I hope we don't have to take human life, but if they go on tramping on our property rights, look out, we're ready to die."[11]

Wally Hickel was still full of big ideas. He began his administration by suing, though unsuccessfully, the federal government for reneging on its promise to allow Alaska to develop its lands as it saw fit. But he did not believe Alaska should secede, and when that became clear to the AIP leadership, they tried to recall him. It wasn't the only recall effort. His administration was rife with controversy. Turnover was constant and dramatic. He famously threw a water glass at a legislator. A nasty rumor campaign began suggesting Hickel was mentally ill. Perhaps this isn't surprising. Until Sarah Palin, he was one of the toughest governors on the oil companies. In his first year, he settled a $1 billion suit over state costs associated with the *Exxon Valdez* oil spill. Against huge opposition, including Bill Allen and his legislative allies, Hickel extracted nearly $4 billion from the companies on back taxes they owed for overcharging the state for shipping its royalty oil on the trans-Alaska pipeline. The fight to get that money was, once again, huge. Bill Allen had his pro-industry Republicans firmly in place, but Hickel fought and fought, and he succeeded. But the battles took their toll. He was so bruised that he decided not to run for a second term, something that he would always regret.

His legislative victories were fleeting. He knew that they would be. He also knew that Alaska would always be under oil industry control unless it owned something of its own. His biggest dream, his biggest idea was to spark another pipeline boom. This time, though, instead of pumping oil, another pipeline would be built that would carry natural gas. The North Slope oil fields were estimated to hold the largest conventional gas reserves in the United States. Since the 1970s, state leaders had hoped someday the oil companies would tap the gas and export via a pipeline. The proposals ran the gamut, from building a pipeline through Canada to running one parallel to the trans-Alaska oil pipeline. Hickel preferred the latter. He also advocated for the state to build the line, rather than wait around for the oil companies. Supporters of this project came to call it the "all-Alaska gas pipeline."

At the end of 1994, his popularity on the decline, the fight with the oil companies and the federal government too hard, the natural gas pipeline too expensive, Hickel left government once and for all. But he kept an eye out for any potential politician with a similar philosophy and continued to push for a state-owned pipeline. In his twilight years, he and former Governor Jay Hammond became allies in this quest, and when Sarah Palin, who had her eyes on the governor's office, offered her support, the three of them posed together for advertisements in support of the line. Standing beside Alaska's two elder and beloved statesmen did wonders for Palin's image. Hickel supported Sarah Palin for Alaska governor, and Hammond might have also had he not died a few months before she announced. She was the one politician Hickel felt had vision and understood that the people owned the resources and the state had to play tough if it ever wanted to realize the next pipeline boom. He co-chaired her campaign and appeared in ads for her. After she was elected, he would grow disenchanted as she moved away from her support of a state-owned gas pipeline. Two weeks before Palin leaped into the 2008 presidential race, Hickel was asked what he thought about her oil and gas policies. All Hickel could say was, "Fuck Palin! Fuck Palin! Fuck Palin! I made her governor . . . Now we've got to replace her."[12] He would have a spark of hope for her when John McCain tapped her, believing that she would serve as a fitting ambassador for Alaska. But then she didn't. Hickel died in 2010 at age 90, raging against Palin, knowing that he helped create her, angry that he helped pry open the bottle that let her out, one that she had no intention of being shoved back into.

In 1994 Matanuska-Susitna borough voters tossed out three longtime Democratic legislators and replaced them with conservative Republicans who had little or no political experience. They'd run on an anti-tax, pro-God, pro-gun, anti-abortion platform. Two years after that, Sarah Palin, then thirty-two years old, decided she wanted Mayor John Stein's seat, and those state legislators were there to help her. Looking back on it, Stein said, she "sandbagged me." They had been friends, but suddenly he became a "good old boy" who was more interested in the "status quo" than in moving Wasilla forward. "I didn't see it coming," he recalled later. "I was shocked. Me, a good old boy? It was absurd." Why did she vote along with most of his proposals, Stein wondered. Why didn't she approach him and say she objected to the way he was governing?[13]

In a questionnaire during the 1996 Wasilla mayoral election published in the local newspaper, Stein said his hobbies included target shooting, gardening, photography, and reading. Palin listed her hobbies as "slaying salmon, hunting, 10-mile runs, the Iron Dog." Asked about issues facing Wasilla, Stein listed "construction of a city collector street grid" and an "architectural planning process." Palin said one issue that needed fixing was how the city interfaced with Wasillans. When residents went to city hall, they encountered "complacency, inaction and even total disregard." She decried the town's "current tax-and-spend mentality" and its "stale leadership." She wrote, "New administration finally allows new input, fresh ideas and ENERGY to work with the public to shape this city!!!"[14]

Part of the new energy moving Wasilla forward involved cultivating a Christian conservative base. "I never thought that my religion would come into play in Wasilla politics. But Palin and her followers began a whisper campaign about needing Wasilla to elect its first 'Christian mayor.' I was shocked," said Stein. "Not that I'm not proud to have a Jewish-sounding name, but I'm Lutheran. I never thought I'd need to say that when I was campaigning, but I did." Another rumor flying around claimed Stein and his wife, who went by her maiden name, weren't really married. He finally produced a marriage certificate, which didn't help matters any. Another rumor: Stein was the kind of guy who would stoop to forging a marriage license, all for political power. Flyers began to appear urging Wasillans to vote for a pro-life candidate. Letters to the editor poured in about guns and God and the evils of liberalism, and how those conservative Republicans elected to the Alaska legislature had campaigned for Sarah Palin. That was another new thing for Wasilla—traditionally mayoral races had been nonpartisan.

Wasilla resident Katie Hurley was chief clerk to the Alaska constitutional convention in 1955–1956 and served in the House. She was the first woman to win a statewide election as the Democratic nominee for lieutenant governor in 1978. She lived in a small house on Wasilla Lake stuffed with newspapers from across the country. Old *New Yorker* and *Harper's* magazines littered her coffee table. Original artwork hung from the walls. On a fall evening in that house, she talked about how the Christian Right had gained a foothold in Wasilla:

> We were all taken by surprise. This is Alaska, a place that's supposed to be immune to Lower 48 politics. Those people who also say, "We don't give a damn how they do it Outside," were the same people who were very much paying attention to how they did it Outside. We used to all be in this together. We could fight over things, sure, like how to develop the resources and how much to give away to the oil companies. But religion? Before the late 1980s, we never fought over religion. We never knew what each other's religion was. We wouldn't even think to ask. We just all assumed that we were in this together.[15]

Palin campaigned tirelessly in the 1994 mayoral race, with her father, Chuck Heath, egging her on. He drove her to one end of a block and she would run from household to household passing out fliers and talking to voters. Then he'd pick her up and take her to another row of houses. Wasilla's haphazard layout is hard on candidates wanting to go door knocking, but Palin and her father were all over that town.

In Sarah Palin's mind, John Stein and Irl Stambaugh and their supporters, which included most city workers, symbolized all that threatened Wasilla—things like community planning, codes, and ordinances.

Elitism. Mainline Protestants. The push to close the bars at 2:00 AM, to post signs prohibiting firearms on city buildings. Just beneath the surface lay a smoldering resentment at the thought that they—the "good old boys" she called them—considered her ill equipped to run a city and made snarky remarks to the papers about her and, as she later put it, "humiliated" her.

When asked why she wanted to be mayor—what exactly she wanted to see changed in Wasilla—Palin's father said in an interview in 2007, "because she thought she could win and wanted to be sure. You know," he said after a pause, "to get rid of the good ol' boys."

After Palin won, Stein penned a good-bye to the community that ran in the newspaper. His prose poem was titled "New Road":

> With but a whisper, barricades fall to open new paths of commerce; Great investments of the public fisc beyond the realm of mere households. Dreamt, planned, consented then built. Thoroughfares materializing, in tortured efforts like icebergs from a glacier. How easily we tread on the perennial labors of our public caste. Often oblivious to all but the faults. Taking for granted the rich utility of our common effort, delighting in movement, yet owing thanks.[16]

Within a few months of Palin taking office, only two of the department heads who had served under Stein still had jobs in the administration. Palin had fired a few of them, including Chief Stambaugh, and others left on their own, including two women in their seventies who ran the museum, citing philosophical differences with Palin. The firings and the walkouts caused a ruckus in the small community. A recall effort was formed but died out. The *Frontiersman,* the local paper, was especially harsh toward Palin, railing against her in editorials, news articles, and columns, referring to her administration as "Kingdom Palin, the land of no accountability."

"The mayor's administration has been one of contradiction, controversy and discord. While she will blame everyone but herself, we see mostly Sarah at the center of the problem," one editorial said. It excoriated her propensity to "roll her eyes or make a face" when someone criticized her during a public meeting, and claimed she was losing the public's faith by "her philosophy that either we're with her or we're against her."[17]

If Stein and Stambaugh were good old boys, what did that make Ted Stevens? If Sarah Palin had been paying attention to current events and reading the local newspapers, she would have known Stevens was the granddaddy of good old boys—those rough-and-tumble white Alaskan males who knew they had power, felt they deserved it, and believed they were the ones best suited to wield it in their state. Only Ted Stevens could threaten his constituents with walking out on the job. And only Alaskans would beg him not to. In a 1988 interview, Stevens famously declared that if he were to continue serving in the U.S. Senate, he wanted Alaskans' full support. "I just want people to understand the commitment I'm making if I stay on," he told an *Anchorage Daily News* writer.[18] "This is a period I could go out and make $1 million a year without any question. I would like to stay. But I think there is a mutual commitment that has to be made," he said. From then on, one of Ted Stevens's many monikers in Alaska was "senator for life." Surely that must have irked Palin—if she read the paper.

Stevens knew what was in store for him and his state if he continued in the Senate—billions and billions of federal dollars. He'd achieved two decades of seniority and Alaskans needed him more than ever. The 1990s saw slow economic growth in Alaska. Oil production had peaked in 1989 at just over 2 million barrels a day. Now production was on the decline and companies weren't searching for new fields with as much gusto as in the 1970s and 1980s. Stevens had already proved a formidable force in steering federal money to Alaska. But his pork barrel powers would reach new levels in the late 1990s when he was named chairman of the U.S. Senate Appropriations Committee, wielding immense influence over federal spending. States with senators chairing the Appropriations Committee historically benefited greatly from an influx of federal spending, and Alaska was no different. Under Stevens's reign, federal spending reached $12,000 per capita in Alaska, double the national average. Stevens took advantage of his chairmanship to create a commission to steer federal dollars to rural Alaska villages and social programs. He used his influence to secure a special, and controversial, program that allowed Alaska Native corporations to go after no-bid federal contracts. To Alaskans, Stevens was known as "Uncle Ted." His legacy was evident everywhere, from runway lights in villages to military bases to fishing and maritime laws to the re-vamped Anchorage International Airport named in his honor. He spent his summers traveling across the state: eating traditional Native food in tiny villages, flying in prop planes over rugged white peaks, the endlessly choppy seas of Alaska's uncharted mountains. He spent days hunting and fishing with wealthy Alaskans, and evenings sipping their red wine by the fire. When he came back home, to Alaska, he breathed deeply. And then he went back to D.C. and fought for his baby, for his state. A part of him knew that he shouldn't. A part of him knew that all that federal money was helping to keep Alaska trapped in a permanent adolescence. But then again, he liked it that way. If Palin's scapegoat was the good old boys, then Stevens's was the Outside's ignorance of Alaska and all the challenges Alaskans faced. The fledgling state adored him.

As mayor, Sarah Palin had no problem philosophically turning to Stevens, or the rest of Alaska's good old boy congressional delegation for that matter, to pump federal dollars into tiny Wasilla. As governor, Palin railed against earmarks and out-of-control federal spending, and during the 2008 presidential campaign she even criticized Alaska's "Bridge to Nowhere," a project she had wholeheartedly supported earlier in her ca-reer. But Mayor Palin in the 1990s and early 2000s, like so many small-town Alaskan leaders, depended on Ted Stevens–sponsored funding for her community, so much so that in her latter years as mayor of Wasilla, she hired an Anchorage law firm to lobby Stevens and Alaska's congres-sional delegation for federal funding. The lobbying was overseen by a former chief of staff for Stevens and partner of the contracted law firm. Wasilla landed a $1 million earmark for a rail and bus project, $500,000 for a mental health center, another half million to purchase federal land, $450,000 to fix up an agriculture processing plant, and the list went on, as reported by the *Washington Post*, which highlighted the earmarks and the Palin-Stevens connection in the days after she was picked in 2008 by John McCain as his running-mate.[19]

For most Alaskans, if Palin and Wasilla benefited from Ted Stevens's power in Washington, that was a nonissue, at least until years later when she started ranting against earmarks, federal spending, and even the senator himself. Alaska was still the Last Frontier, and Stevens—the man who had championed statehood, ushered in the oil boom, and showered Alaska with federal spending—was practically a saint. And Alaskans would need Uncle Ted more than ever at the millennium.

As for John Stein, he ran again for Wasilla mayor in 1999, but lost by a wide margin to Palin. He left Wasilla and settled in Sitka—a picturesque town in southeastern Alaska, where he headed the Sitka Sound Science Center, a local nonprofit. Irl Stambaugh, Wasilla's police chief whom Palin fired when first elected mayor, fought his termination in court. He lost that case when the judge found that his contract, written when Stein was mayor, wasn't legal. During the court proceedings, Palin couldn't specify anything Stambaugh had done wrong except to say she felt he didn't support her. That, the judge ruled, was enough to fire him. Stambaugh left Wasilla and worked for the United Nations as a peacekeeper in Bosnia and Croatia. When he returned to Alaska, he directed the Alaska Police Standards Council before retiring. "I can't tell you how disheartening it was to get fired from the job in Wasilla," he said. "I loved that job."[20]

CHAPTER 6

Bill and Ted's Excellent
Adventure

In the spring of 2000, Bill Allen asked his nephew, Dave Anderson, to drive down to Girdwood, a small ski town about forty minutes south of Anchorage. As Anderson, an oilfield welder employed by the VECO Corporation, headed south from Anchorage, the highway shrank to two lanes hugging the Chugach Mountains to his left, Turnagain Arm to his right. This stretch of Seward Highway is beautiful but treacherous. The road snakes the edges of sheer-faced rock and avalanche chutes, with Dall sheep perched on cliffs watching the steady stream of traffic. Out the other window you may spot beluga whales in late summer or the bore tide of Turnagain Arm, a six-foot wave rushing through this northern corner of Cook Inlet. Mountains, glaciers, and rivers in all directions.

Anderson hung a left at the Girdwood turnoff, catching a glimpse of the Alyeska Ski Resort towering about a mile behind the town, which itself rises from a rain forest. Girdwood is not a big town, and most certainly not a ski resort like a Vail or an Aspen. Resorts evoke rosewood and brandy snifters and smoky perfumes. They evoke men with blindingly white teeth who wear their college rings; women whose lipstick matches their fingernails; likeminded people who live in houses that look alike. That's not Girdwood, or any place in Alaska for that matter. Girdwood is where Alaskans go to get away, but what they find is a microcosm of much of the state: the tipsy houses, the way the dogs have the run of the town, the fresh-faced snowboarders and the hairy hippies, the businessmen and developers sipping cocktails on the decks of their cottages, the oil executives and their wives atop the ski hill, staring longingly toward Houston or Bartlesville or London.

Anderson drove through a tightly packed neighborhood not far from the slopes and turned onto a narrow street. He was headed to "Ted's cabin." Bill Allen had dispatched his nephew to tidy up the senator's yard, a little spring cleaning to help a friend busy holding the purse strings of the federal budget. Not long afterward, Allen sent Anderson back down to Girdwood, along with some other VECO employees, to do more work on Ted's cabin. It was a modest little structure in a state where the size of your home, the kind of car you drive, and the kind of clothes you wear don't matter as much as in the Lower 48. Years later, when they learned about Allen and VECO working on Ted Stevens's house, some Alaskans didn't seem to think much of it. That was the mind-set engrained in old-time Alaskans. It was a small state, after all, and politicians and businessmen were friends and should be friends. Sometimes they helped each other out. As long as Alaska benefited first, what difference did it make? This was a state that still needed to find its purpose, still needed a future. Even in the year 2000, more than forty years after statehood, Uncle Ted was doing all he could to help find that future.

Ted Stevens was now in his late seventies and at the height of his power. He was Senate Appropriations chairman and would in a few years become Senate president pro tempore, making him third in line to the presidency. By now, his legacy was cemented in history. At the millennium, the state legislature named him Alaskan of the Century. More than one historian cited him as the most influential politician in the history of Alaska, besting William H. Seward, the U.S. secretary of state who spearheaded the purchase of Alaska from Russia in 1867. Still, Stevens felt his political career had come with great personal drawbacks, not the least of which was his inability to put his Harvard law degree to good use. After being named Appropriations chairman, he was again grumbling to reporters and friends about the "sacrifices" he'd made for his state. He'd traded time with his family for helping Alaskans and he gave up millions of dollars by not practicing law. If Stevens wanted it, he now had an opportunity to cash in on his seniority and make a few bucks before he retired. There was no shortage of friends and businessmen who'd do a favor for Stevens, especially now that he controlled federal spending in the Senate.

His friends and supporters were Alaska's elite, mostly middle-aged men who'd grown up in the shadow of his stardom. They included Bill Allen, who was now the most powerful oil contractor in Alaska; the state's biggest banker, the head of the state's largest brokerage, and a cadre of colorful characters, including Bob Persons, who owned a New Orleans–style restaurant in Girdwood, where Stevens and his friends dined when he was in Alaska. They shared ownership in a racehorse, helped each other's families, and enjoyed getaways to places like Las Vegas and the Paris air show. Bill Allen might have had a hard time understanding Stevens's world, but Stevens understood Allen's. He always liked the rough-and-tumble, according to former business partner and longtime friend Jack Roderick and others who knew Stevens over the years. They were "self-made men; people who picked themselves up from their bootstraps, like he did."[1]

"Ted was not an idealist," Roderick added. "He didn't want to change the world; there was none of that in him. He wanted to fix the world we already have." And the fixers of that world tended not to convene in Georgetown restaurants or fancy D.C. cocktail parties. They were the builders. The ones who had calluses on their hands and used words not meant for polite company. Stevens and Allen shared rough childhoods. They each had memories of the Great Depression. Both had shaped Alaska. Each was known as "uncle." Although Uncle Ted had graduated from Harvard law school and Uncle Bill dropped out of school to work in the oil patch, they shared a dream for Alaska. They believed the state still had a long way to go with an uncertain economic future. Sometimes they'd head down to the Arizona desert, where they'd drink wine, smoke cigars, and dream of that future. In the process, they'd shed a few pounds.[2] They called it "boot camp."

In 2000, Bill Allen rented a penthouse suite at Girdwood's Alyeska Resort and called Dave Anderson and another VECO worker to a meeting to brainstorm how they could remodel and expand Stevens's house. Stevens and his second wife, Catherine, a D.C. lawyer he married two years after Ann died in a 1978 plane crash, had agreed to take Allen up on his offer to help. As Anderson recalls it, Allen approached the Stevenses and "worked on Cathy more than he did on Ted. He said, 'Let me help you out here . . . We can expand the house and this is how we can do it.'" The plan was to jack up the house and add a floor below, which would roughly double its 1,200 square feet. "Bill started getting excited about the project," Anderson said after Stevens gave the okay. "He started adding on shit, and pretty soon we were talking about fire escapes and balconies and decks."[3] Bob Persons, the Girdwood restaurateur, was to be Stevens's eyes on the ground.

Dave Anderson could be cleaned up for polite company if you could keep him away from the bottle. At the time of the remodel, he was in his forties. Short and stocky, his voice as rough as the Arctic oil fields where he once welded pipelines. (The last time we heard from him, Anderson and his girlfriend, who also happened to be Allen's former girlfriend, had exiled themselves to an apartment that they called "a resort" in Albuquerque, New Mexico, replete with a blender and a pool—far away from Bill Allen, the federal investigation into his uncle's bribery and illegal dealings with Alaska politicians, and Ted's cabin.) He'd say things like, "It's all gone to shit," or "This is some hillbilly shit," or "We're just real people caught in a world of shit." There was less shit when Anderson was a VECO worker in the old fields, before he started climbing the company ladder, before he started organizing political fund-raisers and working on politicians' property.[4]

Anderson's parents separated when he was young and he was largely raised by his grandparents in New Mexico. His grandfather "beat the shit out of me when I was a little kid. I mean, he took the lead ropes off the cows and beat me with them," Anderson recalled. He wondered if his uncle was also beaten when he was a boy. "I don't know if Bill *didn't* go through that shit, but I did." Anderson held jobs in oil and construction around the West before drifting to Alaska in 1975 amid the pipeline boom. It was only when Anderson lasted four years in Alaska that Allen gave his nephew a job at VECO, and then only for the most menial jobs. "They first put me on top of the roof as a roustabout, tarring the roof," Anderson said. "I ate crow on everything," including being the boss's nephew.

He was proud of becoming a skilled welder like Uncle Bill, working at Kuparuk and other North Slope oil fields. The Arctic was a strange and magical place to work in, and harsh as hell: the polar bears lurking around the camps and rigs, the northern lights glowing overhead, the headlights of giant machines fighting the long winter darkness, like ships floating through space. One of his fondest memories on the Slope occurred in 1988. Three gray whales became trapped in Arctic ice, creating an international media event as rescuers tried to free them. Bill Allen donated a VECO hovercraft barge to help break a path in the ice for the whales. Dave Anderson was on the crew. (In 2010 Drew Barrymore and other Hollywood actors would come to Alaska to retell the story of the stranded gray whales in *Everybody Loves Whales,* with Ted Danson signed up to play an oil executive figure.) The next year, in 1989, Anderson was sent to the shores of Prince William Sound to help mop up the *Exxon Valdez* oil spill.

Bill Allen added new duties to Anderson's job description in the 1990s. By this time, it was clear that Allen's son, Mark Allen, was more interested in raising horses than in working for VECO, so Anderson took on some of the role Mark might have filled. As Anderson tells it, he became "Bill's right-hand man." That might be a stretch, but he did play a sensitive role in Allen's quest to please his politician friends.

Ed Dankworth was right: Allen had no idea how to stay in the lines when he mingled with Alaska's politicians. Business and friendship blurred quickly, as did lawful lobbying and flat-out bribery. Dave Anderson's role was simple in all of this. On behalf of his uncle, he worked on politicians' homes, helped organize political fund-raising parties, and contributed thousands of dollars in campaign donations, reimbursed, of course, by the company. Anderson's handy work included building a float plane dock for Rick Halford. A longtime state senator at the time, Halford would later claim he paid Allen $10,000 for it, even though Allen didn't want to take his check. In the 1990s, Halford, a big-game hunting guide, took Allen and some VECO workers on a moose hunt. He charged Allen full price for the trip, about $8,000, but the oilman wanted to pay him $15,000. Halford rejected Allen's offer. "I'm not sure what he thought he would get out of me by doing that, because he knew that I wasn't a strong supporter of the oil companies," Halford recalled. "But that's just Bill. He came from nothing and he wanted to help people."[5] Halford didn't seem concerned to have Allen as a friend while he was a lawmaker, or the perceived conflict of interest it might create; in 1998 he sold VECO his hunting lodge and seventy-four acres. Allen dispatched Dave Anderson on other duties. The nephew installed a stair lift at the home of Ramona Barnes, the first female speaker of the Alaska House of Representatives; welded a rotisserie used for a yearly pig roast fund-raiser for U.S. congressman Don Young; and ran the parking logistics and sound system for the pig roasts and other political fund-raisers. It was all part of Anderson's job, but no assignment was as sensitive as supervising the work on Ted's cabin.

During the first months of the renovation, Anderson and a small crew of VECO workers spent several days a week, on average, working on Stevens's home. By summer, however, it became apparent they needed help finishing the project. They were trained to work on oil modules and pipelines and giant commercial projects. "We weren't residential construction guys," Anderson said. "We did big projects, and we needed to bring in some expertise." In addition, VECO's labor costs were running high because the company's workers were paid top wages by Alaska's largest oil contractor. Residential carpenters could get the job done less expensively and more efficiently. So Allen subcontracted out the framing for the first-floor addition, the new garage, and the interior finishing.

When home owners undertake major renovations, they usually solicit competitive estimates and closely track material and labor costs. That apparently didn't happen on the Stevens job. Ted and Cathy were in Washington, D.C., during most of the renovation. Anderson met several times with the couple when they were in town and they seemed "nonchalant" about the project. Neither they nor Allen ever provided him with a project budget. By Anderson's account, VECO workers supplied more than $150,000 in labor on the renovation and odd jobs at the senator's property. And there were the costs of the subcontractors. The Stevenses would claim they paid at least $160,000. The federal government said that all told, the remodel and other "gifts" he failed to report as a senator totaled at least $250,000. In any case, there wasn't a lot of paperwork to back up what the work actually cost and who was paying whom and for what. Invoices never made their way to Stevens's office, and when Stevens would ask Allen about them, Allen would put him off. Stevens would later recall during a federal trial over whether he should have reported VECO's work on his Senate disclosures that his wife dealt with most of the bills and paperwork.

Even if there was nothing illegal about an oil contractor renovating and expanding Stevens's home, VECO workers were instructed to keep the project on the down-low. At one point, Allen became concerned rumors might start flying about VECO trucks and equipment sporting the firm's black and red logo parked at the senator's home. He called Anderson and told him, "Get the goddamn VECO stuff out of there. Get it out." Looking back on it in 2007, Anderson said, Stevens was probably getting special treatment: "I knew it was underhanded, without a doubt, but Ted didn't have any problem with it, Bill didn't, so why should I? Yeah, morally it wasn't right. But I work for a living. I'm not going to pass judgment on anybody. It's not my duty to judge anybody. We all got our own faults. I work for a living, I draw a paycheck. Work on the senator's house. Okay, not a problem, what do you need done?"[6]

The VECO crew added some special touches to Ted's cabin: a Viking grill, Christmas lights, some old furniture he hauled from Uncle Bill's house in Anchorage, and a bed for the senator and his wife. Did Ted Stevens want all of this stuff, or was Bill Allen just helping his friend? Or was Allen planning on spending more time there than Ted and Catherine? Remember what the former president of ARCO Alaska said about Allen: "He wants pats on the head." And remember that this was Ted Stevens, chair of the Senate Appropriations Committee, working his way to president pro tempore, where if the president, vice president, and speaker of the U.S. House of Representative were all wiped out, Stevens would be running the country. "Wouldn't you want the fourth most powerful man in your pocket?" Dave Anderson recalled seven years later.

VECO Corporation was on its way to becoming a billion-dollar operation, with oil and construction contracts across the world. Federal
prosecutors would imply later that Allen helped Stevens out in return for
his friend's support as a senator for VECO (as an example, the year before
Allen remodeled his home, VECO landed a five-year, $70 million federal
contract to perform logistical work for a polar research program, a program Stevens supported funding for) and the senator's steadfast commitment to oil development in Alaska, which included opening a slice of
the Arctic National Wildlife Refuge to oil exploration and expanding development in the National Petroleum Reserve-Alaska. Stevens would have
probably helped a major Alaska company like VECO land federal contracts, even if Allen hadn't remodeled his house or given him a bed. But
if you weren't part of the club, or were from Outside, or if you were an
FBI agent, the lines could sure seem blurred.

After the VECO workers packed up their gear and headed back to
Anchorage, an old friend visited Ted Stevens at his remodeled two-story
chalet. According to Clem Tillion, a former state lawmaker and an Alaska
legend in his own right, Stevens told him, "You can use this place anytime you want, but check with Bill." He had a twinkle in his eye. He suspected Bill was bringing down his lady friends, Tillion said. "I think it
was a place [Allen] could hide," he added. "Ted made it very clear [to
me] that Bill was putting his furniture and stuff into the building. And
he didn't care."[7]

Ted Stevens might not have cared about furniture, but he certainly cared
about Alaska. He showered Alaska in care. Because of a policy he spearheaded through the U.S. Postal service, airplanes carrying mail also began
to carry groceries and people into some of the impoverished, far-flung villages throughout the state. Stevens led processions of politicians and federal
secretaries through these tiny communities, many of them located hundreds of miles from the nearest road. The politicians saw people struggling,
with no basic services, such as running water, and no airstrip lights. Houses
were rotting and people had no access to medicine or doctors. And when
those dignitaries returned to the Beltway, their eyes were opened and
money began to flow into these outposts. By the end of his career, Stevens

was still working on getting plumbing to 13,000 rural Alaskans.[8] He helped bring telephone and Internet service to rural corners of Alaska, as well as grants and other funds that went toward building new community centers and basketball courts. Retaining walls to prevent an unruly sea agitated by climate change from flooding a town, thank-you senator. A health clinic in a little dot of a village in the middle of nowhere with cutting-edge telemedicine capability, thank-you senator. Federal funding to study everything from whale blubber to berry picking.[9] Thanks to Stevens, villagers now can use food stamps to buy fishing hooks and nets as well as groceries.[10]

In Anchorage, some urban Alaska Natives from those small villages have nice offices in glimmering buildings, buildings housing huge corporations that are the beneficiary of huge federal government contracts. Because of Ted Stevens, the Alaska Native corporations created under the land settlement act he fought for in the early 1970s qualify for no-bid federal contracts, with no limit on the size or number of contracts. This, with the help of slick businessmen from Outside, made sure the corporations had a chance to thrive. And thrive many of them have. When some of the corporations grew too big to qualify for small business loans, Stevens successfully lobbied for an amendment to continue granting Native corporations small business status. When they began to approach the nine-year limit for a single company's participation in the program, Stevens made sure they got a break, allowing the corporations to create subsidiaries to apply for the contracts. As often was the case, the Native corporations' subsidiaries then contracted with other businesses—companies like Lockheed Martin, Halliburton, and Blackwater. And so Alaska Native corporations, funded by federal contracts and contracting with big businesses, provided security in Iraq, monitored seismic activity from a base in Korea in support of the Nuclear Test Ban Treaty, developed "precision measurement services" for the military in Guam, and performed other such unlikely work around the world.[11] From 2000 to 2008, Native corporations landed $12.1 billion under special federal contracting privileges.[12] All because of Ted Stevens.

Did it matter that one of the Native corporations hired Stevens's son, Ben, as a consultant, or that his brother-in-law, a lawyer and a lobbyist, represented some of those Native corporations and their subsidiaries? Or that Stevens owned a racehorse with one of the CEOs of a Native corporation? Or that he made money off a development where one of those Native corporations built its headquarters? Laboratories and military bases and research centers and training centers and telecommunications. All reminders of Ted Stevens. In Gakona, an outpost of a couple hundred people, 180 antennas reach into the sky like gigantic twitching whiskers, gathering information on the energy potential of the aurora borealis, which will, one day and hundreds of millions dollars later, improve military communications. With any luck. Additions to museums. Hundreds of millions on plans to build roads and bridges to nowhere, which have yet to be built.

Stevens tamed the rough waters of the Bering Sea, teaming with Senator Henry "Scoop" Jackson, the Democrat from Washington State, to drive foreign fishermen out of Alaska waters in the 1970s. He continued to shape fisheries policies for the next thirty years. To channel more money to cash-starved rural Alaska, he crafted laws that give some of the Bering Sea's seafood bounty—worth tens of millions of dollars a year—to Alaska villages. Did it matter that his brother-in-law was a lobbyist for the fishing industry? Or that later his son Ben Stevens started a consulting firm into which money from commercial fishing businesses poured, or that he sat on the board and held stock options in one of those companies worth potentially millions of dollars?[13]

When Stevens was questioned about it at a press conference, he responded by threatening the *Anchorage Daily News,* the state's largest newspaper, with congressional action. He noted the paper's owners, Mc-Clatchy Company, had been sued for circulation inflation. "I intend to find out if they're pursuing that activity in our state," Stevens threatened. "And I intend to show them we can fight back . . . I believe there should be a law, a federal law, that requires truthful disclosure of circulation, and we intend to pursue that."

"People who live in glass houses shouldn't throw stones," he said.[14]

And there was more. The Anchorage Nordic Ski Association once unexpectedly ended up with an extra PistenBully grooming vehicle for maintaining cross-country trails. No one was quite sure who asked Stevens for it, but the club was happy to have it.[15] And it was a small thing compared to the $500,000 Stevens obtained to help fund a ski center in Alaska's largest city, helping Anchorage become one of the pre-eminent Nordic ski communities in North America. He also helped secure more than $13 million for the Special Olympics World Winter Games in Anchorage. Son Ben was hired as executive director and was paid $715,000.[16]

The requests to Uncle Ted kept coming: letters, thank-you notes, postcards from all across the state. It was hard on his staff sometimes to figure out who Stevens was shaking hands with and talking to when he'd come into town and draw crowds. They'd scurry behind him, writing notes like, "The guy in the brown suit who talked to you about the railroad."[17] A letter from Stevens's administration would find its way to everyone he talked to, even to the guy in the brown suit who talked about the railroad. In Washington, D.C., Stevens was known for wearing neckties with pictures of the Incredible Hulk. He described himself in Washington as a "mean SOB." He did it all for Alaska, he'd say. Alaska was home, his love. And many Alaskans believed him. He wasn't much of a social conservative. He was pro-choice, and according to one gay staffer who worked for him, didn't care one bit about sexual orientation. But on some of the hot-button issues of the day, he'd vote whatever way his party wanted him to vote, if it was good for Alaska. His motto was, "To hell with politics. Just do what's right for Alaska." And he stuck to it.

Alaska had been a big beneficiary of military spending since World War II and the ensuing cold war, and Ted Stevens secured funding throughout the decades to build up Alaska bases and protect them from closures. Hundreds of millions for a new hospital, an engineering complex, child care centers, buildings to restore corroded aircraft parts, to store fuel and hazardous waste, to store munitions maintenance and equipment, and hundreds of military apartments. By 2004, the federal government was spending more than $8 billion in Alaska. The Defense Department payroll was $1.2 billion in Alaska, and that didn't include the private contracting firms hired for all that building. With Stevens's help, Anchorage developers Jon Rubini and Leonard Hyde landed a $450 million contract to renovate and build housing on Elmendorf Air Force base in Anchorage. At around the same time, the two men offered Stevens a deal: invest $50,000 on a grab bag of properties around Anchorage and they'll grow his money.[18] By 2005, when Stevens sold his stake under increasing media criticism, it was worth more than $1 million.

When the press questioned Stevens about his investment, he reminded them and the rest of the state how much he did for Alaska year after year, and said that such "malicious attacks" against him were harming Alaska. "If I want to invest at home, with the things I've done in thirty-five years, I'd have a conflict in anything that could be reportable," he said in his defense, while acknowledging he'd made "a hell of a return" on his investment.[19] If anybody in Alaska was going to get a hell of a deal, shouldn't it be Ted? Other senators had made much more money than he did. Besides, those military bases were good for all Alaskans, particularly the many Alaskans with construction skills.

Every year Ted Stevens would attend an annual fund-raiser to help sports fishing on the Kenai peninsula in south-central Alaska, where in summer the Kenai River becomes choked with salmon whose flesh is the color of sorbets and sunsets, and where guides and boat dealers and little shops up and down the area rake it in from Alaskans and tourists alike. The money raised from the event went to shoring up eroding river banks so that more fish could spawn, and more fishermen could cast their lines. And there would be Stevens, casting himself, along with members of Congress, cabinet secretaries, and executives from corporations like Lockheed Martin, Northrop Grumman, Raytheon, Boeing, and BP (which had thinned its name down to its initials, dispensing with "British Petroleum" and branding itself "Beyond Petroleum"), and Holland America. Lobbyists and campaign donors of all sorts, including many defense contractors, who apparently cared about Alaska's most popular salmon river as much as Stevens. All there to fish and to get close to the chairman of the Senate Appropriations Committee, who also chaired the subcommittee that wrote the military spending bills. "Frankly, he's the reason I think all of us are here," Ralph Crosby, chairman of EADS North America, one of about a dozen defense contractors who underwrote parts of the tournament, told a reporter in 2003. "Everybody loves Senator Stevens and doing anything to support him."[20]

Usually more than 200 people would show up to the Kenai River event and pay $4,000 or more each for a charity that funded an association to protect and rehabilitate the river, which was responsible for supporting a burgeoning summer tourism industry. It happened to be an association chaired by Ted Stevens's longtime pal Bob Penney, one of the guys he owned the racehorse with. Penney and Stevens were partners in a Utah land deal. Stevens made an initial investment of $15,000. Seven years later he reported that he'd cashed out at $150,000.[21] As in his dealings with Rubini and Hyde, Stevens said it was nobody's business. Penney opened the event, microphone in hand, on the lawn of his riverfront house, amid tents with fresh oysters and Alaska king crab, wine tents and beer tents and vodka tents. The food and the booze were sometimes supplied by VECO. The next day, the congressmen, cabinet secretaries, and corporate executives grabbed fishing poles and jumped on boats. As they waited to feel the pull on their lines, a hospitality boat motoring up and down the river checked on them, making sure they were warm enough, had enough clothing, sandwiches, vodka, Irish cream, and cigars.[22]

And there was more. Ted Stevens flew to Homer, that idyllic little town south of where Bob Penney and the sports fishermen slay salmon, where hippies and halibut fishermen and artists live. That day was for the opening of a $10.4 million marine education and research center that Stevens had championed back in D.C. There's another memory of Stevens on Kodiak Island. Alaska's Emerald Isle, it's called, because in summer, when it's not raining sideways, the isle and landscape sparkle green. He drove for about an hour on the recently paved road to the end of the island, past a herd of buffalo and a surfing beach, to visit the Kodiak launch facility. When the state-owned rocket launcher was conceived in the early 1990s, it was supposed to generate new industry in Alaska as a launch pad for private communication and observation satellites. It was a risky idea, and Kodiak's weather and isolation didn't help. Uncle Ted to the rescue. The rocket launcher benefited from $18 million, thanks to Stevens inserting the funding into a defense spending bill.

Back in Anchorage, there was a party at the airport to honor Uncle Ted. There he was in the cockpit of a vintage twin-engine transport plane like the one he flew over China during World War II. Stevens taxied up

to a hangar, where the celebration was under way to rename the airport
after him—Ted Stevens Anchorage International Airport, in part a trib-
ute to the tens of millions of dollars in federal funding he helped secure
for runway and terminal upgrades—even a brand-new depot linking the
state-owned Alaska Railroad to the airport. Four U.S. Air Force F-15s
raced overhead and everybody sang the national anthem.[23] On hand were
the U.S. Army secretary and the FAA administrator, as well as two of
Stevens's oldest and closest friends in the Senate, who happened to be
Democrats: Fritz Hollings of South Carolina and Daniel Inouye of
Hawaii. Neither questioned Alaska's voracious appetite for pork, unlike
some other senators, such as John McCain. And most of Stevens's hometown buddies, smiling as they listened to a special song written just for
the senator, sung in baritone to the tune of "They Call the Wind Mariah"
from the musical *Paint Your Wagon*. The song was titled "Typhoon
Teddy" and included this verse:[24]

> *There won't be no denyin'* . . .
> *Because he is in Washington*
> *We know they won't forget us*
> *Because we know he has great clout*
> *Outsiders won't sublet us*[25]

Ted Stevens's influence on Alaska's economy was so profound that
some economists referred to it as "Stevens Money." From the 1980s to
the mid-1990s, Alaska received 30–40 percent more federal money per
capita than the national average. At the height of Stevens's reign, that
rate jumped to more than 70 percent. All for keeping Alaska alive until
it could finally maintain itself—someday. Stevens was sure it would succeed, as long as there were people like Bill Allen around, people who
could grow and develop this state; as long as Alaskans believed in themselves and clung to the idea of self-sufficiency. The problem, however,
was that the more money Stevens brought home to keep the state alive,
the more dependent Alaskans became on him and those federal dollars.
The more they wanted, the more he gave. Nearly one-third of working
Alaskans were employed by the federal government. Alaska was a ward of

both big oil and the feds. Residents paid no state income or sales tax and they were still receiving the annual dividend from the Alaska Permanent Fund. A Neverland fueled by oil and Ted Stevens.

But there was one development Ted Stevens couldn't deliver. For decades, he'd yelled and threatened on the Senate floor to allow oil exploration in the Arctic National Wildlife Refuge, a pristine and vast hinterland in the northeastern corner of Alaska protected by the feds from development. By the 1990s, ANWR was believed to be the last big oil reserve on the North Slope. The state didn't control it and would not benefit as much from taxing the oil, but if wildcatters were ever allowed to explore along its coastal plain, ANWR still promised jobs and investment in Alaska's oil industry. But by then, ANWR was a symbol of the national environmental movement. Most Alaskans, including many state Democrats, supported drilling in the refuge's coastal plain, but not the rest of the country. Some of Stevens's angriest moments in the Senate—his eyes bulging, his Hulk tie swinging from his neck—were over that scrap of Arctic land, which to this day remains a wilderness.

Just as uncertainty hung over ANWR and future oil and gas development in Alaska, so it did over Ted Stevens's longevity. His federal pork barrel spending had been like a mini oil boom in the late 1990s, but now he was almost eighty, and Alaskans knew he wouldn't be around forever. In 1999 the U.S. Labor Department ranked the state last on average annual pay growth and second-worst for unemployment in the country. The state's economy had little going for it besides oil and federal spending, a crude fact that hit home to Alaskans when oil prices suddenly crashed under $10 a barrel in 1999. Worse yet, oil production had fallen to about a million barrels a day—the lowest since the late 1970s. One economist began griping that Alaska, which by then had a population of 625,000, was turning into the "Appalachia of the North."[26] At the same time, the state's most recognizable institutions were going through a shakeup. Corporate America was settling into the frontier, and mergers and acquisitions were changing the landscape in 1999 and 2000. Carr-Gottstein Foods, a beloved Alaska grocery chain that had been around for decades, was sold to supermarket giant Safeway; homegrown National

Bank of Alaska, the largest bank in the state, was bought up by Wells Fargo; and perhaps most concerning, BP was taking over Atlantic Rich-field. The two oil companies were the largest in the state. In response to state and federal antitrust concerns and the need to maintain competition, BP eventually agreed to sell off ARCO's Alaska assets but hold on to other holdings in the Lower 48. It assumed operations of Prudhoe Bay, still the largest oil field in the nation, on behalf of itself and other oil companies. ARCO Alaska, in turn, was snatched up by Phillips Petroleum, which then merged with Conoco, resulting in Conoco Phillips, the largest oil producer in Alaska today.

Although oil prices were in the tank, natural gas prices were steadily climbing. In the winter of 2001, Americans paid some of the highest natural gas prices in decades to heat their homes. Prudhoe Bay and other large oil fields contained not only billions of barrels of oil but trillions of cubic feet of natural gas. The gas was re-injected into the fields to push out the oil. Now that the oil reserves were declining, oil companies and state officials were dusting off plans dating back to the mid-1970s to tap the natural gas and build a four-foot-wide pipeline from the Arctic to Chicago, perhaps 3,500 miles. At the same time, Alaska's leaders would make it their mission to do everything possible to encourage industry to pursue gas development.

Bill Allen and VECO executives started making trips down to Juneau to size up lawmakers in the early to mid-2000s, as they had so often before. A gas pipeline would be a boon for VECO, not just because of construction contracts but because it would increase the value of the company. Allen, now in his sixties, could see a time in the near future when he would want to sell VECO. If the state granted concessions, such as low taxes, to the oil industry and the companies committed to building the project, VECO's value would increase substantially.

At the time, Governor Tony Knowles, a Democrat, had less than two years left in his second term. He made the gas line his top priority, a legacy he hoped to capitalize on if he ever decided to run for senator. Knowles was an avid oil supporter—he called the industry a "partner"—and ran in Republican circles from time to time, including with Allen. Instead of turning to the oil industry when times were getting tough in the late 1990s, Knowles wanted to reinstate the income tax or tap the multibillion-dollar Permanent Fund—the state's rainy day savings account—to fund projected budget shortfalls. Allen had served on Knowles's transition team in 1994 and donated to the governor's first election. He worked behind the scenes in the Knowles administration to promote the pipeline. Meantime, a prominent state senator had been appointed to an advisory role in the U.S. Department of Interior. Ben Stevens, who was on VECO's payroll as a consultant, was appointed by Knowles to fill the lawmaker's seat. Later he would ascend to the Senate presidency and support the industry's pipeline. It was all very reminiscent of how Ted Stevens got his start: Uncle Ted appointed to the U.S. Senate and his son to the state Senate.

As the Knowles administration wound down in 2002, the pipeline project was still uncertain, but at least it was on the map. The oil companies held fast that no line would ever be built unless a deal could be struck on taxes. Still, the pieces were coming together, especially after U.S. Senator Frank Murkowski, Ted Stevens's counterpart, announced he was running for governor. Murkowski, a Republican, had served in Stevens's shadow for two decades and now saw an opportunity to return to Alaska and lead the state into the next pipeline boom. As governor, Murkowski would have the power to appoint his Senate replacement and ensure Alaska was represented in D.C. by an industry supporter. It might have worked too. Alaska would give up much, but it would finally land the pipeline project, meaning that it would have a future after the oil wells were nearly sucked dry. But then, seemingly out of nowhere, a young Wasilla mayor jumped into the scene.

PART II

PIPE DREAMS

CHAPTER 7

If You Can't Beat
the Good Ol' Boys,
Become a Good Ol' Girl

In the early 2000s, after Bill Allen had finished expanding and renovating Senator Ted Stevens's home, he sent his oil workers and subcontractors to remodel his own house. Allen lived just around the corner from a part of downtown called Bootlegger Cove, an upscale neighborhood with a view of Cook Inlet. Across the street lived a federal judge who would become a household name in Alaska for presiding over the corruption trials and sentencing Allen to prison. Governor Tony Knowles, who was wrapping up his last term in office, lived in the neighborhood. Ted Stevens's brother-in-law lived nearby too. When Allen's nephew, Dave Anderson, and his VECO crew were through renovating his house, it would be one of the nicest on the block. On a lower roof they built a deck and what looks like a makeshift tree house but is actually a covered hot tub. Bill Allen could soak and stare out at Cook Inlet and Mount Susitna, also known as the Sleeping Lady for the profile she casts. Sometimes he had company: girlfriends, including the daughter of a politician; sometimes girls who later would claim they were underage when they soaked in the hot tub and slept over at Allen's home, and then left richer than they arrived.

Bill Allen was now in his mid-sixties. His hair had faded gray, his middle had thickened, and his sway over Alaskan and U.S. politicians had grown. Not all acted on his behalf, but many Republicans and a few

Democrats took campaign money from him and from VECO. Allen hosted political fund-raisers at his newly remodeled home. There was Congressman Don Young's annual pig roast, a late summer event that packed the narrow streets of the tree-shaded neighborhood with BMWs, Hummers, and Cadillacs. One of the political fund-raisers he threw had a Harley Davidson theme. Dave Anderson recalls the judge across the street complaining about the noise from such parties. "Bill pissed off the whole neighborhood, trust me," Anderson said. "That's how he is—pedal to the metal."[1]

Allen wasn't working for a big oil company. He wasn't flown in from Texas. He belonged to Alaskans. And when he wasn't in Juneau signaling from the floor how a lawmaker should vote, he was actually a little shy, his humble New Mexican roots wrapped around him, making him feel, as those from such roots can, out of his element. An imposter, maybe. But people liked him. His smile wasn't too bright. His nails weren't manicured. Even at his own parties, he didn't work the room and press the flesh. He usually stood unassumingly with his drink, huddling with his closest friends, making plans for Alaska's future.

In 2001 those plans involved lobbying the state to pass legislation for a private prison to be built by VECO and its partners, and funded by the state. VECO's interests in private prisons dated from 1997, when the oil contractor partnered with a privately owned halfway house company to form Corrections Group North. The partnership's goal was to promote a 768-bed private prison, first in South Anchorage and then, after the citizens voted against it, in one of several other towns, all of which shot down the plans. Allen wasn't deterred. He and his partners were now looking to build a prison in Whittier, a tiny town about forty-five miles and a world away from Anchorage. Prisons were such lucrative businesses that VECO eventually would build one in Barbados.

But Allen's biggest plans were reserved for Alaska. He, along with Republican Party chairman Randy Ruedrich, was laying the groundwork for building a GOP majority in the state legislature, which would work in concert with a Republican congressional delegation to go after big projects, fight overzealous regulators, and champion the oil industry's cause. The biggest item on the agenda was to pass legislation supporting, after more than a quarter century in the making, a mega natural gas pipeline project.

The state had been dreaming about the gas pipeline since the oil was discovered—keeping Alaskans hoping for another big boom—but nothing ever came of it. Studies were done about the best routes. Should it run east along the Beaufort Sea and link up to another proposed Arctic gas pipeline on the other side of the Alaska-Canada border? Or should it take the longer, 3,500-mile route through Canada and eventually end in the Midwest? There was also a plan to follow the route of the 800-mile trans-Alaska oil pipeline to Valdez, where the gas would be liquefied and exported on tanker vessels. Throughout the years, conferences were held. Experts brought in. Papers produced by the ream. Fortunes waged and fortunes lost. But still no pipeline. However, natural gas prices had steadily been climbing in recent years, as demand outpaced new gas wells in the Lower 48. The rest of the country needed more of the clean-burning fuel. Natural gas was the rage.

In the early 2000s, Alaskans were cautiously optimistic for the gas pipeline, as well as their economy. Oil prices had climbed steadily since crashing to under $10 a barrel in 1999. By 2002 they were back around $25. The state had dodged a bullet. Alaskans still paid no income tax and still collected a dividend from the multibillion-dollar Permanent Fund, their oil-seeded savings account. The dividend had gotten quite large, with a family of five receiving annually an average of $7,622 in checks between 1996 and 2003. In 2000 alone, the dividend reached $1,963. Alaska still depended on oil royalties and taxes to fund more than 80 percent of state government. But with oil production under a million barrels a day and the low oil prices, Alaskans were not in the clear. With no other industry except oil, budget deficits were on the horizon. Although there were murmurs still of raising taxes on industry, especially after oil prices crashed and the state was facing budget shortfalls, it remained off the table. Lawmakers did look at taxing Alaskans or tapping the Permanent Fund to make up the difference, but none of the plans advanced, in part because the oil companies and the state hoped to make the natural gas pipeline a reality. With the election of President George W. Bush, a Texan who had spent a summer in Alaska in 1974 during the oil boom, and the war on terror, pro-development Alaskans were hoping Congress and the president might finally allow oil drilling on the Arctic National Wildlife

Refuge's coastal plain.[2] And while they waited for all of those things to get straightened out, they knew they could count on Uncle Ted to funnel home billions of dollars.

In 2001 Sarah Palin left her Wasilla home, drove through the downtown streets of Anchorage, and pulled up at Bill Allen's house. She had been in Wasilla city politics for almost a decade, now wrapping up her second term as mayor with higher political aspirations. She was outgrowing the small-town politics, where hour upon hour was spent debating whether or not snowmachines should be allowed on ski trails; whether the library needed $10,000 or $13,000 to install a new furnace; who should win the "Welcome to Wasilla" sign contest; filling potholes and resurfacing roads; refusing to sign a resolution to honor former police chief Irl Stambaugh, whom the former mayor had hired and Palin had fired when she took office. Some small-town mayors would climb the political ladder more cautiously, running for, say, a spot in the state legislature. Palin had her sights on the number 2 job in Alaska, lieutenant governor. In those days for a Republican, it seemed there was only one road to the state capital for a Republican, and it passed through Allen.

Dave Anderson, Allen's nephew, was working on his uncle's house that day in 2001 when Palin pulled up. (He couldn't remember if it was before his uncle's motorcycle accident or after. That same year, Allen slammed his head on the Parks Highway in Wasilla. It left his speech impaired but did not affect his memory, he later said.) In 2008, when she ran for vice president, a Palin spokesman did not deny the meeting happened between Palin and Allen. Everybody went to Bill Allen back in the day, the spokesman said. How was Palin supposed to know any different? And besides, the spokesman said, it's "a silly story," before ending the interview.[3] Silly or not, Palin surely would have known, even in 2001, that Bill Allen had a reputation as an under-the-table political mover and shaker. He still had his special editorial section in the *Anchorage Daily News*—the "Voice of the Times," a mouthpiece for Big Oil and the Republican Party. His questionable lobbying activities and support for an industry-friendly Alaska all preceded him. Palin would have known who Allen was and what he had to offer. That's why she would have knocked on his door.

Dave Anderson fetched a bottle of wine for the two and then left Allen and Palin to talk alone. What was discussed might have gone something like this: Palin told Allen she was planning to run for lieutenant governor, that she wanted a bigger role in the state Republican Party, that she fully supported "progressing development of Alaska's resources." Perhaps she paid lip service to keeping taxes low on industry, knowing Allen's soft spot. Or how she was a fiscal conservative and believed the state should knuckle down and cut government. Palin wasn't saying anything specific or novel as she began her run for lieutenant governor, but she looked good saying it, just as she looked good saying it that day in Allen's house. And she had a certain spark. Valley Republicans had supported her and campaigned hard for her during her mayoral runs in Wasilla, in large part because of her anti-abortion platform and her focus on "family values." Allen didn't care so much about the Christian stuff. He was a big business Republican, not a Christian Right Republican, but he knew he had to keep the Christians happy to get what he wanted.

In late 2001, Allen threw financial support behind Palin's campaign. VECO executives and their spouses gave her campaign $500 a piece, for a total of $5,000. VECO donations accounted for more than 10 percent of Palin's campaign war chest for the lieutenant governor's race. Somewhere along the way Allen got his picture taken with Palin. That photograph floated around his home, depending on what mood his housekeeper was in. Allen's girlfriend and housekeeper didn't get along. Sometimes the housekeeper placed the framed picture of Allen and Palin on his dresser, just to bother his girlfriend.[4]

In Alaska, voters pick lieutenant governors and governors in the primary elections. The candidates who win their primaries then run on the same ticket in the general election. If Sarah Palin won the Republican primary for lieutenant governor in 2002, that would almost certainly mean running with one of Alaska's other well-known good old boys—Frank Murkowski. He'd served in the U.S. Senate since 1980 in the shadow of Ted Stevens. A former banker with a booming voice and a quick temper, Murkowski had a mission to develop the fledging state as he saw fit. Permits, environmentalists, political factions be damned. No one—certainly not the spoiled adolescents who inhabited Alaska—was going to tell him otherwise. He thought big, in the style of Wally Hickel, Jay Hammond, and Ted Stevens. But he lacked their down-home charm, their ability to make Alaskans feel that he was one of them. He was an avid proponent of logging the Tongass National Forest, a temperate rain forest that stretched 17 million acres across Alaska's panhandle, including around Ketchikan, the town where he was raised. He dreamed of the day when a railroad would connect Alaska to Canada and America. "Imagine someday riding the railroad to visit relatives in the Lower 48, enjoying beautiful scenery and spectacular views aboard a train," he said. Never mind that nobody was building new railroads in America in the early twenty-first century, or that the project would cost at least $11 billion. Murkowski shrugged off criticism. The rail line would open up a hinterland of virgin forests and untouched land to log and mine. It would be an economic boon, he declared, if only the government and regulators would get out of the way and let the earth moving begin.

He might not have Alaskans' affection, but Murkowski had name recognition going into the 2002 gubernatorial election. He was never a Ted Stevens, but the sixty-nine-year-old chaired the Senate Energy and Natural Resources Committee and was actively involved in the state's ongoing quest to open the Arctic National Wildlife Refuge to oil exploration, as well as shepherding a national energy policy favorable to Alaska's long-standing natural gas pipe dream. Now running for governor, he told voters he was ready to come home and lead on the front lines for these and other big projects.

Sarah Palin didn't have name recognition going into the 2002 race. She was known in Republican circles as the young and attractive mayor of Wasilla, but she was a stranger to the rest of Alaska. There's only so much attention you can garner when one of your greatest accomplishment was luring a new big-box store to your already jammed strip mall of a town.

Things had settled down in Wasilla after Palin's first tumultuous term as mayor, when she fired the police chief and tried to undo many of the things that former mayor and idealist John Stein had set out to accomplish before she turned on him. She had left some scars, but her critics conceded that by her second term she was an effective mayor who got things done and made good snap decisions. There were more paved roads, more big-box retailers, and a new sports complex, which provided residents a much needed outlet.

State politics was a different arena than Palin was used to, but that was part of her charm. This was a homegrown politician whose day-to-day routine included things like visiting schools, signing ordinances, and even officiating a wedding ceremony at the local Walmart. As she started to appear on the campaign trail in 2002, her good looks and smile were leaving an impression on voters.

Sarah was everywhere in 2002. She traveled to Fairbanks at least five times. She traveled to soggy southeastern Alaska and through the Kenai Peninsula. And everywhere she went, at every forum, at every function, at every barbecue and debate, she said the same thing, over and over: We must develop our resources, get government out of the way, and prioritize the budget. She said, in effect, nothing. But Alaskans loved her fresh face. Soft on the eyes, sexy but not too sexy. Sarah Palin hunted and fished. She wore her hair like a sculpture. Her glasses gave her something that passed for gravitas. She had people on edge at a Fairbanks forum when she said, "I would encourage firing the guys who can't prioritize"[5] the state budget. Letters to the editor poured in saying Palin alone would protect personal freedoms, that she understood the Second Amendment, that she would put the gun control lobbyists in their place. "Sarah is the only candidate who has not been part of the 'status quo.' She will bring new vision, new energy and new direction to state government," said these letters, in one form or another. In 2002 the budget gap was projected to run $500 million to $800 million, depending on oil prices. The governor and state legislature had been dipping into a reserve account to make ends meet. But now the reserve held only $2.3 billion and was projected to run dry in 2004. Palin didn't speak much of the looming budget crisis. No reporter in the state got a good quote from her. But she was a novelty to Alaskans.

Her opponents had dominated Alaska politics for years. And while they lacked Palin's looks and sparkly smiles, they offered specifics. Among them was a five-term legislator who had served four years as state House speaker, a state senator who had served in the legislature since 1984, and Loren Leman, the Republican Senate majority leader. He was the Christian Right candidate. A little like Mr. Rogers meets Jerry Falwell, Leman had been surprisingly tough on the oil companies. In 1996 he almost lost his Senate seat when BP announced it would gun at unseating him by backing a challenger, a former BP lawyer. Leman, then chair of the Senate Resources Committee, had committed that unpardonable sin of questioning tax breaks on new oil fields, even against the wishes of the Democratic governor. The president of BP's Alaska division co-hosted a fund-raiser for Leman's challenger that brought in nearly $15,000. VECO executives held fund-raisers and donated generously too.[6] Had Leman been a maverick when he ran for lieutenant governor in 2002, he might have played up his battle with industry and how he was committed to ensuring Alaskans got their "fair share" for their oil. But Leman didn't have to. By now he had fallen back in line, touting his pro-business credentials and playing to his Christian base. That—and years of experience as a state politician, which she lacked—was good enough for Leman to beat Sarah Palin in the GOP primary of August 2002, though she had come surprisingly close. She lost by about 1,500 votes. Frank Murkowski won his primary handily.

Palin handled defeat well, at least publicly, proving a good and loyal Republican soldier by almost immediately campaigning for the Murkowski-Leman ticket. She zigzagged across the state doing rallies and fund-raisers. She appeared in so many campaign ads that if you weren't paying attention you might have thought she, not Leman, had won the lieutenant governor's race. Frank Murkowski faced Fran Ulmer in the general election. Ulmer was wrapping up two terms as lieutenant governor. A Democrat raised in Wisconsin, she was a true blue intellectual, and she looked more like a professor than a politician. Her hair and shoes were sensible. She spoke with a Midwestern twang. She was gentle and smart, and had served the state since 1975. She'd worked for Jay Hammond, the "bush rat governor," had been mayor of Juneau in the early 1980s, and had served in the Alaska House of Representatives from 1987 to 1994, when she was first elected lieutenant governor. Now in her mid-fifties, she knew the state and all the numbers that mattered; she could rattle off budget deficits and royalty payments and oil prices and production statistics. She understood how much Alaska depended on the federal government. She also knew enough about Alaska politics that she had to shed her liberal label.

Before she went on the campaign trail in 2002—the Tour de Fran, she called it—Ulmer applied for a concealed weapons permit, took the classes, and with reporters in tow, went out shopping for a pistol that would fit in her purse. She said she needed it on the campaign trail for "insurance." She said, "I like that laser sight," as she handled a Glock.[7]

Alaskans might stand for someone who looked and talked like a professor, but not a professor who pretended to be something she wasn't. The backlash was predictable. Ulmer, everyone knew, didn't much care about guns. What she cared about was looming budget deficits; that oil prices had slipped just a few years earlier; that oil production was now less than half its peak back in 1989. What Ulmer cared about was being honest with Alaskans, finally telling them that they might have to make some tough choices. What she cared about was that Alaskans begin to think about paying their own way. What she cared about was that the oil was running out, and there was nothing in sight to replace it.

In previous decades, a politician might have gotten away with proposing some far-fetched plan that would bring another boom: floating icebergs south to thirsty Californians or detonating nuclear bombs to build Arctic harbors; a $30 billion rail and highway tunnel under the Bering Strait to link Alaska with Siberia; a huge Teflon dome in Denali State Park. But such big ideas require confidence in the future—not to mention high oil prices—and that future didn't look so bright to Ulmer. Even some limited ideas to broaden Alaska's economy in recent years were failing, among them a state-funded fish processing plant and a state and federally funded coal plant. Somebody needed to be the grownup. Somebody needed to start making sensible plans, like how to get Alaskans involved in funding their government, or how to grow small businesses in the state's urban centers, or how to develop small economies in the rural parts of the state, which in some places in 2002 still resembled the Third World. But many Alaskans refused to hear it. And they didn't buy the Franny's-going-to-get-herself-a-gun shtick.

While the Tour de Fran chugged along, Frank Murkowski was wrapping up his last term in the U.S. Senate, hoping to leave on a bang that would propel him into the governor's mansion. Part of that effort involved including a provision in the energy bill that year to provide $10 billion in loan guarantees to the builders of a future natural gas pipeline project. He also proposed tax credits for the oil companies should the price of natural gas ever crash, an assurance the industry sought to lessen the risk of what at the time was billed as a $20 billion pipeline—a sum that would increase to more than $40 billion. But the bill wasn't going anywhere in 2002, and Murkowski came back to Alaska still promising the gas pipeline, as well as his other favorite things: railroads, gold mines, timber tracts, and other dirt-turning projects.

They were big ideas—with little behind them. In true senatorial style, it was vision, not cost or practicality, that mattered. The real issue, he told voters, was the environmentalists. They were holding up the mining and logging and oil drilling. His solution was to fight them, just as he did as a senator. The bottom line: Alaska's economy was fine. No way, no how would its citizens need to pay a tax. There might need to be some budget trimming, some service reductions, but nothing major, he said. Bright days were ahead; just wait and see.

Sarah Palin was Frank Murkowski's bulldog on the campaign trail. She played her part well, barnstorming around the state, telling Alaskans that Fran Ulmer's vision for Alaska was all "doom and gloom." "We don't need to look back. We need to go forward," she said during the campaign as it pushed into fall 2002. Nobody really knew what that meant, but it sounded positive and vigorous. Ulmer tried to reason with Alaskans. She told them that Murkowski was running a campaign that basically said, "Don't worry, be happy," and that he was "misleading people and underestimating their intelligence."[8] Perhaps. But it was good politics. Murkowski aired television spots tying Ulmer to former president Bill Clinton, who was against opening the Arctic National Wildlife Refuge to oil exploration. It was a thorny issue, since many still dreamed of drilling in ANWR, with some surveys suggesting that more than two-thirds of Alaskans were for it. Ulmer counterattacked by highlighting Murkowski's Senate voting record on education and minimum wage. Frank Murkowski was clearly winning the battle of the ads.

Then the heavyweights came out for Murkowski. Senator Ted Stevens, U.S. Representative Don Young, and even President George W. Bush implored Alaskans to do the prudent thing and vote for Murkowski. By now tagged as the tax-and-spend liberal, Fran Ulmer saw her poll numbers take a nosedive. In November 2002, Murkowski easily won the governor's race, taking nearly 56 percent of the vote. Moreover, Alaska Republicans had scored big wins in the state legislature. The Republicans held majorities in both the state House and Senate and now had a Republican governor, the first time since 1966. Alaska's congressional delegation was Republican. The president was a Republican. The stars were aligned for the next big boom, as Murkowski, Stevens, and others promised Alaskans.

Before Governor Frank Murkowski could jump-start that big boom, he had one last order of business. As governor, he had final say on who would serve out the two years remaining in his U.S. Senate term, thanks to some careful planning and plotting on the part of state Republican lawmakers. After Murkowski decided to run, they worked to ensure that he, and not outgoing governor Tony Knowles, would have the authority to make appointments to vacant Senate seats. They amended the law so that the seat had to be vacant for five days before an appointment could be made. It was all very reminiscent of when Ted Stevens and his fellow Republicans tweaked the law to ensure Wally Hickel could appoint a Republican to the U.S. Senate, resulting in Uncle Ted going to Washington in late 1968 after Democrat Bob Bartlett died.

Speculation ran rampant as soon as Murkowski took the helm. Would he appoint Fairbanksian John Binkley, longtime Alaska businessman and former state legislator? He was smart, decent, and honest, as well as a licensed pilot and boat captain. Former Teamster head Jerry Hood, who had been a Democrat until he began sucking up to Murkowski, was eyeing the Senate seat too. Good lord, would it be Ben Stevens? He was an ornery cuss who'd recently been appointed to the state Senate. Surely Murkowski wouldn't be so arrogant as to appoint Uncle Ted's son.

What about Sarah Palin? She was young, telegenic, said the right things, and had worked hard to get Murkowski elected. Yet to many Alaskans, she still seemed less than qualified. She had the charisma, the confidence, the charm, and those who knew her said that she wanted badly to be senator. But what about the depth of knowledge of Alaska, the patience to listen and learn and analyze, or the smarts to survive in the Beltway? How could she possibly gain those skills as mayor of Wasilla? Was there really that much to analyze in Wasilla? The whole point of living in Wasilla was that you didn't have to go around analyzing things, not the least being this massive problem-ridden, money pit of a state addicted to oil and Stevens money. Murkowski went ahead and interviewed Palin anyway, along with about ten other candidates. He asked them about their vision, about what they would do in the Senate. He asked them about their family life and warned that D.C. could be tough on spouses and children. He spent more time on the family stuff with Palin, mother of four children at the time, than with other candidates. In the end, however, meeting with Palin was more of a favor to her for the work she'd done on his campaign than a serious interview. "It was a courtesy," Murkowski said later. "I got a list of a bunch of names, and was told that everyone on the list wanted to be interviewed. She was pleasant. She didn't say much. I was carrying the conversation. When you're interviewing people, you check to see if their experience matches what you need. In fairness to her, she didn't have any experience in those areas. On the other hand, she didn't make any excuses for not having that experience. I would be less than honest to say that she was given serious consideration."[9]

Instead, Murkowski looked to his own family for his successor. At a swearing-in ceremony on December 20, 2002, the governor turned to his daughter, Lisa, and said, "I know that you have the capabilities and the desire and the commitment to represent Alaska. Your mother and I are very proud." That was the first of many mistakes Frank Murkowski made. And there was one person that day who began to keep a tally on both Frank and Lisa. A few years later, when Palin was asked at a Democratic function if she had plans to run for U.S. Senate, she said, "I'll do it the Alaska way. I'll wait for my dad to become governor."[10]

CHAPTER 8

Neverland Meets Lord of the Flies on Crack

Frank Murkowski's twenty-two years in the U.S. Senate might have been too many. He grew a paunch extending up to his chin. His suits were a little too nice, and his hands were soft. He'd been a banker before he left Alaska in 1980 to serve in the Senate, but at least he pretended to wield an ax and cast a line, like he was supposed to do, being as he grew up in the panhandle rain forest. Now Murkowski was getting reacquainted with Alaskans, and there were signs of disconnect. He'd come rolling back to his beloved state like a king, having appointed his daughter to finish out the two years left in his Senate term and now presiding over his people from the governor's mansion. Murkowski had forgotten how much stock Alaskans place in their governor, how hard they could be on their governor. Alaskans do not cow to governors. They do not automatically laugh at their jokes. They do not clear the floor when the governor walks into the room. Murkowski had forgotten that Alaskans tend to watch their governor as closely as those in the Lower 48 watch the president. Perhaps even more closely because the population is so small. It's not unusual for an average citizen to go to the same party the governor is invited to. It's not unusual for the governor to be on a first-name basis with constituents. The problem with such intimacy is that when you start breaking campaign promises—or when you appear to be using the state as a stepping stool for higher aspirations—people take it personally. Sarah Palin would find this out soon enough. For now, it was Frank Murkowski's turn.

He didn't have these problems when he was a senator, 3,700 miles from the people he represented. He'd come back occasionally and vow to fight for things: opening the Arctic National Wildlife Refuge to oil drilling, for instance, or logging in the Tongass National Forest. They took him for granted when he was in Washington, paying more attention to Ted Stevens and Don Young, Alaska's lone U.S. congressman. But now Murkowski was here all the time, and although he promised he would "keep Alaska open for business" and land the state a mega natural gas pipeline project, his fiefdom wasn't sure they didn't like it the way it used to be.

First, realizing that Alaska did indeed have a budget problem, he attacked it with a hacksaw. He had said during the campaign that he would tighten state services but was never specific. But now he was suddenly very specific. First to go: the longevity bonus, a $250 monthly state check sent to many Alaskans over 65. The bonus was draining the coffers, and even well-off people qualified for it. Frank proposed replacing the longevity bonus with a check based on income level and assets. But if seniors in the Lower 48 are loud when dissatisfied, in Alaska they're doubly so. They'd helped create the state; some actually had a hand in writing the constitution. They'd been through countless seven-month winters, dug themselves out of endless snowbanks. They'd come all the way up here and sacrificed real milk for the powdered stuff, fresh steak for grizzled pieces of gray meat. They lived in little shacks with moss for insulation. They pickled noses of moose and ate canned salmon all winter. They organized community meetings and built churches. They felled trees by hand and planted turnips and built roads through terrifying mountain passes. They'd been gorged by bears and fought off charging moose. They'd brought the Bible to Eskimo villages, and were sometimes run out of those communities. Their hands were twisted from all of the hard work and the arthritis that came with it; some were missing a few digits from frostbite. They made this state and would not tolerate somebody messing with them. And Frank Murkowski, a senior himself, had messed with them.

He wanted to cut all sorts of state services and programs, and asked Alaskans to sacrifice by paying higher user fees—those little charges on things like visiting state parks or changing from winter to summer tires. It all started to sound a lot like taxes, which Murkowski had promised he'd stay away from as governor. Murkowski was unapologetic for breaking campaign promises, as if there was something wrong with Alaskans for taking offense, as if the state was full of spoiled children who needed a time-out. He stomped out of press conferences when asked about it and grew impatient at public forums.

Frank Murkowski would bring back aerial wolf hunting, a government program designed to thin the predator population to increase caribou and moose numbers in some parts of the state so that other hunters had a better chance of filling their freezers. Wildlife lovers howled. More shocking, perhaps, was his proposal in 2003 to abolish the Alaska Public Offices Commission, the state agency that regulates campaign financing and lobbying—a primary line of defense to prevent things like oil policy and politics from getting blurred. APOC was a notoriously underfunded agency, as well as a thorn in the side of those who liked to push the bounds of the law, guys like Bill Allen. In the early 1980s, it was APOC that levied the fines against VECO for its illegal campaign contributions. And in 2002 the agency was again investigating Allen and VECO, this time over alleged lobbying activities in the state capital. Neither had registered as a lobbyist, a requirement for anyone who spends more than four hours a month trying to influence legislation. Such a violation could carry penalties for Allen and his oil company, including being barred from making political donations, when Allen and VECO employees were the biggest political donors in the state. But nothing came of it. Although Murkowski did not succeed in dismantling APOC, the Alaska legislature in 2003 revised the state guidelines to allow Allen to lobby up to forty hours a month.[1] In the halls of the Capitol, it was referred to as the "Bill Allen bill."

In 2003 Sarah Palin was still on favorable terms with Frank Murkowski and the good old boys. She'd labored hard to get him elected and was now under consideration for an appointment. She was a good Republican but make no mistake: she wasn't one of "them." Although she had recently left her church where people speak in tongues—a move that coincided nicely with her lieutenant governor campaign the previous year—for a more mainstream nondenominational church, she was still a different kind of Republican. She was a Wasilla Republican, a Christian Republican. The Murkowski Republicans—the big business GOP—didn't socialize much with Christian Republicans between election years. They didn't really understand them. But they needed them and the passion they inspired.

Murkowski's chief of staff, the iron-fisted Jim Clark, dealt with Palin. A Cornell law school graduate, Clark, like his boss, had a big temper. Analytical and arrogant, a lousy communicator who nonetheless assumed that results led to respect, he was a red-faced table thumper and an old and dear friend of Murkowski's. And he wielded extraordinary power in the administration. "I didn't know Sarah Palin from Adam," Clark recalled in a 2010 interview.[2] "But the governor had been very impressed with her, and wanted to make sure she had a place in the administration." As they discussed a job for Palin, she had a few nonnegotiable demands: "The governor had already announced that all commissioners had to live in Juneau. She told me, 'I can't do that. I've got four kids and a husband on the Slope. Any job I take has to be in Anchorage.' And she told me that, 'Any job I take has to pay well.'"

There were two commissioner posts open at the Alaska Oil and Gas Conservation Commission, a state agency charged with regulating oil wells, drilling, and production. Clark offered her one of the commissioner jobs that included ethics supervisor for the agency. "It was the only thing I found in the $100,000 range, which seemed to be her criteria," Clark said. "I told her that [the job] required using her intelligence to think like the public, and that she needed to make herself aware of oil and gas issues." The job might have seemed a stretch for Palin; the Alaska Oil and Gas Conservation Commission was a complex agency that oversaw thousands of wells and valves in the aging Arctic oil fields in an effort to ensure that oil and gas companies were developing the resources for the maximum benefit of the state. It was on the forefront of regulatory battles with industry, and at times lawmakers sympathetic to the burdens of regulation had slaughtered the agency's budget.

Palin might have seemed an odd pick, but her lack of credentials was nothing compared to those of the other commissioner appointed to the

Alaska Oil and Gas Conservation Commission. Murkowski chose the chair of the Alaska Republican Party, Randy Ruedrich, to serve as the petroleum engineer commissioner. In the early 2000s, Ruedrich, who had a doctorate in chemical engineering, was the Karl Rove of Alaska politics. A Texas native and former ARCO drilling manager, with the requisite slow drawl, pot belly, and big swatch of gray hair, he took over the Alaska Republican Party in 2000, and was now behind the scenes building a coalition. He remapped voting districts and closed the primary to Democrats. He raised loads of cash and brought discipline to a party that, much like in the Lower 48, was trying to reconcile big business Republicans with Christian Right Republicans. Ruedrich was from the libertarian side of the party but understood the need to bring in value voters, somehow convincing them that low taxes and loosened regulation on industry also meant fewer abortions and fewer divorces. He understood how regulations could stymie development; that was one of the reasons he was appointed to his position.

Both Ruedrich and Palin needed to be confirmed by the legislature. Only three lawmakers voted against Palin's nomination, saying they wanted someone with more technical expertise. All of the Democrats voted against Ruedrich. They were apoplectic about it. How could the chair of the Republican Party also be in charge of regulating the industries that gave the most money to the Republican Party? "I don't know how you can take propriety information at the same time you're serving as political party chairperson. The conflicts are inherent and omnipresent," one Democrat lawmaker said.[3]

Of all the things that Murkowski did wrong during his four years as governor—appointing his daughter to finish out his U.S. Senate term, gutting funding for seniors, raising user fees, hiring his personal politico to be attorney general, buying himself a jet, turning a blind eye while his chief of staff got close to Bill Allen, failing to win the confidence of the public when he was conducting less than transparent tax and pipeline negotiations with the oil companies—the one thing that perhaps had the most impact on the state, and later the country, was pairing Randy Ruedrich with Sarah Palin. That one unforeseen blunder would catapult Palin into the limelight and deem her a savior of Alaska politics.

"It was one of my biggest mistakes," said Jim Clark, who oversaw the pairing. "I should not have done it. I take total responsibility for it," he said, anguish in his voice.[4]

Sarah Palin worked at the Alaska Oil and Gas Conservation Commission in downtown Anchorage in 2003 during one of the most glorious summers city residents could remember. They experienced a true heat wave, with temperatures reaching 84 degrees. Blue skies hovered over the city. People talked about the sunshine in grocery stores, in bars, in parks. This is the way they live in California, like all the time, they said. They got sunburned while fishing, dipped their white bodies into lakes, sweated under the midnight sun. They boated and camped and frolicked and climbed mountains and ran with arms swirling through fields of tundra. They got freckles in places they didn't know they could get freckles, and they grew tomatoes, actual real tomatoes that turned red and burst when you bit into them. Toby Keith came that summer and played his new hit about loving a certain bar to a stomping, flag-waving, sweaty crowd, who loved the bars and the state and everything about it.

In the south end of town, inside a large house with views of Cook Inlet, another tale was unfolding in 2003. If you were just moving to Anchorage from a suburb in the Lower 48, looking for a neighborhood that might remind you of the one you left behind, you might choose to live in Oceanview, in a place where your kids would be in good hands. Mature trees. Large homes. A place to keep the wild out. Josef Boehm, the fifty-nine-year-old owner of a hardware store chain in Alaska, lived in one of those Oceanview homes, a five-bedroom, 4,000-square-foot house. Boehm was an Alaska success story. He started with little, and now he had eight stores scattered throughout the state. When he worked, he worked hard. Neighbors didn't see much of him in the summer of 2003, but there were signs of life at his house: cars and teenagers showing up in the middle of the night, lights on at all hours, shouting in the driveway. Boehm himself looked pale, skinny, and disheveled. Was he sick and having a bunch of teenagers take care of him, teens who came and went at all hours? Something had to be wrong, but neighbors shrugged their shoulders and got going about their day. Alaskans can be like that. It's a state that attracts the best and the worst from Outside, a place where you can come and be anything you want. You can go as high as you want and as low as you want. No limits to ambition, in either direction. A state whose history is built on the backs of castaways. A state where a man with an idea and a dime can become a top businessman. A place where a woman who went to five colleges, charmed a state by saying nothing, but looked good saying it can be governor. A place where successful citizens can disintegrate right before everyone's eyes and nobody has much to say about it.

Some of Boehm's friends knew he had a problem with a certain drug. They knew that he had been locked up in his house for months, and that he had plenty of company. A few of his friends tried to get him help. One called his daughter, who lived in Florida, to try to do something. She came up a few times but her father's girlfriend—a woman in her early twenties with steely blue eyes and long dark hair—never let her into the house and kept Boehm away from her.[5]

The girlfriend, Bambi Tyree, knew all about what went on at Joe Boehm's house. She was a ringleader of the group, the Lord of the Flies on Crack. She found the teenage runaways—girls as young as thirteen— for him, many of them like Tyree having grown up in Wasilla. The lost children: pubescent outcasts in a rugged land, a land without borders and rules. Boehm, in return, gave Tyree money. And while he was holed up in his bedroom, strung out on crack and sleeping with the girls, Tyree had the run of his house, along with the runaways, ghetto boys, pimps, prostitutes, and drag queens. "Joe Millionaire," the young Alaska castaways called him, would do anything if you kept a pipe between his lips with a naked girl next to him. When he tried to kick everyone out, they'd threaten to call the cops. They did things like dangle his cell phone and car keys in front of him and demand money for them. When he handed over the money, they'd do it again. He was so stoned he'd forget. If he didn't, all they needed to tell him was that he was crazy. Joe Millionaire, dressed in a bathrobe, bags under his eyes, would scratch his head and eventually retreat to his bedroom. One time he had enough energy to try to escape his house. He sneaked downstairs in the middle of the night, tried to clog all the drains downstairs, and turned on the water. He thought he would flood the place and everybody inside would finally leave. But they caught him in the act and took him back upstairs. He tried to sneak out of a window, but Tyree caught him and again threatened him with the cops. She got another girl to lie next to him and keep him busy until he forgot about everything.[6]

Bambi Tyree knew money and power didn't inoculate rich men like Joe Boehm from their weaknesses. She learned this from none other than Bill Allen, when she was fifteen years old, as she would later tell authorities. It would all start to seep out between mid-2003 and early 2004, when the cops finally busted Boehm. Allen, though, wouldn't know just how much trouble he was in until three years later. The events that would unfold—the downfall of Murkowski, the corruption and the federal indictments, Sarah Palin's spectacular rise, and Senator Ted Stevens's dramatic downfall—would in part stem from Bambi Tyree, another raven-haired beauty from Wasilla who would leave her mark on Alaska.

Day after day, Sarah Palin, wearing outdated suit jackets with shoulder pads, drove from Wasilla to Anchorage and did her job at the Alaska Oil and Gas Conservation Commission. She was cramped up with the head of the Alaska GOP in a small, chilly office, its cement walls and fluorescent lights making it feel like a prison. She had to drink hot water to keep herself warm. She spent many days in the conference room sitting next to Randy Ruedrich, in one of the three commissioners chairs, listening to oil engineers explain how they planned to inject gas and water into wells, how much natural gas was needed to increase oil production, about packers and rams and top seals, fluids and well bores, disposal-injection orders, disposal wells, safety-value system tests, mechanical integrity tests, flaring, and aquifer exemption orders. While the industry men talked, she could eye the maps on the wall. There was the North Slope, with the outlines of the various oil fields: Kuparuk, Milini Point, Alpine, Endicott, Badami, and so on. On one map was Prudhoe Bay, the biggest of the fields, the one that made everything possible. She must have thought about that 1968 discovery, about how it changed the state for the better and in some ways made it worse. How it attracted people like Randy Ruedrich, whom she was beginning to loathe. Ruedrich was buddy-buddy with the oil executives and condescending toward her, rolling his eyes and ceasing conversation when she walked into the room. It was humiliating, particularly given that she didn't feel up to the job, and justifiably so. Her job was to give an informed citizen point of view of the agency's actions, but that meant knowing what rams and top seals actually do, what a multilateral well actually is, how a blowout preventer works, the difference between a gas-cap drive and a water drive. Her predecessor was a former state assistant attorney general who went on to be a petroleum manager for the Alaska Department of Natural Resources. This was a job for someone who loves to dive into details. She might be a quick study, and she definitely could view a situation and make a talking point out of it. But Palin was a politician. Sitting in a small office, grinding over such details, was not her calling.

It was not only Ruedrich and her job she was starting to disdain. Palin was growing more dubious about the Alaska Republican Party, especially Frank Murkowski and his administration. She read the papers avidly at the time, paying attention to the letters to the editor. She noticed a change in tone in those letters. Murkowski's luster was wearing off. How could she work for an increasingly unpopular Murkowski and keep her distance at the same time? The state's top political jobs were locked up; the U.S. Senate seats were taken by Ted Stevens and Frank's daughter, Lisa Murkowski. And Lisa had already declared her intentions of running in 2004 to hold on to the seat her father had bestowed on her. She had the full support of the Republican Party, already raising more than $1 million; even Vice President Dick Cheney showed up to speak at a $1,000-a-plate fund-raiser for Lisa Murkowski and other Republicans in Dallas.[7] Frank was less than one year into his first term as governor. Would Palin be told to shut up like a good girl and wait her turn for a big spot on the ticket? That might be eight years, nearly a lifetime. Would she be stuck in this shabby office talking about valves, drilling mud, and corrosion for all that time? Working for an increasingly unpopular Murkowski administration?

The answer came to Palin over the summer and fall of 2003, when she saw the crack in the door. She began to hear things about Randy

Ruedrich, like how he had attended a fund-raiser for a politician, how he'd sent emails to GOP members on his state computer, the very thing that he promised not to do. She was getting phone calls from Mat-Su Valley residents about Ruedrich blurring the lines between state and party business. The press started picking up the scent. In September 2003, there was a newspaper cartoon of Ruedrich wearing two hats. A staffer at the Alaska Oil and Gas Conservation Commission pinned it on the bulletin board and employees chuckled around it, according to notes Palin started to methodically keep as her suspicions widened. She kept track of every negative thing written in the newspapers about the agency, Ruedrich, and Murkowski, and it was coming at a greater speed. Ruedrich didn't pay much attention to it. At one point, according to Palin, she told Ruedrich, "You're like a duck . . . like this is water that just rolls off your back." He reminded her that he'd been around a long time, and like a "Jewish wall . . . the harder you push, the taller it grows."[8]

It was a proposed coal bed methane development, natural gas that's relatively shallow and found in coal seams, that she was hearing most about from her former Mat-Su Valley constituents. Many Alaskans are pro-development, including those in the Valley, as long as that development doesn't happen under their homes. The state owned the subsurface rights and wasn't required to notify owners prior to gas drilling on private land, even though it might poison the water. Evergreen Resources, a Denver-based company at the time, had made sure of that by hiring a state legislator as a consultant. Palin gave a nod to local control, but she went so far as to lend her name as campaign chair to a mayoral candidate who was one of Evergreen's biggest boosters. Yet when the coal bed methane issue started causing a ruckus in the Valley, Palin began to distance herself. Hordes of angry Valley residents were showing up at community meetings to protest the development. They heckled Evergreen representatives and held signs with pictures of what such drilling looked like in the Rocky Mountains, and it wasn't pretty.

Ruedrich talked to one group in his capacity at the Alaska Oil and Gas Conservation Commission, which would be involved in regulating Evergreen Resources if it moved ahead with its project. But he didn't sound like a state representative. He sounded like a company man. Even a Power Point presentation he gave at a public forum looked suspiciously similar to one given by Evergreen Resources just days earlier. Some Valley residents began to accuse Palin of supporting Ruedrich and his industry-sponsored push for coal bed methane. Letters began to appear in the local paper, questioning her role in the deal. A coworker of Palin's at the Alaska Oil and Gas Conservation Commission showed her an email sent from Ruedrich to an Evergreen Resources lawyer and lobbyist. It contained a confidential state legal memo about coal bed methane.

Palin called the governor's office to express her concerns, and in the meantime leaked information about what was going on in the agency to the press. Media began asking questions and eventually honed on Palin, the whistleblower. Later, after Palin was deemed a hero for blowing it up, she told local reporters that sometimes she had to wait for weeks to get a response from Murkowski's staff, that his administration was ignoring and failing to communicate with her. The media ate it up and pretty much reprinted what she said verbatim. But the truth was more complicated. According to her own notes, Palin first talked to Jim Clark, Murkowski's chief of staff, about Randy Ruedrich's conflicts of interest on September 27, 2003.[9] It took the administration seven weeks from that point to ask for Ruedrich's resignation. During that period, Palin noted that the administration contacted her at least seven times; three times in person. One contact she doesn't note was a trip she took to Juneau, where she talked to Clark about Ruedrich. She wrote a letter to the governor about her concerns but never gave it to him. She finally talked to him about Ruedrich on October 26, 2003. The attorney general visited her and Ruedrich the next day. Twelve days later, Ruedrich was no longer at the Alaska Oil and Gas Conservation Commission. Clark recalled later that the administration should have paid attention to Palin's concerns earlier, and that she was right to question the ethics of the situation. But it was a new administration. Every time Clark spoke to him, Ruedrich offered a plausible excuse for his actions. Still, Clark stuck up for Palin, saying that she did the right thing and that Ruedrich should never have been appointed to the commission. "I made a terrible mistake," he said in an interview.[10]

On January 16, 2004, Palin abruptly announced her resignation. The people working there, the people she left behind, had generally supported her effort to oust Ruedrich. They didn't like him, wanted him gone, and applauded her for blowing the whistle. However, some were confused by her resignation. Ruedrich had already left. The problem, as far as they were concerned, was solved. Now there were two empty commissioner positions. Decisions needed to be made. The agency was in disarray, its reputation bruised. Why did Palin have to quit? they wondered. Why not stay on and help them through the crisis?

The local media didn't focus on why Palin resigned, instead lionizing her as the young Republican female who took on Murkowski and the head of the state GOP. They cheered her on as she embraced the role and continued to inflict damage on the Murkowski administration. Palin and a state Democrat lawmaker later lodged an ethics complaint against Murkowski's attorney general, who was embroiled over owning stock in a company that stood to benefit from a trade deal he was working on for the state. Reporters again interviewed her, her picture appearing on TV and in the newspapers. Still, the Murkowski administration discounted the threat she posed to them and the Republican establishment. By some accounts, they'd written her off as a wannabe state politician turned gadfly.

The Alaska Public Offices Commission—the agency Murkowski had proposed abolishing—fined Randy Ruedrich $12,000 for engaging in partisan activity in his office, improperly disclosing the confidential legal document to the lobbyist, and improperly running the party after he promised he wouldn't. Ruedrich continued to run the state GOP. It was all a big story then, the beginning of the breakdown of Alaska's GOP, the party that promised Alaska another boom. The arrogant party, the one that didn't listen to regular folks like Sarah Palin. The party that people were beginning to love to hate. Soon, however, it would all seem relatively minor, a little tremor before the big one.

In the early 2000s, the FBI was ramping up its efforts to weed out public corruption across the country. As was happening from New Jersey to Washington, D.C., Las Vegas to San Diego, agents were nosing around in Alaska. In 2003 a female FBI agent in Juneau was laying the groundwork for Polar Pen, an investigation into the dealings of state officials and lawmakers with private prison companies, construction contractors, and others. For years, the state had been talking to contractors about a private prison project somewhere in Alaska. The state was paying hundreds of millions of dollars sending more than 800 inmates to the Lower 48 because it lacked prison beds. A partnership of private prison companies, builders, and Bill Allen's VECO lobbied the legislature for support in building a private prison in Alaska and bringing the inmates home. They saw the potential for hundreds of millions of dollars in state contracts, and the group's partners spent more than $1 million between the mid-1990s and early 2000s in campaign donations on lawmakers they hoped would support the effort.[11] The FBI cultivated sources and leveraged questionable players in a game to see how deep corruption ran in Alaska. Private prisons were only the tip of the iceberg.

In early 2004 a young fugitive knocked on Bill Allen's door. Bambi Tyree, then 23, was on the run after Joe "Millionaire" Boehm's home had been raided by police, busting up one of the most notorious sex and drug rings in recent Anchorage history. Tyree came to Allen looking for help. Allen, through his lawyer, would later say he was friends with Tyree and knew her father, Mark, a plumber who had helped VECO remodel Senator Ted Stevens's home four years earlier. Before Mark died in 2005, Allen pledged he would look out for his daughter and family, according to Allen's lawyer. Bambi Tyree, who had a warrant out for her arrest, asked Allen if she could stay at his house. She was in trouble and she was going to the only person she thought could help her. He turned her away but did not report her to police.[12] She turned herself in shortly thereafter and agreed to cooperate with the feds—including one of the lead prosecutors in Alaska's corruption probe—against Boehm for a reduced sentence. That cooperation involved telling them everything she knew. All the teenagers in Boehm's house. Everything that they did to him. All the drugs. All of her past associations, including her relationship with Allen.

Nobody would have thought that a street girl from Wasilla could cause so many problems, least of all the feds. Allen would later go to great lengths to hide his relationship with Tyree, and the feds would help him along. They needed him, after all. Their star witness in Alaska's biggest corruption investigation could not be sullied by some sordid sex crime that involved a girl who would trade teenagers for crack. It would be devastating for their case. For his part, Allen always maintained his innocence through statements by his lawyer, denying having a sexual relationship with Tyree. And as of this writing, he was never charged with a sex crime. "Bill has done nothing but help Bambi," Bob Bundy, Allen's lawyer, later said. But the investigations and accusations against him are documented in court filings, as well as by those who claimed to know about Allen's transgressions.

It's a convoluted story, in the way that stories involving drugs and crime can be, particularly in a small town like Anchorage, where everyone seems connected. Particularly in a state like Alaska, where perceptions of class distinctions don't exist as much as in the Lower 48. In other states, people know where the bad side of town is, who you should and should not mingle with. In Alaska, it's all jumbled, and so are its people, for better and for worse. It might be unlikely in other places that a street girl like Bambi Tyree could hook up with someone like Joe Boehm. It might be unlikely that someone like Bill Allen would become the state's political kingmaker. It would certainly be unlikely that such a man would rub shoulders with the presidents of some of the largest corporations in the world, just as it would be unlikely that the same man would consider one of his best friends to be one of the most powerful senators in the country. But given the right circumstances, this could perhaps happen. What would be nearly inconceivable in another place is that the same man, the same kingmaker, the same political powerhouse, would become smitten by a teenage crack addict.

According to federal and local investigative interviews and other documents filed in federal court, Allen allegedly met Tyree when she was fifteen years old through a prostitute, Lisa Moore, with whom Allen had a relationship. Moore was nineteen years old when she and Allen first met in 1996. He gave Moore money and jewelry and an apartment. She slept

with him and introduced Allen to Tyree, who was just getting out of ju-
venile jail for running cocaine for a "pimp." Tyree, according to Moore
and others who knew her, was highly manipulative. A friend said that
she was the "best hustler I have ever seen." Her "scams," a former
boyfriend said in a deposition, "were furthered through physical intimi-
dation, black mail and threats of calling law enforcement."[13] Other
women who later did prison time with Tyree when she was in her twenties confirmed those traits. But they also said Tyree had a touch of vul-
nerability to her. You could see it when she smiled, her blue eyes sparkled,
surprising considering how badly she had been used as a child. If they
shined when she was in her twenties, imagine what they looked like when
she was fifteen, even though by then she was already struggling with a
crack addiction.[14]

Allen drank and cussed and was attracted to young girls, but he didn't
approve of drugs. In this way he was old school, and he tried to help
wean Tyree from her crack addiction. He also did something else that, in
another life, another dimension, could be perceived as gallant. Perhaps by
the standards he was raised with it was. He allegedly approached Tyree's
mom and asked if it was okay if he dated her fifteen-year-old daughter.
She gave him her blessing, and in exchange got cars and gifts.[15] Later,
Allen would hire Bambi's father as the plumber for the renovation of Ted
Stevens's cabin.

Sometime before 1997, Allen had enough of Moore. He liked Tyree
better, and Moore got upset. This, Moore told both federal and local
investigators, led to a "falling out." Allen called Moore and her mother
in for a meeting with his lawyers. They tried to get Moore to sign an affidavit, swearing that neither she nor Tyree ever had sex with Allen.
They offered her $5,000 to keep her mouth shut. She refused to sign it,
thinking she could probably get more. For some reason, Allen also
asked Tyree to sign a similar statement. Tyree did so, she told the feds
in 2004 when she had to spill her guts over the Boehm affair, because
she cared for Allen and didn't want anything bad to happen to him.
Assistant U.S. Attorney Joe Bottini was one of three in the room when
Bambi told the feds this. Bottini would later help prosecute the Alaska
corruption trials.[16]

Moore began dating another man and told him the story. When Moore found out that this other man was having sex with another fifteen-year-old girl, she called the cops on him. He, in turn, threatened to call her to the stand during his trial and expose the Tyree-Allen connection. Allen got wind of this and persuaded Moore to move to Bakersfield, California, setting her up with an apartment and Moore's brother with a job. It didn't last. Moore came back and wanted more money from Allen but he refused, which angered Moore and her mother.

In 2004, when the media was reporting on Bambi Tyree and her role in the Boehm sex-drug ring, Moore's mother called Allen and left a message on his answering machine. "It looks like your secrets are about to come out," she said, according to court documents.[17] Indeed they were, but it would take awhile. Moore told much of this and more to FBI agents and local cops who were investigating the Boehm case. She even dropped off diaries, plane ticket stubs, a rental lease, receipts, and pictures to back up her claims, information that would later mysteriously disappear. Frank Russo, an assistant U.S. attorney general in Alaska co-prosecuting the Boehm case, listened to Moore's story. Although he didn't deny the veracity, Russo thought it was best to leave the Bill Allen–Bambi Tyree connection out of the investigation. It was complicated enough as it was, he said, and he told a local police detective that he should also back off of Allen. This didn't sit well with the local cop.

In the meantime, Boehm's lawyers had gotten word about Allen and Tyree. They wanted to portray Boehm as a doddering drug addict who had been manipulated by Tyree. They wanted to cast Tyree as a hustler with a history of seducing older men with money, men like Bill Allen. If they could convince a jury that Tyree was a central figure in the sex-drug ring, then perhaps Boehm might get less prison time. Prosecutors, which included at least one who would later be heavily involved in the Polar Pen investigation, fought bringing Allen into the mix. "To be clear, the United States does not have any interest in protecting Allen from what he did," wrote Russo in a July 26, 2004, sealed statement. "Indeed, he may still face charges for statutory rape. However, the United States is concerned about the potential distraction introduction of such evidence may create. Because Allen is a well-known figure in the community, there is danger of 'the sideshow taking over the circus.'" Within a month, the FBI was debriefing at least one witness in its separate political corruption probe.[18]

Bill Allen's name was not made public in relation to the Boehm case. But this is a small town, and inevitably the information would get out. Perhaps the FBI and Alaska's federal prosecutors spearheading Polar Pen, an investigation that would depend on Allen's cooperation and testimony, didn't understand this. Or perhaps the feds were thinking ahead. If Bill Allen was indeed a key player in Alaska corruption, the fact that he'd actively covered up his sexual relationship with an underage prostitute could become leverage to flip him on other suspects.

After Bambi Tyree appeared on his doorstep, Allen was paranoid. He hired a private investigator to sweep his house for bugs, as his nephew Dave Anderson recalled. As the months passed in 2004, Allen watched and waited, but nothing happened. His neighbor, the federal judge, presided over the Boehm-Tyree case, which hit a little close to home. But the cops never showed up on Allen's doorstep, and he went on with his life.

Bill Allen had reached the pinnacle of his power. He'd fulfilled his dream of creating an international oil company. VECO now operated in Russia, Abu Dhabi, Sudan, and other countries, with annual revenues of $1 billion and a workforce of more than 4,000. It had expanded into commercial construction and landed a contract to build a $200 million prison in Barbados. Yet Allen's personal life seemed to be unraveling around him in 2004. Bambi Tyree was just one loose end that threatened to embarrass him or worse, land him in prison.

Dave Anderson, who once considered himself his uncle's "right-hand man," a trusted employee, and heavily involved in his pet political projects, suddenly fell out of favor with Allen. The issue was personal: Allen's girlfriend left him and started dating Anderson, and the love triangle triggered a family feud. Allen's pride was wounded, Anderson recalled, and his uncle fired him from VECO and ordered him to leave Alaska. Except for a brief trip to New Mexico, Anderson stayed in Anchorage as Allen continued to threaten him and his girlfriend. In December 2004, an Anchorage police officer responded to a call made by Allen's ex-girlfriend, who said he was allegedly drunk threatening to come to her house where Anderson was staying. Around the same time, there were more problems. A reporter had asked Ted Stevens's staff if VECO had worked on his home and if he had paid the company. Word got back to Allen, and he accused his nephew of snitching to the media. Nothing ended up in the papers, but the oilman's troubles weren't over.[19]

During the last month of 2004, the FBI began secretly investigating Bill Allen as part of Polar Pen, which soon would have less to do with private prisons and more to do with oil.

CHAPTER 9

Oinkers, Pit Bulls, and Frank

In the mid-2000s, as the national debt soared, the wars in Iraq and Afghanistan raged on, and the price of North Slope crude climbed past $60 a barrel, Alaska's congressional delegation was doing what it did best—keeping the federal funnels open. At the helm, of course, was Senator Ted Stevens. The state's congressman, Don Young, also demonstrated tremendous pork-wielding abilities while chairing the House Transportation and Infrastructure Committee. Young almost seemed to be competing with Stevens to see who could dive deepest into the federal cookie jar. This may have been okay back in the day, but the country was getting concerned with the growing national debt, and eyes were looking northward. It didn't help when Young declared, "I'd like to be a little oinker, myself" at a 2004 luncheon in the panhandle city of Ketchikan. A *New York Times* reporter quoted Young making fun of the criticism he and Stevens had been taking over federal spending for their state. "If he's the chief porker, I'm upset," added Young, referring to Uncle Ted.[1] Young was in Ketchikan to tout his commitment to securing hundreds of millions of dollars for what would become a black eye for Alaska—the Bridge to Nowhere. The *Times* described the project like this: The bridge "would be among the biggest in the United States: a mile long, with a top clearance of 200 feet from the water—80 feet higher than the Brooklyn Bridge and just 20 feet short of the Golden Gate Bridge. It would connect this economically depressed, rain-soaked town of 7,845 people to an island that has about 50 residents and the area's airport, which offers six flights a day (a few more in summer)." Another bridge was also on the drawing table, which would connect Anchorage to a vast and mostly un-developed wilderness that stretched from the shores of Knik Arm to Wasilla and other towns in the Matanuska Valley. Young unabashedly summed up the power he and Stevens commanded in the Beltway. "This is the time to take advantage of the position I'm in, along with Senator Stevens," Young said.[2]

Truly it was now or never, not just for the bridges to nowhere but for other big projects, like the natural gas pipeline, offshore oil drilling, and opening ANWR to exploration. The times were changing in ways that were not favorable to Alaska's power structure. Young was seventy-two, Stevens, eighty-two. Lisa Murkowski had been in Washington less than three years and didn't yet have the clout or seniority to carry the torch. Both Stevens and Young felt a sense of urgency to continue their mis-sion to develop Alaska, a state, they argued, still young and with more needs than other places around the country; that was the justification for all of the earmarks, all of the federal money coming home to Alaska, as well as other things like no-bid federal contracting privileges for Alaska Native–owned corporations. When Hurricane Katrina pulverized New Orleans, lawmakers from other states suggested Alaska do its part to help Louisiana by giving back funding that'd been earmarked for the Bridge to Nowhere. "They can kiss my ear! That is the dumbest thing I've ever heard," Young told a *Fairbanks Daily News-Miner* reporter.[3]

Alaska was becoming a national symbol of government waste, and the state's breadwinners were finding it difficult to justify Alaska's appetite for federal funds. Indeed, Alaskans had grown even more dependent on the government. Federal spending in the state had more than doubled between 1995 and 2005, reaching past $9 billion annually.[4] One-third of all jobs in Alaska could be traced to it, from the military to government-funded construction projects to the agencies that managed the wilder-ness and fisheries and skies across Alaska. In the coming years, it was estimated that the state might lose 7,000 to 20,000 jobs as a result of federal spending cutbacks, which could range from $450 million to $1.2 billion a year.[5] The problem for Alaska was the same as it had always been: its remote location, its undeveloped lands and sparse population, its undiversified economy. Oil and mining, fishing and tourism—along with federal spending—were pretty much all Alaska had going for it. Other states had small businesses and factories. Alaska still depended on making money off its lands and waters.

Although state founders had vowed to develop those resources and do their best to not live off the federal dole, that commitment seemed long forgotten. A generation of young leaders, including Sarah Palin— "pipeline kids," they are sometimes called—had grown up in a world where they paid no state income tax or sales tax, collected a dividend each year from the Permanent Fund, waited for the next big boom that would save them, or took high-paying oil industry jobs on the Slope, where you could, like Todd Palin, not have a college degree and still make six figures as a production manager at Prudhoe Bay. Even though their federal taxes were going to projects in Alaska—funding that increasingly was being labeled "pork" by senators and congressmen from other states—not all Alaskans saw it as such a bad thing. This was still a state that refers to the world beyond its borders as "Outside," as though Alaska is its own nation. What went on within Alaska's borders, some argued, was nobody else's business. Cynics pounced on Alaskans' addiction to the oil funding their state government and the federal dollars padding their economy. "Alaskans have a ridiculous conception of representative democracy now visible to the entire nation," longtime *Anchorage Daily News* columnist Michael Carey noted in 2005. "We expect the men and women we send to Washington to loot the federal treasury on our behalf: That's our definition of statesmanship. From the Alaska perspective, Congress is not a deliberative forum but a bulging bank ripe for robbery, and earmarks are but a refined way of saying, 'Stick 'em up.'"[6]

While his old colleagues in Washington tried to defend Alaska's appetite for federal dollars in 2005, back in Juneau Governor Frank Murkowski was having his own problems. His approval ratings were in the dumps, with one national poll ranking him the second least popular governor in the country. He just couldn't get a break. Every time he opened the newspaper, there was some scathing story about ethical questions or his breaking campaign promises. Mostly they criticized his dealings with oil companies and the closed-door negotiations his administration were having with them to encourage construction of a natural gas pipeline. It just didn't seem right. He had spent more than two decades in the U.S. Senate, trying to appease East Coast blowhards, West Coast loonies, and the religious nuts in between, and now he was being crushed by a state of adolescent ingrates. He truly believed he was saving Alaska. Oil was running out. The companies were finally ready to play ball on the gas pipeline. Murkowski needed them to stay at the table, and to do that, he told Alaskans, they needed privacy to hash out a deal. Murkowski was trying to save Alaska the only way he knew how.

The natural gas pipeline was a thirty-year-old pipe dream—Jimmy Carter was the first president to endorse the project—long deemed financially risky for three reasons. First, the pipeline was estimated to be the most costly private energy project in North American history (in 2011 dollars, pipeline construction was estimated at more than $40 billion). The line would be so long that it would cross land owned by more than 10,000 public and private entities. The sheer size of the pipe itself was mind-boggling. One forty-foot-long segment would weigh 56,000 pounds. Second, natural gas prices weren't nearly as high, and fluctuated even more wildly than oil prices. The concern among industry leaders was that tapping Alaska's vast reserves could flood the U.S. market and depress natural gas prices. And the third reason oil companies were reluctant to pursue the project was uncertainty over how much the state would tax them on developing the gas, which, like much of the North Slope's oil reserves, was owned by the state. Exxon, BP, and Conoco Phillips—which held leases to develop much of the North Slope's gas—didn't have much control over price swings in the natural gas markets, but cutting a favorable tax deal with the state could wipe away some of the financial risks plaguing the project. Without long-term guarantees on the tax structure and rate, the companies would likely never commit to the project.

For the oil companies, the North Slope's natural gas was an unrealized asset. They'd reinjected the gas into the oil fields, using it increasingly to push more crude to the surface. The question for the companies was identifying the right time—the most profitable window—to tap the reserves. Each company had its own timetable and benchmarks, in part because it had other developments and investments around the globe. As businessmen often told Alaskans, the state's oil patch had to compete with their other projects. Back in 2002, when the three big oil companies released the results of a $125 million study looking at whether the pipeline made financial sense, they concluded they could make money on it but the project remained too risky. The issue was how much profit was necessary. For Conoco—the biggest oil producer in the state and the smallest of the three oil giants in Alaska—the profit expectation was said to be smaller. BP fell somewhere in the middle. And Exxon, which held leases to develop the majority of the Slope's natural gas, was looking for a bigger margin, with speculation running as high as 20 percent.

For Alaska, developing the gas fields was a matter of urgency, or at least that is how Frank Murkowski portrayed it. Ted Stevens was still kicking in Washington, a derrick of federal funds flowing back to his state. Oil prices were steadily climbing, with the companies earning more than $5 billion, after expenses, from North Slope oil production between mid-2004 and mid-2005. That year the state collected more than $3 billion in taxes and royalties, thanks to high oil prices—the most it had earned from its oil since 1991 after the Gulf War.[7] But how long would it all last? Alaskans might have felt like they were living large, but underlying it all was one crude fact—oil production at Prudhoe Bay and other North Slope fields was slipping, and fast. Since the trans-Alaska pipeline began operating in 1977, it had transported about 15 billion barrels of oil. By the mid-2000s, the pipeline's output was down about 60 percent compared to the 2.1 million barrels a day it carried at its peak in the late 1980s. In 2011 the pipeline would carry roughly 619,000 barrels a day, with some experts warning that in the coming years there might not be enough oil flowing through the line to keep it running. What would happen then? Would the oil companies pack up and leave, taking thousands of jobs along with 90 percent of the tax base funding state government with them?

Murkowski had initiated closed-door talks with the three oil majors in Alaska and, at least in the beginning, he seemed intent on negotiating hard with them. The conversations ranged from the state taking an ownership stake in the gas pipeline to locking in oil and gas tax rates for decades. One of Murkowski's first acts was signing an administrative order to end a tax break on some oil fields. With his signature, Murkowski generated at least $150 million a year in new tax revenue. Executives from Conoco, BP, and their contractor, Bill Allen and VECO, expressed outrage and warned Murkowski, lawmakers, and average Alaskans, as they had so often in the past, that overtaxing industry could lead them to invest less in the state.

But another tale was shaping up behind closed doors as members of the Murkowski administration continued meeting with the same oil players to discuss how the state and industry could work together to make the proposed natural gas pipeline a reality, a new era of petroleum development in Alaska. The state couldn't control natural gas prices or supply and demand, but it did have the power to encourage Exxon, Conoco, and BP to build the project through favorable tax policies and terms. Murkowski believed the pipeline would give industry a renewed stake in Alaska's oil patch. If the companies were developing natural gas, they'd be inclined to explore for more oil.

Throughout 2005, Alaskans had little way to gauge how close Murkowski was to striking a deal, let alone whether it would be a good one for them. There was mounting dissent over the governor's closed-door meetings with oil executives, led by Democrats and fueled by Sarah Palin, who was making strong statements for transparent government, her eventual stump speech when she ran against Murkowski in 2006. "Secret negotiations" was how people started describing the talks. It wasn't a term coined by Palin, but when she said it, it stuck. "Secret negotiations," kind of a had a ring like "death panels," which she also didn't coin. But look at what that did.

When Sarah Palin resigned from the oil and gas commission after outing the state GOP chairman, Randy Ruedrich, for doing party business on state time, she didn't go quietly. To her, Frank Murkowski symbolized the arrogance of the Alaska Republican Party. The governor had humiliated her, had all but patted her on the head and told her that she had a promising future, someday. Palin began to see vindication within reach. Months earlier, she'd been part of an effort to draw attention to questionable dealings by Murkowski's attorney general, Gregg Renkes, who owned stock in a coal-related company that Renkes had promoted in state negotiations. While an independent prosecutor looked into charges of malfeasance, Palin teamed with a Democrat lawmaker, Eric Croft, who also had his eyes set on the governor's mansion, and filed a state ethics complaint against the attorney general. When Murkowski said the whole thing was politically motivated, Palin fired back: "It's said the only difference between a hockey mom and a pit bull is lipstick. So with lipstick on, the gloves come off in answering administration accusations." She continued, using her favorite sports metaphors:

> I voted for Frank! I campaigned for him and put my reputation on the line speaking for him, promising he'd do right by Alaskans. I've given him the benefit of the doubt and I'm not politically motivated, but I am getting annoyed, so Croft and I will do the right thing by asking appropriate questions. Though answers may result in another player joining Ruedrich in the penalty box, or even getting DQ'd, questions must include: Was this an unassisted play by Renkes, or should refs look at other teammates, and do we need a line change?[8]

First Sarah Palin had taken on the state Republican Party chairman, and now she was targeting the attorney general and the governor himself. Frank Murkowski's hope for finagling a deal with the oil companies to build a natural gas pipeline was getting lost in the Palin-Renkes-Ruedrich media coverage. Murkowski was sure that if everyone would just quit yammering, he could explain that all of this was nothing compared to what he was going to bring to the state. But every time he tried, he got red faced and blustery.

When Renkes resigned, Jim Clark, Murkowski's chief of staff, replaced him at the table, and the negotiations with Big Oil continued throughout 2005. And so did the drama in the administration—over an airplane, of all things. Murkowski had made the unpopular decision to purchase a $2.7 million jet. The jet would get him around faster, especially now that he was flying to oil capitals like Calgary and Houston for conferences and meetings. And besides, state troopers could use it too, in a state where airplanes are needed to get around. The jet was faster than the state's turboprops and it would save its passengers the indignity of having to pull a partition for privacy and use a funnel-and-bottle when they had to relieve themselves in flight. Murkowski was in his early seventies and his wife, Nancy, often flew with him. What was she supposed to do? Murkowski gave a wide berth to that reasoning and focused instead on how the jet could be used to take prisoners from Alaska to the Lower 48, where, because the state didn't have a big prison, it paid a private company to house them. But how to pay for the jet at a time when seniors' money was getting slashed, when the public was paying extra just to get their tires changed? First, Murkowski proposed using Homeland Security funds to buy the jet, but the federal agency nixed the idea. Then he added funding for it in the state budget, and lawmakers told him no. Then, to the astonishment of all, he chose to use discretionary funds to buy the plane.

When the news broke, a Republican lawmaker could be heard singing "Come Fly with Me" in the halls of the Capitol.[9] A radio station had a "name the jet" contest: "The Bald Ego" and "Incontinent Express" tied for first.

In mid-2005, Murkowski was not saying whether he would run for re-election the next year. Some close to him say he never wanted to serve a second term as governor. His plan from the start was to zoom into the state, land the biggest construction project in history, get Alaska under control, and then spend his winters in Palm Springs, as he does now, his summers fishing in Ketchikan, his legacy secured. He thought he could do all of this in one term, but the talks with the oil companies were far-ranging and dragged on. He kept on telling Alaskans that things were moving along, that soon he'd reveal what went on behind those closed doors. But then weeks would go by, months, and still nothing. He would occasionally drop hints at chamber luncheons and press conferences, saying things like the state would own a piece of the pipeline. Or that the industry's demand for fiscal certainty meant locking oil and gas tax rates for years. But he was light on specifics, and Alaskans were becoming increasingly dubious.

Behind closed doors, Murkowski staffers and oil company executives were spending day and night in conference rooms around Anchorage. The best minds in the state, plus dozens of attorneys and consultants; the state spent $25 million on outside lawyers and experts. The deal that would eventually be proposed called for the state to spend around $4 billion to own 20 percent of the pipeline and to collect its royalty payments in the form of natural gas, which the state would either sell or use in Alaska. Murkowski thought that owning a piece of the pipeline would reduce some of the upfront costs and risks to the oil companies. It would also allow Alaska more access to confidential information on the tariffs and fees of transporting natural gas on the pipeline. Knowing those costs would ensure the companies weren't overcharging to move the gas— important because the state would be making its money from natural gas, as would other companies that didn't own a piece of the pipeline. Since the trans-Alaska oil pipeline was completed in 1977, the state had struggled with knowing the actual cost of shipping crude on the line. The state had spent millions of dollars challenging the owners of the oil pipeline over the costs, sometimes winning billion-dollar settlements. Frank Murkowski figured that at the very least, owning equity in the natural gas pipeline would help the state avoid costly legal battles with Big Oil.

It sounded reasonable until you read the fine print, which said that a state company or agency would be entrusted with the information garnered from its ownership interest in the gas pipeline but that it would remain confidential, even from the state. Marty Rutherford, deputy commissioner at the Alaska Department of Natural Resource, took note of these details and objected strenuously behind closed doors in 2005. Rutherford was born and raised "on the knees of the people who created this state," in Valdez, where the oil pipeline ends. She was the daughter of the town's mayor during the pipeline boom. Her family was in the oil wholesale distribution business. They were "all about oil," as she tells it, and all about the politics of oil, particularly pipeline politics.[10] Rutherford had worked for the Department of Natural Resources since 1992. During that time, she'd seen how oil politics seeped into the department, how governors and oil executives influenced the DNR. For example, while serving under Governor Tony Knowles several years earlier, she'd been instructed to consider Bill Allen's former son-in-law, John Kerrigan, for a job in the agency. Allen had suggested his son-in-law to Knowles at a party. Initially the governor asked that Kerrigan, a former VECO executive, be considered for director of the oil and gas division, a position that, among other things, oversees leasing lands for oil and gas development, as well as royalties collected from leases. Rutherford and her boss didn't like that idea. "I was extremely uncomfortable of putting him in charge of Oil and Gas," she recalled. "To me it is one of the most important jobs in state government. It has to be somebody who understands managing the state resources—the state's oil wealth. I would have quit over that." Instead, Rutherford found Kerrigan another job: state pipeline coordinator, a key official who helped manage a state-federal agency overseeing the 800-mile trans-Alaska oil pipeline, the conduit that supplied some 13 percent of the nation's oil. The last job listed on Kerrigan's resume before Rutherford hired him was working as a Century 21 property manager. Rutherford kept a close eye on him, but even then there were issues with Kerrigan. "He had problems with not understanding that you don't act like you're in private industry when you're serving the public," she said. Among other things, Kerrigan was caught borrowing a pickup truck from Alyeska Pipeline Service, the consortium that runs the oil pipeline and that Kerrigan was supposed to be regulating. In 2004, he resigned from the agency.[11]

Now serving under Murkowski, Rutherford and others from the Department of Natural Resources felt the state needed to negotiate hard with Exxon Mobil, BP, and Conoco Phillips because they essentially held a monopoly on the North Slope. They believed the state needed to learn from its past dealings with the oil industry to structure the best arrangements for the state to develop the natural gas. The three companies owned the lease rights to the oil and gas. They owned all the equipment to extract the crude. They owned most of the trans-Alaska pipeline, as well as the tankers that carried the oil to the market. That grip on Alaska oil, Rutherford and others argued, prevented new players from investing in the state and reduced competition. The state, as the owner of a resource that funded much of its government, was caught in the middle but had no control over how and when the oil and gas were developed.

As Murkowski pursued the gas pipeline, he also wanted the industry to agree to an overhaul of the existing oil tax structure in the state. For the industry to go for that, it wanted a reasonable tax rate that could be locked in for decades. The oil companies feared then, as they had in the past, that the state would continue to raise taxes. They wanted one final tax hike and then no more. That, to the oil companies, was fiscal certainty. In mid- to late 2005, dissent over the state's agreement was starting to show in the ranks of the Murkowski camp.

Daniel Johnston, an independent oil and gas consultant, came to Alaska in 2005 to consult for Murkowski's gas pipeline team. One thing he does when he's called by a government to negotiate taxes and leases is to size up the power of the companies in the particular oil province. In Alaska, he found out quickly that industry had an upper hand. Murkowski fired him when Johnston objected to how the negotiations were going. Johnston was particularly worried about the state fixing tax rates for years—a policy decision that would give up Alaska's negotiating tool with industry: raising or lowering taxes. The oil companies "have it pretty good up in Alaska. It's almost embarrassing how good they have it," Johnston would say later. "The companies can and will manipulate data when they have so much power, when they own so much. The one trump card that Alaska has, though, is to levy taxes. The governor was going to give that away! It was unprecedented," he said.[12] He wasn't the only one who thought so. Rutherford and others from DNR were increasingly uncomfortable with the negotiations, and they began to let their discomfort show.

As the negotiations dragged into fall 2005, coffee cups and newspapers littered the conference room table. Fists thumped. Time-outs were called. Groups huddled and then went back at it. Those responsible for the more technical aspects of the pipeline, like Rutherford, often stayed up well past midnight, reading about natural gas, regulatory requirements, upstream and midstream credits, processing subsidies, and ownership terms. Lots of bad food. Lots of stress. Little exercise. Many of those at the negotiating table gained weight. Rutherford got as skinny as she had been in high school. The fifteen-hour days were taking a toll. She and her husband divorced during the negotiations. To be sure, everyone from the state who sat around the table thought they were doing their best for Alaska. But they all had different ideas of how to do that.

Rutherford and others from the DNR began voicing objections to what Murkowski was giving up to the oil companies. Little by little, the critics claimed, concessions from the state were weakening Alaska's sovereignty. Little by little the oil companies were wearing down Murkowski's team. Rutherford, the brains of the group and the person who was still respected amongst even those who were advocating for Murkowski's plan, was the point person for these objections. And the more she pointed them out, the more resistance she got from Murkowski and Jim Clark, the governor's chief of staff. "There were so many problems that began to evolve," Rutherford recalled. "At some point in time, they just got tired of hearing about them." Soon she was labeled a troublemaker, the one for whom nothing was good enough. "She was going for the perfect at the detriment of the good," Clark recalled. "They had such a negative view of the producers. It was an attitude like, 'They've screwed us in the past, and we have to make sure they don't screw us in the future.' They were relentless in their objections."[13]

As for Rutherford, she said, "We were outgunned, outmanned, and outclassed." There were only a dozen or so oil executives on the other side of the table, but they had hundreds helping them back in their offices. "This was their business," she said. "This is not our business." Rutherford and other DNR officials involved in the pipeline talks began protesting Murkowski and Clark's handling of the negotiations. They did so by not showing up.[14]

As quickly as Alaskans can turn on you, they can embrace you. It's a big dysfunctional family. And family members tend to forgive each other. Second lives and second chances litter this state like the ghosts of big dreams. This could have worked for Murkowski. He could have reached out to Alaskans, told them what he was doing with the negotiations, and what they truly meant for the state before things got out of hand. But as events unfolded in October 2005—including Sarah Palin's an-

nouncement that she was running for governor in the 2006 election—
he was quickly running out of time to change the perception Alaskans
had of him and his dealings with oil companies. In late October,
Murkowski made an attempt to show the people that his negotiations
were "advancing" the gas pipeline. At a press conference, the governor
stood beside Jim Bowles, the president of Conoco Phillip's Alaska division, and announced the company planned to sign Murkowski's pipeline
contract—a document that the governor still had not released to the
public. "The journey has started" Bowles said. What was the journey
and where would it take the state? Murkowski said those details would
come later.

That same day a memo to the state attorney general written by Department of Natural Resources Commissioner Tom Irwin expressing concern over the contract was released to the public. "I must point out that
putting members of the Department of Natural Resources in a work environment where they seriously question the legality of administrative
actions they are asked to participate in is so troubling that it could result
in the resignation of exceedingly valuable members of our gas pipeline
team," Irwin wrote.

Less than a week later, Murkowski fired Irwin. Rutherford and five
other DNR employees resigned amid huge drama, whispers, meetings,
and weeping secretaries. As they were leaving the building, their coworkers lined the halls, whistling the tune to *The Magnificent Seven,* a 1960
movie about a group of seven men heroically saving a village from ban-
dits.[15] It was a nice touch. Made great headlines. The outgoing group
was quickly dubbed the "Magnificent Seven" by Murkowski's critics. A
couple of days later, there was a rally in downtown Anchorage, with
dozens of people demanding that Murkowski not fire Irwin and that the
governor cease his "secret negotiations" with Big Oil. Three candidates
hoping to unseat Murkowski were at the rally, including Republican gubernatorial candidate Sarah Palin. She talked about the bravery of the
"Magnificent Seven" and called their demise "a defining moment in our
state . . . a perfect example of things that are amiss in Juneau."[16] Tom
Irwin was suddenly an Alaska folk hero. Palin could see it. If she won
the governor's race, she would hire Irwin, Rutherford, and others who'd

stood up to Murkowski. She would be the anti-Murkowski, the "Joan of Arc" of Alaska politics, for as long as it worked.

In 2006, just months before facing Sarah Palin in the Republican primary, Murkowski would release the fruits of his secret negotiations. His proposal called for a host of incentives, including freezing natural gas taxes for up to forty-five years and oil taxes up to thirty years. Murkowski tried to make the deal more palatable to Alaskans by getting the companies to agree to revamping the state's petroleum tax structure to generate more revenue, but the Alaska legislature would have to sign off on the deal. Meantime, Palin was building support. Her future depended on how the legislature would receive Murkowski's proposal. If rejected, Palin would almost certainly beat Murkowski in the GOP primary. But her onetime supporter, Bill Allen, was gearing up for an all-out effort to make sure that didn't happen. Allen was ready to wage the mother of all oil tax battles in Juneau.

Now in his late sixties, Bill Allen was still involved in the day-to-day dealings of VECO, perhaps even more than ever. He was looking to sell the company. Allen had shaped VECO's reputation over thirty years, making it a preferred oil contractor in Alaska, with long-standing relationships with Conoco Phillips, BP, and Exxon Mobil. If Allen could help his oil company clients land a natural gas pipeline—or at least be perceived as helping—that could only help raise VECO's profile. That meant making sure his friends in the Alaska legislature voted the right way.

Allen had the ear of the Alaska executives for BP and Conoco, along with lobbyists from Exxon and other oil companies. Some of them actively rooted him on, looking past his bribing and boozing of state lawmakers. But going into the oil tax battle, he wasn't on top of his game. He was distracted. Murkowski might have had troublemakers to deal with, but Allen had his personal life to contend with.

Bambi Tyree was safely off in a California prison doing time for her role in the Joe Millionaire scandal, so he didn't have to worry much about her. But his nephew, Dave Anderson, was still causing all kinds of grief. Allen had various girlfriends throughout the years who were age appropriate. The most recent was Kirsten Deacon, the daughter of a former state legislator, who had been supportive of Allen's private prison push. She was pretty. Blonde. Wore coral lipstick. A good Republican gal who had adopted children and could also throw back a few.

Deacon and Anderson, whom Allen had dispatched to do work on Deacon's house, had become lovers. Allen was furious when he found out, and he ordered his nephew to leave the state. This had the effect of bringing Deacon and Anderson closer, both fearing for their safety, both drawn by the danger of crossing one of the most powerful men in the state. Anderson couldn't bear to leave Deacon. So he stuck around off and on in Alaska, and soon Allen was accusing his nephew of blackmailing him. As the good old-fashioned family feud unfolded, the FBI was watching and listening. Operation Polar Pen was in full swing, and Allen was now a target.

A series of letters and other correspondence provided by Anderson showed the dispute reaching a boil in fall 2005. The documents also revealed that at least Anderson thought the remodeling of Ted Stevens's house five years earlier and other work he did for his uncle might raise questions and should be kept quiet. And he nodded to knowing about Bambi Tyree, Allen's alleged teen prostitute from years earlier. Anderson claimed he never blackmailed Allen over such issues. He was seeking only a "proper severance" for his twenty-five years at VECO. But that's not how Allen took it.

In an October 3, 2005, letter to his uncle's lawyer, Anderson wrote he was worried for his life: "Before I was fired from VECO Bill spent months threatening me with physical harm and beyond . . . I was told by Bill personally and repeatedly that I was not allowed to live in Alaska. And if I was in Alaska—anywhere in Alaska—he would 'stomp me into a mud hole.'"

"My house was packed up in August of last year by VECO employees," Anderson continued. "Bill personally oversaw the project. People took my personal property and rummaged through my home. He 'allowed' me to come to Alaska just to pick my things up and to head back out to New Mexico . . . About two weeks ago I drove by my home which I lived in and paid on for fifteen years and guess what? VECO employees demolished my home and removed it."

In the same letter, Anderson told Allen's lawyer that he'd been a loyal employee who managed many of his uncle's inside political jobs.

> As you may or may not be aware of Bill had me doing a lot of different work for VECO and yes it is true I worked on Senator Stevens house in Girdwood and other peoples personal projects as well. I made political contributions on behalf of Bill by him giving me the cash, me depositing it and then writing a check. I have never mentioned him helping Bambi out in the Boehm situation or any of that. I never once have disclosed ANY sensitive information I have . . . political, business or personal . . . although of course as you know I have been accused of doing just that. I am now labeled a 'troublemaker'—people are afraid to hire me because of the backlash from Bill. That is not right.

While the FBI had Bill Allen under surveillance, his lawyer drafted a ten-page document, "Settlement Agreement and Release of All Claims." Allen and Anderson vowed to neither speak to one another ever again nor discuss their VECO work with any federal, state, or local government authorities, including the Internal Revenue Service, Alaska Public Offices Commission, and the Federal Election Commission. For signing the document, Anderson said, he was paid $30,000 by his multimillionaire uncle.[17]

In early 2006, FBI agents hunkered down in a hotel room in downtown Juneau. The Baranof Hotel was one of the oldest and most distinguished in Juneau, just three blocks from the state Capitol. They had moved onto the sixth floor, home to Suite 604, known among pols as the "Animal House"—the war room from which Bill Allen monitored and pulled the strings of the Alaska legislature. The agents hooked up video cameras and microphones, along with recording equipment, and settled in for the coming months to watch what happened in the Animal House. Their investigation had started a few years earlier looking into the state's dealings with private prison companies. Now they were focused on the state's relationship with the oil industry, particularly the interactions Bill Allen and VECO executives had with lawmakers. Did Uncle Bill really control the legislature? And if so, how did he do it?

FBI special agent Mary Beth Kepner ran Polar Pen. At the time a fourteen-year veteran of the agency, she worked out of Juneau, where her husband was a cop.[18] She had aspirations of working for the bureau overseas. Kepner was the one who would eventually cultivate Bill Allen into a cooperating witness. The FBI had profiled Allen and figured he would be more comfortable talking to a woman.[19] Her partner, Chad Joy, would later accuse Kepner of, among other things, getting overly friendly with Allen: visiting him alone in a hotel room when he was preparing to testify against Ted Stevens and wearing a skirt for him during that trial, and warning Allen about reporters digging into his alleged past relationships with underage prostitutes. In 2008 Kepner described Allen as charming and cooperative, a man who might love his women but would never sleep with girls. Allen told her he never slept with Bambi Tyree, and she took him at his word. It's unclear how much Kepner probed Allen, but she believed him, she later told a reporter from *Alaska Dispatch*. Besides, Kepner and federal prosecutors did not want to go there. Allen was their chief witness. The sex stuff could taint him on the stand if defense attorneys caught wind of the allegations against him.

All of that would come later. Then, in the winter of 2005–2006, as the snow turned to ice, then to snow, and then to ice, as the politicians and lobbyists filled the halls of the state Capitol, a team of FBI agents eavesdropped on what happened in the Baranof's Suite 604. Cigarette smoke wafted, wine and whiskey flowed, politicians talked and promised, and Allen and his sidekick, Rick Smith, VECO's vice president of governmental affairs, laughed and patted backs, drank and swore, and strategized or didn't, depending on who was visiting the Animal House.

Kepner was onto a case that could propel her career in the agency. It was going to be a big story. Not only was she going to nab some state legislators for taking bribes, but those bribes were going to be the result of Bill Allen doing the bidding for the world's largest energy companies. Then bigger yet, maybe Allen would lead the FBI to Ted Stevens, the longest-serving Republican in Senate history and third in line to the presidency. The wire was up and the party was on at the Animal House.

CHAPTER 10

The Corrupt Bastards

It was almost eleven o'clock on the night of March 4, 2006. Tensions were running high in the Animal House. Bill Allen and Rick Smith lounged in worn chairs in the hotel suite, slugging wine and plotting their course. They'd spent all day talking to legislators and lobbyists, and the oil tax battle unfolding a few blocks away at the Capitol was intensifying. This session wasn't going to be easy. The Capitol building was thick with the oilies—executives and lobbyists for the companies. Nobody could remember there being so many. At stake were billions of dollars in profits for oil companies or tax revenue for the state, depending on the outcome. The fate of the deal for the natural gas pipeline, which the Murkowski administration had still not released to the public, weighed in the balance. All along, Murkowski continued to be his worst enemy. Most Alaskans had given up on him.

Lounging in his chair, Allen lectured Smith: "We have to produce. Me and you, we have to fucking produce. Right now."

"Have to get dirty and have to produce. I understand that," Smith said.

"Right here, right here in this motherfucking place," Allen said. "We have to fucking to do it . . . "

" . . . We have to do it, but we have to be careful how we do it," Smith said.

"But our clients have to know what we've done," Allen said. "Somewhere here with Jim Mulva [Conoco Phillips chairman and CEO] and with the big wheel with BP and Exxon and all that stuff, we got to

147

fucking produce . . . And I don't give a fuck whose ass we have to fucking kiss . . . whether you like it or you don't. Really, really Rick, we're down to the . . . "

"Because it's so important to us—your life and my life," Allen said a few moments later. "And whatever the fuck I got to do, I'll do it."

"We have to produce," said Smith, as he stood up and walked a few steps to the bathroom, leaving the door open. "Otherwise, they are going to realize how old you are and where the company's at and . . . "

"I know," Allen cut him off. "That's why I'm doing it."[1]

There was a long pause as Smith urinated. Then the toilet flushed. And that's the end of the clip secretly recorded by the FBI inside the Animal House. The agents who edited the hundreds of hours of footage from Suite 604 caught lots of hazy and drunken moments like this. At the clubhouse, the doors were open to certain legislators, certain oil lobbyists, certain members of the governor's administration. Knock. Rick Smith would often answer the door, "Howdy partner," offering a glass of Silver Oak or something stronger. Some of those who visited the Animal House knew they shouldn't be there, or at least claimed to later. They were uncomfortable. They tried to swear and cuss and slap backs, but it didn't come off right. There would have been fewer qualms a couple decades ago, when the oil industry was full of men who spoke and drank like Bill Allen and Rick Smith. When it was still full of men who did business the way Alaska did business. But they'd since been professionalized and old school Alaska hadn't. They'd been through diversity training, having sat through seminars on "best ethical business practices." Alaska is a world away from Houston, from the headquarters and conference rooms, but still some of the talk, the expletives, the booze, the references to owning certain lawmakers, flew too much in the face of the things they'd learned in corporate headquarters. Some would know enough to leave early when the chatter in 604 turned cheap.

But plenty didn't leave. One who hung around was Pete Kott, a state representative for fourteen years and former House speaker. Kott was perhaps the closest of any state legislator to Allen in 2006. He called Allen "Uncle Bill" and considered him a best friend, or at least he'd say so in drunken late-night conversations. "If I can go home and sleep at night, and

I have a friend in the world, that's all I need," he slurred to Allen. "Uncle Bill's my best friend. You're my best friend, Uncle Bill." Kott, fifty-seven years old, was a moderate Republican. Pockmarked, mustached, tall, he was a ringer for a Hollywood cowboy when he got a certain buckaroo twang in his voice after he'd thrown a few back. And he drank a lot. He'd spent twenty-two years in the U.S. Air Force. He had a master's degree in public administration. When the legislature was not in session, Kott ran a flooring business. A "hard-working man who puts in hardwood floors," is how his lawyer later described him to a jury when he stood trial for allegedly taking bribes from Allen, who'd testify they paid him nearly $8,000 for phony work on his hardwood floors. The oilmen also gave Kott other kickbacks, the feds would claim, in return for the senior lawmaker pushing VECO's oil tax agenda, which, of course, was that of Big Oil. At one point, Kott was famously recorded by the FBI saying, "I sold my soul to the devil." Another time he'd say, "I had to cheat, steal, beg, borrow, and lie," to which Bill Allen replied, "I own your ass."[2] Kott had aspirations beyond his flooring business and serving in the Alaska legislature. He'd expressed interest in getting out of politics and becoming a lobbyist for VECO. Or perhaps a warden at the VECO-built prison in Barbados, or maybe a towel boy on the beach, as he often joked with Uncle Bill.

The same month in early 2006 that Bill Allen and Rick Smith talked about the need to produce and get dirty, a newspaper op-ed implicated certain legislators for being in oil company pockets. It detailed campaign contributions from VECO to eleven lawmakers, all of whom supported Murkowski's pipeline and tax deal. A handful of those legislators were having drinks in the bar in the Baranof when someone walked up to them with a smile on his face, waving the column. He called them all, with slaps on the back, "corrupt bastards."[3] They talked about being part of the club. The Corrupt Bastards Club. It was Pete Kott who came up with the idea to take the joke a step further. He had his girlfriend make baseball caps embroidered with VECO on the back and "CBC" on the front. As the FBI listened, Kott called Rick Smith and asked him how many he should have made. Smith suggested fifteen or twenty; Bill Allen would certainly want some extras. And then Smith said, "We gotta figure out who the club is."

Surely Ben Stevens was a member of the Corrupt Bastards Club. The son of Senator Ted Stevens, Ben was state Senate president and had been elected two years earlier to represent Alaska on the Republican National Committee. He held sway over votes in the Senate, and Allen often referred to him in the same breath with Pete Kott as one of two lawmakers he could count on being in the oil industry's camp—his pillars in the Alaska House and Senate. Most legislators didn't care for Ben Stevens. Unlike his father, who, though cranky and arrogant, had earned Alaskans' support through more than three decades of action, Ben Stevens seemed to have nobody's interest at heart but his own.

Some in Alaska's business and political circles suspected him of having taken advantage of his father's fisheries legislation by milking lucrative consulting contracts with companies that processed Alaska seafood (also investigated by the FBI). Critics cried nepotism when he was appointed by a charity to head the 2001 Special Olympics World Winter Games in Anchorage, earning more than $715,000 over three years. Also in 2001, Governor Tony Knowles appointed Ben Stevens to his state Senate seat. During his time in politics, he made more than $240,000 from VECO for what, no one we really knew. There'd been grumblings about Stevens's work for the oil contractor, but nothing came of it. He rode on his father's coattails; lawmakers and businessmen alike dared never cross him for fear of retribution from Uncle Ted.

On March 5, 2006, the FBI listened in on a call between Bill Allen and Ben Stevens. They talked about getting lawmakers on their side. They talked about how another lawmaker stood on the proposed oil tax. Stevens advised Allen about who to trust and who not in the legislature. "He's no friend of mine, I can tell you that," Stevens said about one lawmaker. These and most of the conversations and video footage from the Animal House were cryptic, full of inside baseball about the oil tax legislation under debate in the Alaska Senate and House. Sometimes the conversations were sprinkled with promises by Bill Allen and Rick Smith—including cash— apparently in exchange for lawmakers' support. Mary Beth Kepner and the other FBI agents struggled to make sense of it all. The terms and acronyms were complicated: PPT (petroleum profits tax), ELF (economic limit factor), SGDA (stranded gas development act), and other terms. The tax rates and credits being talked about by lawmakers—20/20, 22.5/20, 25/20. The drunken chatter emanating from the Animal House.

What the FBI agents were listening to was the grinding of the sausage that amounted to a rewrite of how the state taxed the oil companies. They needed help interpreting what they were hearing, the nuances of the oil tax legislation, the alliances between factions in the legislature, the goal of Bill Allen's game. So they enlisted a state senator named Fred Dyson, who was on friendly terms with Allen but wasn't corrupt. Dyson was a rough-and-tumble former commercial fisherman who had spent his time in the oil patch as an engineer for BP. A born-again Christian but not the button-up type. Bearded. Gravelly voice, wafting cigarette smoke. He and his wife had spent a year in Berkeley in 1968 being Jesus freaks among the freaks. It was one of the more profound experiences of their lives. He fed junkies and teenage prostitutes. He joined in the protests, got to know some of the more radical student groups, and ran from tear gas. A man was shot by a sheriff thirty feet from him. Dyson held him until he could get help. The man died a few days later. All of which confirmed that he needed to do God's work, in his own way. He came back to Alaska in the 1970s and joined the oil patch. He also worked in the commercial fishing industry, which was no stranger to excess, and Dyson was in the thick of all of that too. He liked the oil patch Okies and Texans, who worked twelve-hour days for two weeks, then spent a blessed two weeks off with naked girls in strip clubs, throwing up in back alleys, sodden stays in Hawaii. He talked to them about God, and was respected because Dyson had seen a lot. And he could tolerate a lot. He was staunchly anti-abortion but not an absolute moralist. So people talked and listened to him. The FBI and the federal prosecutors would make many mistakes, but of all the legislators they could have turned to, they were smart in picking Dyson. He wasn't part of Allen's inner circle, not one of the good old boys. He didn't own a hat with "CBC" embroidered on it. But he wasn't completely outside the loop, either. He was a Republican and he was friends with Allen.

Dyson could be merciful when it came to drugs and sex and human folly of all sorts, as he suspected Jesus could and would. But bribes for votes? That he couldn't tolerate. He felt a moral obligation to try to stop it. Dyson grew up on the wrong side of the tracks; his father was an ex-con.

But he still found what he was learning from the feds jarring. He was shocked at the conspirators' utter contempt for the democratic process. He knew these people. They were his friends, and they were selling out the state of Alaska. So he willingly assisted the FBI. Most of the time he talked to agents over the phone but met with them a few times in the Federal Building in Juneau. He would take the elevator up to the Coast Guard office, and then take the stairs down to where FBI agents were waiting.[4]

On the one hand there were tens of billions of dollars that would go to either the state treasury or the oil companies. On the other there was the fabled natural gas pipeline, replete with a lock on oil and gas tax rates for thirty or more years. Lawmakers knew the pipeline contract would have some kind of provision that would prevent raising taxes in the future, but they didn't know the exact details because Governor Frank Murkowski still hadn't released the contract in the spring of 2006. Neither had Murkowski declared whether he would run for a second term as governor, even though the election was five months away. Legislators were being asked to vote on the oil tax revision first, then the pipeline contract would be next. The oil companies had agreed to no more than a 20 percent tax on their net profits, while receiving tax credits on 20 percent of the companies' capital investments in the state: the "20/20" plan, as it was known.

But by April, some in the legislature were contemplating a much higher tax increase, ranging from 21 percent to 30 percent. Democrats in particular didn't like the profit part of the 20/20 plan, doubting there was any way for the state to truly know how much the oil companies earned in Alaska. Others thought Murkowski was selling out Alaska. They argued that 20/20 should be more like 25/25, or 30/20, or 23.5/15. It was, after all, Alaska's oil, and every additional percentage point meant as much as an additional $150 million a year in the state coffers. The difference between 20 and 30 was more than a billion dollars. And that number would continue to rise as the price of oil went up. Still, the oil companies would make billions of dollars. Even at a 30 percent tax on profits at $60 a barrel, a state study found, the companies would take home $5.8 billion.[5] But how far were lawmakers willing to take it? And how would their actions influence the oil industry moving forward on the natural gas pipeline? If the companies were taxed too much, would they commit to a $20 billion project, perhaps Alaska's last chance at another pipeline boom? The fight raged on, not only in the Capitol but also on talk shows and in newspapers and bars and coffee shops and around dining room tables. The oil companies were spending hundreds of thousands of dollars on lobbying lawmakers and TV commercials extolling all the great things the oil industry had done for Alaska. And some top executives were in communication with Bill Allen over the necessity of keeping the tax at 20 percent of profits. Allen may or may not have shared his strategy with these executives, but they were complicit.

Daniel Johnston, the oil tax consultant fired by Murkowski in 2005, was back in Juneau, this time hired by the Alaska legislature. He assured them that 22.5 percent was fine, but a higher tax rate might be better, especially if the state was planning to lock in the rates for years. He'd worked with oil-producing countries around the world—Algeria and Australia, Jordan and India, Indonesia, Equatorial Guinea, and East Timor. He usually knew what to expect, but in Alaska, he realized, things were different. "Vicious and weird," he later described it. "I've been in many disputes where I've testified against the oil companies. It was all very civil." But not in Alaska. After one of his presentations, a BP executive got red-faced and started to yell at him: "Why don't you go back to New Hampshire. We know more than you do." Johnston was flabbergasted. He'd never been treated like this anywhere else around the world. Johnston also tried to meet with state senator Ben Stevens and other Republican legislators who were pushing for the 20 percent tax. Stevens quickly rebuffed Johnston, saying something to the effect of, "You don't understand how things work in Alaska. If you want to do business here, you better get with the program." He walked away, thinking, "Is this some sort of movie? A remake of *The Godfather*?" This led Johnston to conclude that he was not wanted. Which led him to conclude that there was a reason that he wasn't wanted. The oil companies "treat Alaskans like they're a bunch of children. Alaska's their cash-cow and they don't want anybody messing with it."[6]

Children, Alaskans may be, and they may be outmanned and outclassed, but Sarah Palin had the answer. It was all in what she took to calling, "the good book." Alaska, she wrote in spring 2006, may be "out-gunned at the table, but thankfully we can compete because we've got supremely powerful ammunition. It's called the Alaska Constitution, and it provides our strength as we deal with corporations whose ultimate goal is to make themselves maximum profit."[7]

It was March 30, 2006. Somebody was knocking on the door of the Animal House. It was Representative Vic Kohring, another "corrupt bastard," although really not so much. Kohring, a state representative from Wasilla, didn't drink much and didn't smoke or curse; he was unfailingly polite. Standing about 6 foot 5, Kohring could play the part of the hapless ex-high school football star, one who might have had great promise, if life had only delivered. His swath of blond hair was constantly falling in his face. He seemed to trip over his big feet. He stood stick straight and he bowed slightly when introduced to women and important people. He was always broke and always hungry, would take any morsel offered to him and was known for piling his plate high at the buffet. He slept in his Capitol office to save his state per diem, keeping food in his filing cabinet and a hot plate on his desk. At home in Wasilla, he often slept in a motor home behind his office. His wife was a Russian classical musician. She was living with his daughter in Portland, Oregon, and Kohring was trying to provide for them.

Kohring was a friend and neighbor of the Palin family who campaigned for Sarah's mayoral race. He was a staunch conservative who would prefer no taxes at all. He was so against taxes that if it were up to him, he would have voted against Murkowski's proposal to tweak the tax structure, ranting all the way about the evils of big government, socialism, the nanny state, and for good measure, the big city media. But Bill Allen didn't need that. He needed to keep Kohring off his no-tax rant.

Kohring sat down on the couch in Suite 604, facing Allen and Smith. He made polite conversation, looked a little nervous, and then got down to business: "I've got a situation where, ah, a financial matter, a personal financial matter that could hurt me politically." He told the VECO executives that he owed $17,000 in credit card debt and a collection agency was after him for full payment. Kohring asked them as friends if there was any work for him with VECO. "Some sort of project?" he suggested. The debt came from back surgery at the Mayo Clinic. Allen and Smith asked him why his state insurance wasn't covering it. He told them that Mayo was not a preferred provider under the health plan, and so he had to pay much of it himself.

"I'm doing this, if I can get it done, because you're a friend," Allen said. The oilman warned that if they were going to help Kohring, it must be kept off the books. "Anything that has VECO on it, oh, shit. It'll go right to the fucking *Daily News*."

They talked more about ways to get Kohring money without anybody knowing about it, especially the Alaska Public Offices Commission. Perhaps a loan of some kind, with $500 monthly payments, Allen wondered aloud. Kohring said he was thinking more like $400 a month. Kohring mentioned he might run it by a state ethics adviser to see whether there would be any issue. Allen didn't like that idea much. Better not to say anything to anybody. Kohring suggested maybe he could do "some work" for VECO. If he was hired by VECO, Kohring told Allen, "I don't want any freebies. I want to bust my butt."

"I want it to be above board," Kohring added. "I don't want anybody to ever criticize our relationship and imply that somehow you're giving me some big benefit that I don't deserve."

"Don't say anything," Allen said, "until I can figure out where it won't come back and bite me and bite your ass and my ass."

The conversation drifted and soon they were talking about Easter, which was coming up in two weeks. Kohring had never spent the holiday with his daughter. He'd always been too busy with the wrap-up of the legislative session. This time would be a first, he explained. This seemed to please both Allen and Smith. Allen had an idea. He told Kohring: "Here's what I want you to do, with uh . . . what I usually do . . . on . . . Christ . . . I mean . . . and uh . . . "

"For holidays?" Kohring suggested.

" . . . and Easters . . . I always take a, when I got kids. And always, I really, I go hide . . . "

Smith came up with the word. "Eggs."

" . . . an egg with . . . "

"With money in it?" Kohring asked, hopefully.

"Money or . . . " Allen said.

"Or candy!" Kohring said. "Oh yeah, Nuka [his daughter] said, 'Daddy Daddy, can we do an Easter egg hunt?'"

The three men chuckled.

Allen turned to Smith and asked, "Did you get any hundreds?"

Smith stood up and reached into his pocket.

"Give me a hundred," Allen said to Smith, "and that way you can . . . "

"Put those in the Easter eggs!" Kohring said. "All right. I shall do that. Thank-you very much."

Kohring and Allen shook hands. "And let her find the egg," Allen told him.

"I will," Kohring said. "We're going to have an Easter egg hunt right at the house, and I'll put money in, I promise . . . and she'll be thrilled. I just sent her some money for her mom to buy her a Girl Scout uniform. She's thrilled about that, and I sent her a card telling her about how much I love and miss her and twenty bucks was included in that and . . . "

Allen interrupted: "All right, well then, let me help you on her little uniform." He reached for his wallet, pulled out money, and handed it to Kohring, who thanked him profusely.

"On the uniform," Kohring repeated. "The [money] I sent was a little short, so thank-you. Said she needs about $100. I appreciate that, Bill, thank-you so much." They shook hands again.

"Well, just in closing" Kohring said, "I know you guys got things to do. What can I do at this point to help you guys? Anything? Just keep lobbying my colleagues for the governor's plan?"

They speculated on how other lawmakers might vote on the tax bill. Allen told Kohring to keep him and Smith up-to-date on "where they're really at."

"Okay, okay. Just get an honest, straightforward opinion from them, right?" Kohring asked.

"Yeah," Allen said, "and then you can tell us where they're at, and then maybe you can push 'em over on your column."

"Yes. Well, I'll make every effort to do that," Kohring said. "My first effort will be to figure out where they're at, and then secondly I'll politely and gently and carefully as I can influence them in a positive way to see that the governor's bill is the vehicle they consider. I know that's very important to you. I know that's key to the gas line, and I know that's why you're here. I want nothing better than the governor's bill to pass and that gas line to come to fruition. Even though I'm . . . "

Allen cut in. "Or if you think of anybody else that we could get."

"Okay, all right," Kohring said. "You know my position is an antitax position, and I'd just as soon the industry not be taxed any, we give credits, but I understand that this is an integral part of the whole deal here."[8]

It was that last statement, more than the money for the Easter egg hunt, or the Girl Scout uniform, or asking for money to pay off his credit card debt, that would be the reason why Kohring would two years later find himself on the roadside about halfway between Anchorage and Wasilla, waving a sign to morning commuters that read, "Good-bye Alaska." His hair, which he didn't have the money to cut, flopping in the breeze. Passersby honked and waved. Others rolled down their windows and gave him the finger.[9] What infuriated many Alaskans was the fact that he sold out for so little, for Easter eggs of all things. Kohring's mother would be waiting in the car to take him to the federal courthouse so he could turn himself in to the U.S. marshals.

During the day oil executives gave presentations to legislators on how much other nations and states were taxing companies, teasing them with how much more oil might be produced if the state didn't make the taxes too high. Independent experts produced other graphs, showing how much more money Alaska could get if it went beyond a 20 percent tax rate, that the state could go higher and still keep the industry's attention. Where do the twain meet? Committee meetings lasted for hours, the windows all foggy. Outside the snow turned to sleet turned to rain, and then the sun. The birds were starting to come back: northern harriers, semipalmated sandpipers, western sandpipers, Arctic terns. The first cruise ship arrived, depositing a load of windbreaker-wearing tourists. They inhaled the glacier-tinged air. They bought up miniature totem poles from cruise ship–owned shops, gold nugget-filled snow globes, chocolate-covered caramels shaped in little balls and called "moose droppings." Much of it made in China.

They ate in the restaurants and took walks on Juneau's steep sidewalks. They stared at the governor's mansion and then the Capitol building, oblivious to the battle being waged inside, the wheeling and dealing, threatening, pleading, cajoling; the oil men heckling lawmakers in the hallways; the fortitude of many who resisted the pressure; the weakness of others who couldn't.

In early May 2006, with only days remaining in the legislative session, Murkowski's 20/20 oil tax had not been passed. The governor was still holding back on releasing the proposed contract for the natural gas pipeline, despite a court challenge to make the several hundred pages of provisions available to lawmakers and Alaskans. Sparks were flying in the Capitol building. Fights and caucuses. Promises and threats. The oil companies were still adamant that the tax had to be 20 percent—at current prices, $1 billion more than they were currently paying—but on May 7 an amendment was introduced in the House that would push the rate to 21.5 percent—which would equate to an additional $120 million to $200 million more in taxes than the oil industry would have to pay annually to the state than under 20/20. VECO executives were consulting with Pete Kott on how he could influence the vote.

The debate over the amendment raged on into the evening, and when a vote was finally taken on the 21.5 percent tax rate, one legislator, Bruce Weyhrauch, a Republican from Juneau, voted the wrong way. Weyhrauch was assumed to be in VECO's camp, for he had allegedly been scouting out a job with the company during the session. He must have made a mistake. Smith called Kott to ask him what was going on, and Kott quickly took control of the situation. The amendment was tossed and the proposed tax rate remained at 20 percent. Outraged by what he just saw occur, Democrat Representative Ethan Berkowitz stood up on the House floor: "This is our floor. Our floor. No telephone call is supposed to change what we're doing. No lobbyist is supposed to peer over the railing and tell us to change our mind. It never should happen. I'm frankly dismayed about the course this debate has taken. I expect more from this legislature."

At around 11:30 that same night, Pete Kott was back at the Animal House, bragging to Rick Smith and a VECO lobbyist how he'd pulled the strings, how he'd "outsmarted the fox" and delivered a "sucker punch." "I use 'em and abuse 'em," Kott said. "Fuck 'em."[10] "That was like watching a maestro at work," VECO lobbyist Bob McManus said of Kott's handiwork on the House floor.

"That's exactly right," Smith said. "This guy's pretty good, right? Boy, I'll tell you what, it's every, every year, I mean, I've been with Pete and coming down to crunch time, he, he makes this shit happen."

Two days later, the legislative session ended without approval of Murkowski's 20 percent petroleum profits tax. Murkowski called a special session to resolve the tax and shortly thereafter introduced his pipeline contract with the oil companies. Alaskans and lawmakers alike quickly took note that the contract locked in oil tax rates for thirty years and natural gas rates for forty-five years. Moreover, the contract did not require Exxon, BP, or Conoco to commit to building the pipeline. As long as the companies pursued the project "as diligently as is prudent under the circumstances," they would get taxes frozen for decades and a commitment from the state to own 20 percent of the pipeline—an investment in 2006 of at least $4 billion by the state.[11]

While Governor Frank Murkowski and lawmakers and nearly anyone who had anything to do with politics was bogged down with the oil tax legislation, Sharon and Don Benson spent much of the spring and summer of 2006 driving around the Mat-Su Valley, putting up yard signs that said "Take a Stand," with Sarah Palin's name below the message. Before long, an area the size of West Virginia was littered with the signs. They, as well as a handful of others, spent their mornings on the computer, sharing ideas about how to get Palin's name out. Often the former Wasilla mayor would chime in with ideas. Places she could go, things that she could say. Ways to reach out and press the flesh. Getting instructions from a team set up by Palin, the Bensons hand-delivered many of those signs. Shaking hands as they did so. Talking up their candidate. Both from Palmer, the Bensons were Republicans, but they didn't get involved in the social issues that had created divisions within the party. They didn't belong to the avid Christian Right or to the establishment that rose around the pipeline, the one controlled by Alaska GOP chairman Randy Ruedrich. They didn't get invited to the fancy dinner parties, the wine tastings, the political fund-raisers featuring smoked salmon and cucumber sandwiches and drinks served in crystal glasses. The executive fishing and hunting trips. They didn't want to pray before meetings. They didn't want to picket abortion centers. They didn't want government involved in social issues, period. Sarah Palin had so far been careful not to define herself as a Christian conservative. She focused on tending to the economy and reforming the Republican establishment. It was a message that appealed to folks like Sharon and Bob Benson. They cared most about economic issues, about common sense and being a part of the political process.[12]

"Sarah isn't owned by the oil companies, I'll tell you that," said Bob Benson in a 2007 interview of why he supported Palin in the race. "She's as honest as the day is long."

"The most honest person you'll ever meet," Sharon Benson added.

"That's why we wanted her in office so bad," Bob said. "Before she decided to run for governor, I called Todd and I said, 'Todd, you gotta talk some sense into her. Tell her to run.' He said, 'I almost got her convinced.' It's just that nobody else was as honest as her. Nobody else was talking commonsense solutions, about cutting spending and such. Frank, well, he promised it, but he broke that promise the minute he stepped into office. We can't keep just spending like we are."

The Bensons were invited to Palin's strategy sessions. Sometimes Todd and Sarah would call them to ask how they thought things were going. It was heady for them, mostly because they loved Sarah and were convinced that a new day was dawning in Alaska politics. That Alaska was going to finally act like the state the founders promised it would be, back before the oil and everyone got fat and lazy. How to do that? Kick the bums out and get new blood in the party. Blood untainted by the good old boys and the oil money. Sarah Palin "treated us like real people," said Sharon.

"You just wait," Bob said. "Before our lives are over she'll be president or vice president some day. Mark my words."

"But we need her here," said Sharon.

While Murkowski still hadn't decided whether to seek reelection, Sarah Palin was speaking at rallies and forums, at any public event that would have her. She'd amassed her army of Alaskans from all walks of life, like the Bensons, telling them they needed to take back their state. She cited the state constitution over and over again. Her mantra was that the resources belong to the people, not to the oil companies. Like moles, people squinted into the springtime sun at these rallies, holding signs that read, "Pass the petroleum: We're getting screwed," and "The deal's too Murky," and "What would Jay Hammond do?"[13]

At some rallies, Palin was joined by eighty-six-year-old Wally Hickel. A beloved elder statesman in some circles, Hickel had long believed Alaska should own and build the natural gas pipeline itself. Over the past year, Palin had appeared with Hickel, as well as former governor Jay Hammond before he died in August 2005, in an advertising blitz to support the idea. Though the proposal itself never got much traction, her face alongside those two did.

Formerly old rivals, Hickel and Hammond in their old age had become friends, realizing that they had more in common than they thought. Neither was much trusted by the oil industry, and through the years, that distrust had spread into Alaska's business community. Hickel was seen as too volatile and Hammond as too environmental. In those circles, if you weren't pro-oil, then you were a little socialist, a little Democrat, a little, well, bonkers. But as skepticism of the oil industry grew, ordinary Alaskans began to feel differently. People remembered that Hickel and Hammond were of the people. They fought for the people. They had gotten things done for the people. Palin posed for photos with the two former governors and they lent her the name recognition she needed in winning over the people. Her timing was perfect.

By the end of May 2006, Frank Murkowski finally decided to run for reelection. He didn't really want to, however. He'd hoped to nail down a commitment to build the gas pipeline in his first term and then move on with his life. But at this point, the deal was far from certain. And if he didn't declare, he'd have no political power as the special legislative sessions dragged through the summer leading up to the August primary election. Few gave Murkowski much of a chance. The field was crowded, with all sorts of candidates running on an anti-Murkowski platform, which was rather easy to do, given all of the governor's foibles over the pipeline contract, the expensive jet he bought himself, the Randy Ruedrich affair, and the resignation of his attorney general. The Murkowski administration had been cast as a disaster. His opponents had a field day.

Among them was Republican John Binkley, a former state legislator and well-known businessman from Fairbanks. Former governor Tony Knowles, a Democrat, had also jumped into the race and wasted no time pouncing on Murkowski. Meantime, Sarah Palin peppered her stump speeches with references to "good old boys" and the corrupt GOP, urging her supporters to take back the party. And the people listened.

In early June 2006, the first of what would be two special legislative sessions was winding down. The FBI was still running its secret surveillance of the Animal House and the phone lines of key players. In the state House, Pete Kott had lost control of the situation. Legislators had now moved to pass a tax of 23.5 percent—about a half billion dollars a year more than what Murkowski had proposed and the oil companies agreed to. Bill Allen was frustrated. Kott, the legislator who "uses and abuses 'em," didn't use and abuse enough. The Polar Pen investigation was becoming juicer as agents listened to calls between Allen and a top oil executive, Jim Bowles, the Alaska president of Conoco Phillips. The company doing the most business in the state was closely watching the lawmakers as they debated the tax. On June 6, Allen called Bowles to discuss the looming 23.5 percent profit tax before the House. They settled on the nuclear option. Bowles told Allen that the best outcome would be for the House and Senate to adjourn this special session without voting on the tax. They could start from scratch if Murkowski called another special session.

"Uh, we want to just see if we can't stop this thing, don't we Jim?"

"Yes sir," Bowles said. "If there's any way we can get this thing stopped, that's the best possible outcome."

"Okay. Well, I got working, and it's just between me and you, but I got Pete Kott and uh Jim—uh I meant Ben (Stevens)—doing it," Allen said.

"Well, Bill, one thing that I think what we had talked about is that probably the best outcome for us is to get the House to go ahead and gavel out and finish up and get them out of town," Bowles said.

"Right, that's what I'm trying to do."

"Okay, well, good. I think we're supportive of that. Because if we can get them out of town, we've got a better chance. Then all we've got to do is just work the Senate by themselves."

Allen told Bowles that he'd been hearing Murkowski might support the legislature on a 22.5 percent tax in order to get the bill passed. "We met with the governor yesterday and we told him, 22.5 is not a good answer to this," Bowles said. "No one's gonna be happy with 22.5. And, I mean, actually Bill, I think our belief is 23.5 is better than 22.5 because it just provides us the basis to say we've just really got a terrible, you know, terrible answer . . . We're not trying to push to get this thing moved to 22.5 right now."

"Yeah," Allen responded. "What I'm just trying to tell you, Jim, is that you can bet that [Murkowski chief of staff] Jim Clark and them are gonna try to get a PPT [petroleum profits tax] somehow."

"Well, you know, we've talked with Clark," Bowles said, "several times about don't push through 22.5. That's not what we want to see as an outcome. So if he's doing that, he's doing it against conversations we've had."

"Do you think that's what he's doing, Bill?" Bowles asked slyly in an interrogator's voice.

"Yes. Yes. He tried this morning." Allen said.

Allen tried to reassure Bowles that things wouldn't get out of hand, that the tax would not pass at 22.5 percent on the watch of Representative Pete Kott or Senate President Ben Stevens: "Pete Kott and Ben, they're gonna do it so they don't know who, who it came from."

"Well, that's ideal," Bowles said. "And it needs to catch them by surprise, because otherwise [the legislature will] stay in session just so they can, you know, cause problems."

"Maybe they can't get it done," Allen said, "but they think, they told me they thought they could."

"Okay, well that's good news."[14]

But two days later, Allen was upset. The tax was still alive. He called up Kott, the lawmaker who liked to joke with Allen about someday working for the VECO-built prison in Barbados, and told him, "We just got a contract in Siberia. You're not going to fucking Barbados. You're going to Siberia." That was like telling an Alaskan he must move from Anchorage to Fairbanks.

"Good. I always wanted to go there," Kott laughed.

"You and Ben didn't get this motherfucker dead," Allen said in a very different kind of voice. A deadly serious voice.

"Well, it ain't over yet," Kott told Allen, suddenly serious himself.[15]

Later that night the legislature adjourned without passing a tax. Allen was in the Animal House when he called Bowles to crow, leaving a message on the Conoco executive's voicemail: "I told you we would, uh, between . . . Pete Kott and with Ben, we wouldn't have a bill. . . . Remember what I told you, that we got it done." Allen turned to Kott and Rick Smith, who were in Suite 604 too. "I told Jim Bowles, I said between Pete Kott and Ben, they . . . won't even have their fingerprints on the son of a bitch."[16]

Jim Bowles, the president of the Conoco Phillips Alaska division, was never indicted in Alaska's oil and politics corruption scandal. The feds stopped short of tying any oil executives beyond VECO's to bribing lawmakers over the oil tax vote and pipeline contract. Bowles said little publicly about his appearance in the corruption scandal. He continued on as head of Conoco's Alaska operation until February 2010, when he was killed by an avalanche while snowmobiling on Alaska's Kenai peninsula.

The legislature had been in Juneau for more than five months in 2006 and still hadn't passed an oil tax bill, the first step toward making Frank Murkowski's pipeline proposal come true. It was now late June and the primary elections were two months away. If Murkowski failed on the tax pipeline legislation, he'd almost certainly lose the GOP primary. Time was running out when Murkowski called a second special legislative session.

CHAPTER 11

Republican
Death Picnic

On June 25, 2006, the FBI secretly recorded Bill Allen and Senator Ted Stevens discussing ways to convince the state legislature to act on Governor Frank Murkowski's pipeline contract with the oil companies. "I'm gonna try to see if I can get some bigwigs from back here and say, 'Look . . . you gotta get this done,'" Stevens told Allen. The senator turned to Vice President Dick Cheney, who two days later wrote a letter to state lawmakers urging members to "promptly enact" the pipeline legislation. "Currently, the Alaska Legislature is the government entity that holds the fate of the Alaska Gas Pipeline in its hands," Cheney wrote. He even invoked the Alaska constitution, the much quoted clause that mandates "the development of its resources by making them available for maximum use consistent with the public interest." In the vice president's view, that meant getting the natural gas out of the ground. "You have it in your hands to help ensure that the Alaska Gas Pipeline ultimately furnishes dependable, affordable, and environmentally-sound energy for America's future . . . Time is of the essence in this process. Thank you for your cooperation."

The letter was highly unusual, since the White House rarely contacts state lawmakers about pending legislative matters. But Cheney's meddling in state politics far from the Beltway had the opposite effect on many in the Alaska legislature. State Democrats accused Cheney of pushing oil company interests, something he had long been identified with.

Some Republicans were upset with anybody from Outside telling them what to do. They tossed Cheney's letter to the side and pressed on with the oil tax and pipeline debate.[1]

In the North Slope oil fields, far from Juneau, another event was unfolding that left some lawmakers skeptical of the oil industry. On August 6, 2006, BP was forced to temporarily shut down its Prudhoe Bay facilities after discovering that a corroded pipe, peppered with small holes, was oozing crude onto the spongy tundra. It had been the second of two spills at the oil field that year. In March, a worker had been driving around Prudhoe Bay when he discovered the frozen tundra drenched with several thousand barrels of the black stuff. Unbeknownst to BP management, one of the company's transit pipelines had become corroded and leaked more than 200,000 gallons of oil. The result was the biggest spill ever recorded in an Alaska oil field. In Juneau, lawmakers grumbled that the oil companies were essentially threatening to reduce investment if the legislature raised taxes too high, yet they apparently didn't see fit to repair their rusty pipes. Was that because the aging Prudhoe Bay oil field was like an old Buick, with only a few miles left on it and not worth putting much money in? Maybe it was better to raise the tax now and earn more revenue off the state's oil while there was still some left in the ground.

As lawmakers met for a second special session, summer was slipping away. Two women disappeared while climbing Mount McKinley. Their names were added to the long list of those missing on North America's tallest mountain. Bears attacked campers and anglers, as well as a tent with a tourist sleeping in it. When the tent collapsed and the bear bit the man's shoulder, he yelled and the bear ran away. A handful of fishermen were charged by brown bears at one of Alaska's most popular fishing spots. The bears like the fish. So do the fisherman. A bear was shot. The perennial debate raged about whether or not to allow people to shoot aggressive bears. Some said it was their right to protect themselves. Animal lovers said that it's the bear's right to protect its space, a space that humans have increasingly encroached upon. The Alaska Department of Fish and Game spent months coming up with a solution, to be implemented the following year. They wanted to tranquilize the bears and then dye their hair various colors—yellow, green, orange, or blue—to identify which ones were aggressive. "Clown bears," they would be called, to the amusement of wildlife managers all across the country, and to the horror of animal rights activists, who said that the state was intent on humiliating the bears. It made new headlines when Fish and Game officials swore they weren't trying to "embarrass the bears."[2] A salmon run on the Russian River was the weakest in recent memory. At first, anyway. Near the end of July, when the salmon should have been chocking the river, only a few trickled upstream. The state ordered the river closed, and almost immediately they came with a bang. The state had been hoping for 650,000 salmon. More than 1.5 million made it back to the Russian.

None of this helped the mood of the legislators cooped up in the Capitol since January. They should have been out in May. They should have been spending their summer climbing mountains, frolicking with bears, slaying salmon by the dozens. Instead, the fate of Alaska was in their hands, or so they were told. Should the tax rate be 20 percent? 21.5? 22.5? Or more? There was little chance now that the pipeline contract would get a vote; there simply wasn't enough time before the special session ended. But the oil tax legislation was still in the running.

Two weeks before the Republican primary, polls were showing Sarah Palin and John Binkley, the other Republican gubernatorial candidate, far ahead of Frank Murkowski. Binkley was a third-generation Alaskan; his grandfather came north during the Klondike gold rush of 1898, working as a riverboat pilot. He was raised in the family's riverboat business, but Binkley didn't look like he spent much time on the water. Hair peppered nicely with some gray and an eager smile that made you think Kansas bank manager, spending his mornings at Rotary, weekends at softball, grilling on Sundays. Not a man navigating rough Alaska rivers or living in a town where beards thick with frost routinely touch bellies, where living in a cabin without electricity and running water is the real way to live, where it gets so cold in the winter that the pollution crystallizes into a fog that smothers the city. There was nothing about him, in either style or substance, attaching him to the good old boy network, except that he was a good Republican. But even though Binkley led Murkowski in polls, he wouldn't prove much of a factor. And neither would Murkowski get traction. By this time the governor was resorting to ads like, "It's hard for people to admit their faults and I'm not different. It's become painfully obvious to me that many of you are questioning your support for me. Whatever, the reason, I admit, I'm not perfect." His face was appearing on full-page newspaper ads, with the words, "I agree. I admit it. I'm a long, long way from perfect. Maybe I need a personality transplant."[3] The mood was against the old-guard Republicans and their relationship to Big Oil. It was now on Sarah Palin's side. Even the weather seemed to be on her side.

August in Anchorage is often wet but on August 8, 2006, the day of the annual Republican Party picnic (which local gossip columnist Sheila Toomey would dub the "Republican death picnic"), it was glorious. The sun hovered over the city like a warm uncle, urging the already huge cabbages to grow to the size of boulders, pumpkins as big as fairy tale carriages. Smiling tourists. Happy dogs. Softball games in the parks. It's days like this that make the long Alaska winters worth the wait. Days where winter seems a world away and where nothing bad could happen to this blessed state. Alaskans don't pay taxes, live in the richest state in the union, and the sun is here to stay. The oil and the greed, the long history of exploitation, of people who would lock up the resources or use them for their own wealth and power, far away—days like this that keep Alaska in a perpetual stage of amnesia.

Sarah Palin started that day by meeting with a group of women at a restaurant. She listened and nodded and took notes at the table as they discussed education, health care, and creating good jobs that their children would have someday. She never disagreed, never told the women that they might not get all the things they wanted. She promised that she would work to make their concerns heard and work for them. Many of them, after all, were mothers. And mothers knew best how a state should be run. As they went around the room, she looked each of the women in the eye and when they spoke she nodded her head, as if she were on their side and their side alone. Her suits weren't tailored then.

Her shoes came from discount stores. But her nails were French manicured and her lipstick always fresh; it was hard to keep your eyes off her.
There was something about Palin that even Alaska women recognized
well before she took the national stage: Although she's very pretty, she
doesn't have that thing about her that makes other women nervous or
jealous. Maybe it's those long vowels, the "golly gees" and the "oh mans,"
that prove she's anything but the kind of sophisticate who will lure your
husband away.

At the restaurant, the most profound thing she said was, "Man, oh
man, our next generation is Alaska's most precious resource. We have got
to allow them to reap the benefits of this great state and our great constitution." She left with more votes than she arrived with. Later that day
she stopped by an advertising agency that helped her campaign. She
knew the name of the receptionist and freely bantered with the guys producing her campaign commercials. She disapproved of one but was re-
luctant to say why. Was it the light? They wanted to know. No, that
wasn't quite it. The way she spoke? Nope, not that either. The camera
angle? Finally, someone mentioned that maybe she was uncomfortable
with how tight her shirt fit across her chest. "Exactly," she said. "Bob and
Mark would have a heyday with that."

Bob and Mark were morning FM radio jocks. Alaskans like their radio
personalities, especially talk radio. There is Dan Fagan, Steve Heimel,
Rick Rydell, Shannyn Moore, and Mike Porcaro, to name a few, names
as familiar to Alaskans as Rush Limbaugh, Amy Goodman, Bill O'Reilly,
and Dennis Miller are to those in the Lower 48. In 2006, you heard lots
of yelling and arguing on the radio, mostly about oil taxes and the legislature and what Alaskans would do when the oil ran out. And of course
the natural gas pipeline. That afternoon, the king of Alaska's right-wing
talk radio, Dan Fagan, was trying to nail Sarah Palin down on her support of the "anti-oil populist crowd," he called it, that supported a gas
pipeline from the North Slope to Valdez, rather than to Chicago or Al-
berta, Canada, as Murkowski and the oil companies wanted. Although
she was part of the crowd—in her office was a sign that read "Canada my
ass, it's Alaska's gas"—she wouldn't publicly say which pipeline route or
project she supported over another. Palin was the only candidate who

wouldn't say where she stood. All of the others supported the Canadian route, but Palin danced around the question.

At the ad agency, where radios and Fagan's voice were ubiquitous, Palin had enough and decided to call in herself. "Dan!" she said into her cell phone. "Get the wax out of your ears!" She repeated to him very slowly and very playfully, and a little (but not overly) flirtatiously, that she was keeping all options on the table, and would eventually do what was best for Alaska, as dictated by the Alaska constitution. Fagan was confused. They had been good friends for a few years, the kind who could stop by her house and have coffee. A born-again Christian, he and Palin talked sometimes about politics, but mostly about religion and their personal lives. However, until the race, he had never heard her take an anti-industry stance. He was surprised by it. She had always been a conservative, and now she was talking like a populist, even a liberal. At a fund-raiser that same day, Palin was asked what her plans were for schools and education if elected. She put her hand on her questioner's sleeve, looked him in the eyes and said, "Bless your heart. Thanks for asking that great question." Every child deserves a good education, she told the man. She had respect for educators, she said; her father had been a teacher in Wasilla, and her mother worked for the school. She supported technical schools and local control and municipal revenue sharing, believed in competition, and respected Alaska's constitution, and it would be an honor to serve him and the rest of Alaska.

Another interlocutor wanted to know about transportation, or Alaska's lack of transportation infrastructure. "That's a great question," Palin responded, "Thanks for asking it." She talked about keeping all options on the table and getting the best minds involved in the debate and doing what's right for Alaskans, and respecting Alaska's constitution, and the importance of small government and local control, and what an honor it would be to serve her questioner and Alaska.

What about what Mitt Romney was doing in Massachusetts on health care? She blinked hard, took a few seconds, and paused. "You know, Mitt Romney, the governor of Massachusetts?" a reporter helped. Still, she looked confused. Either she hadn't known who Romney was or she hadn't heard about his plan, or maybe both. "I'd get a group together," she said.

"The best minds around the table and we'd talk about health care," she said. "I'll support anything that lowers costs, puts the power in private industry, and respects the Alaska state constitution," she added.[4]

The Alaska state constitution, that beautiful document written for Alaska's children, the children who, the framers wrote, "could see visions we do not see." At the Republican Party picnic on that beautiful day in early August 2006, here came those children with visions that the framers definitely didn't see. Here was Sarah Palin's army, armed with "Take a Stand" signs and chanting "Sa-rah, Sa-rah," their cars and bicycles adorned with Palin bumper stickers. They had come to take over the Alaska Republican Party. They didn't have a name for themselves yet. A little later, they would be called Palinistas, or Palinbots. And later yet, in the wake of Palin's national debut, they would affiliate with a group called the tea party. They might have been the first of them. But on that day, they just knew something had gone wrong with the Grand Old Party and they were there to help elect a woman who would fix it.

The first order of business? Surround the old guard at the usually harmonious event held at a park chalet, on the edge of town, atop a hill with mountain views. Candidates in booths gave out candy, ate salmon and pig, while a band played country songs about loving America and their houses and their wives and their kids. Hundreds of freedom-loving Alaskans attended the 2006 picnic. Candidates who had labored over oil taxes in Juneau flew in for the occasion.

Sarah Palin's army showed up armed with their signs and their chants. Establishment Republicans knew these people existed. They had heard them on talk radio, had envisioned them in their cabins, cleaning their guns and tying their fishing knots. Ragtag, many of them. Not the sort who usually show up for the annual picnic. Not all, of course—the army had its share of well-respected and "normal" citizens: teachers and oil workers, carpenters, and a few eccentric lawyers. Many of them lived in the Matanuska Valley—Palin's stomping ground—and in cabins and makeshift houses along windy dirt roads, the occasional glint of steel the only sign of their existence. Establishment Republicans courted them come election time. The rest of the year, however, they tended to give them a wide berth. Ben Stevens, Ted's son, one of the leaders of the establishment, went as far to publicly call these people "Valley Trash." Others were more circumspect, though still rolling their eyes behind their backs, and Palin's army knew it.

It might have been a peaceful invasion had not Bill Large, the party's lawyer, who is usually very nice but also, unfortunately for him in this case, happens to be very large, not gotten so incensed with it all. By this time, he had enough of it. He and his fellow Republicans had been attacked for months on talk radio. They had been called corrupt bastards, ugly, greedy, piggish, oil company stooges, disgusting, disgraceful, opportunists, and any other kind of insult that the Palin folks could think of. The tipping point had come just recently, when a columnist for the Voice of the Times, the quasi-journalistic opinion page space on which the *Anchorage Daily News* allowed Bill Allen to run editorials, took up the Palin issue.

Voice of the Times columns revealed that as mayor of Wasilla, Palin had sent emails from her mayoral account and held meetings in her office that were related to her bid for lieutenant governor in the 2002 election. Allen and his company might have helped Palin with campaign donations during her run back then but not in 2006. She'd since gone off the reservation. Voice of the Times editor Paul Jenkins, squarely in the ranks of the old-guard Republicans, wondered how that was so different from what Palin had caught Randy Ruedrich doing when they worked together at the Alaska Oil and Gas Conservation Commission. They actually had her on something. She did, in fact, use her mayor's office for her 2002 campaign, something she knew was wrong. When she was running for mayor in 1996, she criticized her opponent for putting his mayor's office phone number on his campaign literature. "If it's not illegal, it's unethical," she said at the time.[5]

And this might have had an effect on her campaign and her pure image had the Voice of Times stopped there. But they didn't, and it couldn't have been better for Palin. Jenkins called Palin "a lightweight" and "maybe not the brightest bulb in the box." And he still wasn't done: "When her goody-two-shoes act starts to crumble—and going nuts because of a few obvious questions seems a first crack—folks may see her for the rank politician she is," Jenkins wrote, "and not necessarily a good one at that." He subsequently likened Palin to Jesse Ventura in a skirt and suggested she suffered from "vapors" and "a touch of paranoia." For good measure, he also accused her of getting in a "tizzy."

It backfired. Not only were establishment Republicans owned by the oil companies, they were sexist to boot. In response, Palin said that when you take a stand, you make "powerful enemies."

"I've got no skeletons," she said. "No affairs. No porn. Nothing." She did admit to experimenting with pot when she was young, but what Alaskan hadn't? Small amounts are practically legal here. But that was it. And, she said, she got a D in macroeconomics.[6]

Bill Large tried to defend the Republican Party. He counterattacked on the radio and continued the war in emails sent to Palin's lawyer, demanding that she retract her "false" and "reckless" statements about Ruedrich and the integrity of the Republican Party. Palin's lawyer, Wayne Anthony Ross, responded to Large by quoting Thoreau, Jefferson, and Reagan. Then he got down to business: If "you are a gentleman," Ross wrote to Large, "and I have yet to be convinced you are, it is you who should be making an apology." Ross drove a red Hummer with license plates that read WAR, his initials. In his house, beside the rec room in the basement, was a locked door, behind which was a long room filled with enough guns to outfit a small army. Keep walking and you'd find a firing range.

Then Wev Shea, acting as Ross's attorney, got involved. Shea, a former U.S. attorney for Alaska, a maverick conservative, and a diehard Palin supporter at the time, accused Large of fanning "a public spectacle by personally attacking our leading Republican gubernatorial candidate."

"You and Mr. Ruedrich are quite a team," Shea wrote to Large. "You have placed yourselves above what is best for Alaska and 'our' Republican Party. It is very sad."

It was a war of words that Large found himself squarely in the middle of before coming to the normally mellow Republican Party picnic. Except it wasn't a normal event in 2006. Hordes of people were outside, causing a ruckus. Shortly after he arrived, someone from the Alaska Republican Party whispered into Large's ear about the people outside, exhorting him as their lawyer to do something about the situation. So he made his way past the booths, past the tables covered with salmon and rolls and sheet cake, and went outside to ask the people who were chanting "Sa-rah" to quiet down. He did so, he said, because they were too loud, and nobody inside could hear anything else.

When that had the opposite effect, he conferred with Ruedrich, and they decided they would pull out some rule from somewhere that said signs were not allowed outside of the chalet, where most of them had congregated. The problem with this was that there were plenty of other campaign signs outside of the chalet. Why were they treated differently? Was it a conspiracy to silence them? Inside, Palin manned her booth, passed out fliers, and smiled, while a few of her supporters were running in and out of the building, keeping her updated on the injustices Large visited upon them and how it was just more proof of Republican old-guard malfeasance. She nodded knowingly when they spoke, shook her head sadly. Put her hand on their arms and thanked them for all that they were doing to make Alaska a better place to live. She assured them she would continue the fight. Bill Large went back inside to confer with Ruedrich. When he came back outside, he told them they could put their signs in the ground but couldn't hold them. Palin's people were too smart for that one. Nobody was going to deprive them of their God-given right to wave their signs and take a stand. That's when they began to surround Large, the chanting becoming increasingly loud and menacing. "Take a stand," they went. "Sa-rah, Sa-rah." Palin's father, Chuck Heath, was one of them. He grabbed Large's arm and told him that he better stop trying to hurt his daughter. Large shrugged him off and screamed at the crowd, "You're all a bunch of brown shirts!" The group quieted down some and looked at each other, confused. That moment of confusion and relative quiet could have provided the opportunity for Large to slip out, his dignity and perhaps even Republican unity somewhat intact. But he must have felt that if he was going to stoop as low as to call them a name, he might as well use a term that they understood.

"Communists!" he yelled. His face was red. He was sweating.

They knew what that meant, and at least one of them, a senior citizen named Bev Perdew, a Wasilla Palin supporter, said that she wasn't just going to stand there and do nothing about that. So she poked Large, hard, with one of the large "Take a Stand" signs. At that, Large began to push his way out of the group, which wasn't easy. And in doing so, he unfortunately pushed Perdew rather hard into a glass door. The next day was not a good one for the Republican Party or for Bill Large. The storyline: Bill Large, representing the Republican Party machine, pushed and knocked down a seventy-year-old Palin supporter. That's how far the Republican Party will go to keep Sarah out of the governor's race. Palin didn't need to wait for the postmortems, however. She knew what had happened at the picnic and what it meant. When the jostling was done, she stood watching the crowd, her arms crossed. "Gosh," she said of Large, "he was really upset, wasn't he?" She and Todd shared a look across the room. Then she smiled.[7]

Later that night, Palin penned an email to her supporters:

> You missed a very bizarre Republican Party picnic tonight . . . one of my supporters, a 70-yr-old lady wearing a Palin t-shirt, was told to get off the sidewalk by [Republican Party of Alaska] attorney Bill Large. He pushed her. He called my group of supporters "communists" and demanded they leave the public sidewalk area of the picnic pavilion. When later told he needed to apologize to the lady for pushing her and calling her a communist (I was there—I saw it), he said he didn't call her a communist— he "called all of you communists" . . . Large told me to "get your people away from the door and get your signs down," I had never met Large before so I asked him who he was—he said "you know who I am . . . and what are you going to do now? Start crying like you did on the Mike Pocaro [talk] show?" It was very strange. He was so mad and confrontational he was shaking and sweating.

Three days after the picnic, and much to the dismay of the oil companies, the Alaska legislature passed a tax hike of 22.5 percent of profits, which would rise 0.25 percent for every $1 increase in oil prices above $55 a barrel. Oil then was hovering at about $70 a barrel. At that price it amounted to a more than $2 billion increase, the highest tax, oil industry executives said, in the nation.[8]

State Democrats still didn't like it. They called it a giveaway. Conoco Phillips, BP, and Exxon Mobil hated it. The legislature adjourned without voting on Frank Murkowski's contract with the companies to build the natural gas pipeline. For the oil industry, the pipeline was the least of it. They had gotten nothing. The taxes were never locked in. Worse, lawmakers had jacked the rate above what they had agreed to under Murkowski's plan. They had lost.

Two weeks later, Sarah Palin swept the GOP primary. At a downtown Anchorage convention center where candidates amassed on election night, "Good-bye Frank!" stickers abounded. "Take a Stand" signs were raised high. Words like "fascist" were hurled at Murkowski, who stood among a small group, his U.S. senator daughter, Lisa, by his side. When someone hurled an invective at Murkowski, Lisa said, "That man has served this state for twenty-six years. Why can't you let him lose with dignity?"[9] A week after the primary, Palin would again benefit from another blow to the good old boys, and especially for Bill Allen. A death blow, really. And Allen's downfall, along with those who'd associated with him, would ensure Palin's victory in the general election.

PART III

BREAKUP

Sarah Palin's campaign touts the phrase, "Taking a stand for all Alaskans," but her actions speak louder than her words. She was appointed to the Alaska Oil and Gas Conservation Commission, a credential she refers to as a reason she is qualified to lead the state. What she doesn't mention is the fact that she quit less than a year into her term; this is not taking a stand . . . Will she quit again?

—TRACI L. CURRY,
letter to the editor, *Anchorage Daily News,*
August 8, 2006, about two weeks before Palin
won the GOP gubernatorial primary

CHAPTER 12

Glittering Generalities and Pipe Dreams

On August 30, 2006, Alaska state representative Fred Dyson drove into Anchorage from his home in Eagle River, a suburb that climbs up the mountainsides in a glacially carved valley about ten miles north of the state's largest city. He picked up Bill Allen at the latter's cedar shingled house near downtown. Dyson, who had been working with the FBI during the legislative session on the oil tax bill, knew Allen from way back. They'd first met in the oil fields in the 1970s when Dyson was working for BP and Allen was running pipeline camps. Dyson was fond of Allen. They both liked horses and classic cars. He found him charming, but he had reservations. He had accepted campaign contributions from Allen and VECO, but still he kept him at arm's length.

Dyson had watched for years as Allen put pressure on lawmakers. He didn't know whether Allen had ever broken the law, but Allen's tactics didn't sit right. Dyson had seen Allen getting increasingly bold, increasingly willing to show off his power. Dyson had talked to Steve Marshall, then president of BP's Alaska division, during the oil tax debate several months earlier. Dyson told him that Allen was giving everyone the impression that he carried BP's water in exchange for contracts. The BP president denied it to Dyson. "In fact, he scares us," Dyson recalled Marshall saying. "We're afraid in that in his clumsiness, he's going to get us all in trouble." (However, they weren't apparently worried enough to keep

179

their lobbyists from visiting the Animal House.) Dyson later called that conversation "prophetic."

The feds wanted Dyson to wear a wire and take Allen out for break-fast at a restaurant just down the street from the FBI's Alaska headquar-ters. Agents would be waiting at a table nearby. The plan was for Dyson to tell Allen that the agents were there and ask if he'd talk to them. They wanted to get him unaware, before he had time to contact a lawyer. If Allen said yes, the agents would approach. If Allen said no, they would leave him alone. Dyson didn't like the plan. He thought it too great a betrayal of his friend to have government operatives swarm in on him in public. So a compromise was brokered. Dyson, wearing a wire, would pull up to the restaurant and let Allen know that agents were waiting for him nearby. If Allen wanted to talk, great. If not, Dyson and Allen would have breakfast as planned.[1]

On that fateful morning, Allen hopped into Dyson's pickup and the two headed for the Kodiak Café. (Later, after the Alaska corruption case exploded into public view, one of Dyson's daughters had T-shirts made that read, "Whatever you do, don't get into Fred Dyson's truck.") On Fifth Avenue, across from Office Depot, Dyson pulled over in front of the diner. He pointed to the FBI agents in a Suburban parked nearby. He told Allen there was an investigation going on and that his name had come up. He said agents wanted to talk to him. When they heard him tell Dyson he would, they walked toward Dyson's truck and took Allen away.

Only nine days earlier Sarah Palin had upset the GOP establishment by becoming the Republican gubernatorial candidate in the November general election. Fall, which comes early in Alaska and ends quickly, was right around the corner. Political campaigns were in full swing, and there was a sense of busy optimism in the air. Alaskans knew that whatever happened on Election Day—whether Democrat Tony Knowles took the reins again, or the governor's job went to Palin or independent candidate Andrew Halcro—there would be a regime change and a new day. No more secret negotiations with oil companies. No more private jets for the state's chief executive. No more daughters appointed to Senate seats. No more Frank Murkowski, period.

It was a new day for Bill Allen too. Inside an FBI office in downtown Anchorage on that day, a titan of Alaska oil and politics vowed to betray people he loved.

When Bill Allen met with the FBI agents that day, they screened a "best hits" video in the "shock room," a montage of him allegedly bribing lawmakers. It didn't take long for Mary Beth Kepner, who was heading up the Polar Pen investigation, and other agents to get Allen talking. Various accounts put the time range from ten minutes to under two hours, which seemed strange to most who knew the recalcitrant VECO founder. The official line was that Allen knew he'd been caught, and the feds promised leniency if he helped them nail lawmakers and other suspects in the investigation. Eventually they would promise not to prosecute his three adult children, who may or may not have been suspected of crimes, and would allow Allen to move forward with selling VECO. (In 2007 a Denver-based engineering firm bought Allen's VECO for a cut-rate price of about $380 million, far lower than he would have gotten for a company earning about $1 billion in annual revenue had he not gotten caught up in the corruption scandal.) Many Alaskans, as well as lawyers for the future defendants, would come to question how much the oilman's relationship with Bambi Tyree and other underage girls might have factored into the discussions over whether he would roll. Bob Bundy, Allen's lawyer, would say in a 2007 interview that the oilman never had sex with Tyree. "If there was an investigation, it was small and limited, and I can tell you unequivocally that it played no part in the talks of Bill cooperating with the government," Bundy said. One of the federal prosecutors who had worked on the 2004 Joe "Millionaire" Boehm bust also helped on Polar Pen. FBI agents and federal prosecutors denied to local reporters that they'd used the sex allegations to flip Allen, but it would later be revealed that neither agents nor prosecutors were always forthright in sharing information with defense lawyers. Nor were they always prone to hand over evidence that might help exonerate the people they were prosecuting. Senator Ted Stevens learned this the hard way after he was tried, convicted, and voted out of office. Only later would evidence emerge that might well have helped him avoid the conviction.

Whether or not they brought up the sexual misconduct allegations, the agents did threaten Allen with prison time and told him he might get a reduced sentence if he helped prosecute others. Then they gave him the phone and instructed him to make some calls to loosen some tongues. Get politicians to incriminate themselves, they told him. The agents briefed him on what to expect the next day too, when they would bear down on state legislative offices brandishing search warrants. They made him promise that he wouldn't tell anyone he was cooperating. When the searches started, agents instructed Allen, act as surprised as anyone. He did. The day after his meeting with the FBI, he called Ted Stevens and acted surprised about offices being searched.

"And uh, the FBI got a warrant and searched my house and . . . and the office," Allen told Stevens.

For what? Stevens wanted to know. Allen told him that the agents were asking questions about the remodel.

"And I said, well, he's paid for everything and uh, you know, you don't . . . need this problem again, Ted, but that's what they're, uh, talk-ing me . . . and I just told 'em I wouldn't talk to 'em," Allen told Stevens.

In another conversation, Allen called Stevens and said, "Hey Ted, uh, I love ya, you know."[2]

On that August 31, the Alaska State Fair was in full swing in Palmer, the old home of Matanuska Valley colonist farmers just down the road from rapidly growing Wasilla. The leaves were already turning and starting to flutter to the ground. Some of them swept across the roads like miniature flags of a cold, invading army. The tops of the Chugach Mountains that loom over the fairgrounds were dusted with fresh snow, the first sign of the oncoming winter. "Termination dust," Alaskans call this white mantle.

At the fairgrounds, little shacks lining a dirt path sold smoked salmon chowder and enchiladas, deep-fried halibut and Kodiak scallops, turkey drumsticks and funnel cakes. A disproportionate amount of space was taken up by businesses selling hot tubs, snowmobiles, propane heaters, and wood stoves. Compared to most other state fairs, the 4-H farm ani-mal display looked positively quaint. There were a couple dozen head of cattle, some goats and llamas, a few pig pens, and a bunch of rabbits and chickens. The amusement park rides nearby belonged to a simpler era. But there was a spectacular wood-carving competition and a few uniquely Alaska events: a Carhartt fashion show, a Spam cook-off, and a game called the "Rat Race." The latter featured a roulette wheel and a rat. Fairgoers could bet a quarter on which hole the rat would run down as the wheel spun. There was a giant vegetable competition too, featuring the gargantuan growths fueled by the midnight sun. A pumpkin weighed over 1,000 pounds, a cabbage 73 pounds. There were five-foot gourds and hundred-pound kohlrabis.

The fair, however, was not immune from the culture wars. Next to one path was a booth decorated with gory pictures of aborted fetuses and a cutout of a pregnant woman. In the late 1980s, the abortion war was heating up in Wasilla, led by Palin's old church. State fair organizers had tried to exclude the Alaska Right to Life group and its pictures. A court battle over free speech ensued. Alaska Right to Life won, and its booth had been a presence at the Alaska State Fair ever since. Those who walked inside the booth found pamphlets about the evils of abortion and saw pictures of happy children living life to the fullest. One of the children in the photographs was Piper Palin, daughter of the former Wasilla mayor.[3] (Two years later, Palin, with the real Piper on her hip, entered that booth and shoved some dollars in the jar when her Blackberry buzzed. It was John McCain.)

Thousands of Alaskans were enjoying their state fair that day as FBI agents readied for raids that would rock the state. At about the time women were preparing to get on stage for the Great Alaskan Husband Holler competition, pitting screeching woman against screeching woman, FBI agents began serving search warrants across the forty-ninth state. They descended on Anchorage, Juneau, Wasilla, Eagle River, and Girdwood, the small ski town near the end of Turnagain Arm where Bill Allen had remodeled Uncle Ted's cabin. Twenty search warrants were issued that day, and more would follow. The FBI was looking for, among other things, financial ties between Alaska politicians and Allen or his company, VECO. They wanted documents related to the proposed natural gas pipeline and the petroleum production tax, and hats with the CBC label on them—Corrupt Bastards Club.

Phones all across Alaska began ringing as the warrants were served. FBI agents swarmed state offices in Anchorage, hunting for evidence in the desks and filing cabinets of legislators and their staff. Across the street stood the Pioneer Bar, one of the oldest in town. Black-and-white photographs on the walls chart the history of Anchorage: the railroad town it once was, the earthquake-shattered town of 1964, a town on the mend, and an oil boom town, smelling of stale beer, sweaty men, and women on the make. Significant events can be hard to see when they're happening right outside your window in a place with bitterly cold winter nights and ever so short winter days, a place so demanding of human toil merely to survive, a place so far away from the eyes of the rest of the country. Sometimes somebody needs to tap you on the shoulder and say, "Pay attention. This is important. This means something. This is what right is. This is what wrong is. This is where the two meet, or don't. Snap this picture. Save it for later. It will mean something."

Dan Fagan, a radio talk show host and Sarah Palin's old friend, was broadcasting from the Alaska State Fair when he heard of the FBI raids. He understood the significance, predicting then that Palin, the only anti–Big Oil candidate, would be Alaska's next governor. This cinched it, he told his listeners. Some of them thought she wasn't just lucky; she'd been ordained. This had to have come straight from above.

Sarah Palin would not, however, skate through the general election. She faced some tough candidates. Tony Knowles was one of them. He was the consummate Alaska politician, with two terms as governor to prove he could handle a third. Born in Oklahoma, an Army veteran with an economics degree from Yale, he came to Alaska in the late 1960s and worked in the oil patch before opening a restaurant. Tall and handsome, he was an avid runner, cross-country skier, and fisherman. Before becoming governor for the first time in 1994, he served two terms as Anchorage mayor. He ran the state during a tough period of low oil prices, a time when Alaskans actually thought of taxing themselves to make ends meet. Still, there were some who thought he'd been too cozy with the oil industry, including Bill Allen, as well as too compromising with Republicans. Knowles was the one who appointed Ted Stevens's son, Ben, to the Alaska Senate. Knowles was a Democrat to be sure, but a pro-gun, pro-business, pro-oil Democrat. Two out of the three were good, but the last one for the first time in his political career didn't do him any favors, and Palin made people aware of those ties.

Independent candidate Andrew Halcro, Palin's other competition, gave her a run, even though he didn't stand a chance of winning. A socially liberal Republican, he didn't have party support and ran as an independent. The Alaska Republican mainstream was troubled by his support of gay marriage and abortion rights. A lifelong Alaskan, a former state legislator, and one of the brightest minds in northern politics, Halcro always dressed well, usually in suit and tie, sometimes with a square peeping from his breast pocket. His hair was stylishly cut. If he really owned the jeans and flannel shirts that he swore were hanging in his closet, they didn't get out much during his campaign. He didn't like snow. He didn't ski like Knowles or ride snowmobiles like Palin or her husband, Todd, the snowmobile racing champ. There were no photographs of him posing with a fish or walking through the woods with a rifle. Actually, he said that he'd never even held a gun, and he once remarked that he was a fan of Federico Fellini's films.

Halcro was not the warmest guy in the room, either. But he was the smartest one, and he added a much needed voice in the campaign. "Smarty pants," Palin's people called him, particularly after debates where he spouted facts and figures in his infuriating Seattle-tech like, smarty pants inflection, repeatedly telling Alaskans not to listen to Palin's "glittering generalities" and warning them to ignore Knowles's homespun, feel-good riffs.

The three of them—Halcro, Palin, and Knowles—on stage in front of crowds at debates were a spectacle to watch: Palin, always talking about the Alaska constitution, the state's rosy future, and her conservative values and how hard she'd work to put Alaska first; Knowles echoing Alaska's rosy future and promising a government that wouldn't leave its people stranded as he underlined his prior experience that made him the best choice. And then there was Halcro. He simply told Alaskans the truth. Things might seem okay now, but the state was facing tough times. He wouldn't take a personal income tax off the table if oil revenues declined, and neither would he rule out tapping the sacrosanct Alaska Permanent Fund. In response, Palin would stare straight at the gloomy-looking Halcro and, taking her eyes momentarily off her color-coded note cards, say, "Alaskans want hope and opportunity, leaders with vision. They don't want leaders and candidates who are looking at everything as doom and gloom."[4]

At one debate, Halcro asked Palin what percentage of the state budget was taken up by the constitutionally mandated services she always talked about, and what she would be willing to cut. Palin answered by saying she would make sure the state funded constitutionally mandated services. "Sarah," Halcro said, "I didn't hear an answer to my question, so let me repeat it, and I'll say it slower: What percentage of the budget goes to constitutionally mandated services?" Each word was emphasized, the way one might speak to a naughty four-year-old. An uncomfortable silence followed, long enough for a narrative to be spun in the eyes of the public: the boys, Halcro and Knowles, were beating up on the girl. "Give her a break," some Alaskans thought. "She's new at this. She's a fresh face. And she makes us feel good."

At every debate the candidates were asked how they would promote construction of a natural gas pipeline, that long-sought-after next project, the hope for new boom. Halcro maintained that if the project was going to happen at all, it would develop only under the kinds of terms Murkowski negotiated. In the present, though, Halcro thought the pipeline a convenient way for Alaskans to avoid talking about more practical ways to pay for police and roads and schools as the state waited for oil companies to commit billions of dollars to a gas pipeline plan. While Palin and Knowles advocated scrapping Murkowski's pipeline contract and starting fresh, Halcro thought that it merely needed some tweaking. Knowles and Palin were more optimistic. The pipeline would happen under their watch, they both promised. They would get it built by opening negotiations with oil companies other than the major Prudhoe Bay producers—Conoco Phillips, Exxon, and BP. This would break the stranglehold the three big companies had on developing Alaska's resources. Knowles had always said that the best plan would be for the oil producers to build a gas pipeline along the

Alaska Highway into Canada and south to the Lower 48. Palin liked that idea too but didn't rule out a line from the North Slope to Valdez paralleling the existing trans-Alaska pipeline. Neither did she rule out the possibility of state involvement in funding construction. This was the dream of her mentor and campaign co-chairman, former governor Wally Hickel.

If the Palin and Knowles platforms sounded oddly similar—take back the state, don't preclude an independent company from building the pipeline—there was a reason for it. There were operatives in the background who made sure that there were supporters in both campaigns who had an entirely different views of how to get a gas pipeline built. At least three of the original Magnificent Seven—those state workers who got sideways with Murkowski during his negotiations for a gas pipeline—had worked their way into the campaigns. Mark Myers, director of the DNR oil and gas division, and Tom Irwin courted Palin, and Marty Rutherford moved close to Knowles. And they maintained contact with someone on the outside as well. Pat Galvin didn't walk out with the rest of the Seven, but he was on their side. He sat now in his office at the DNR biding his time. Few could have guessed that Galvin was destined to become the face of the Palin administration. It helped that he was smart, articulate, and had a knack for understanding politics. A Democrat and an all-American boy armed with an MBA from San Diego State and a law degree from the University of San Diego, he'd found himself in the thick of the fight at DNR over the gas line. He and Rutherford were friends. She brought him into the fold and told him what was wrong with Murkowski's deal. Convinced that at long last it was time for Alaska to stick up for itself, Galvin, Rutherford, Irwin, and a few others, with the help of a charismatic governor, dreamed a big dream: taking the state back from the oil companies.

Going into the election, the oil companies and many in the Alaska business community supported Knowles, but the corruption raids and the clouds of suspicion hanging over the lawmakers and VECO were too much for most Alaska voters. Longing for a clean start, they went for Palin, the reformer, and voted her into office on November 7, 2006, with 48.3 percent of the vote.

Around that time, Palin met Murkowski and his chief of staff, Jim Clark, for lunch in Fairbanks. They told her they hoped she would continue the work they had done on the gas line. Murkowski lectured her on gas economics and on the state's looming fiscal crisis. He stressed to her the necessity of getting a contract signed. Palin nodded her head. She smiled. She hardly said a word. She had heard Murkowski lecture before. He had used the same voice, the same condescending tone when she sat in his office in downtown Anchorage in 2002 interviewing for his old job as a U.S. senator from Alaska. Being a U.S. senator wasn't as cushy a job as it sounded, he said; living in D.C. was hard on families, particularly young children. Murkowski decided the job wasn't for Palin; he gave it to his daughter, who had two teenagers.[5]

Palin would never forget, and now the tables were turned. This time she was in the seat of power. She had won. She was in charge.

She was sworn in as Alaska's ninth governor on a cold day in December in Fairbanks, fifty years after the Alaska state constitution was written, and a love affair blossomed. Alaskans adored the woman who promised a new start, who would protect them like a "nanook protecting her cubs," the woman who embraced the state constitution and promised she would fight for the strange, small, intimate country called Alaska. The blissful honeymoon, aided by Palin's oil and gas policies passed in part as a reaction to the political corruption scandal, seemed to go on forever. The love affair lasted nearly until she left Alaska with the flickering flame of a possible gas pipeline still burning.

By early 2007, the price of steel had gone up. The cost of building the pipeline was by then estimated to be at least $26 billion, but the price of natural gas was also up. The economics appeared to favor construction. Palin brought back members of the Magnificent Seven, including Marty Rutherford as DNR deputy commissioner and later Tom Irwin as head of the agency. Pat Galvin was appointed commissioner of the Department of Revenue. Historically there had been some tension between the Revenue Department and DNR, but no more. Now they were a team, loyal to each other and their dreams to the end. Galvin and Rutherford and a few others began work on what would come to be called the Alaska Gasline Inducement Act, AGIA for short, a piece of legislation that was going to get Alaska its pipeline. Once again for Rutherford and the rest of the team, there were long nights, little food, and lots of stress. On a whiteboard, they sketched out the history of Alaska oil and gas, marking where Alaska went wrong and where it went right. Then they began developing their own plan and selling it even as it was developing. The team seemed to be everywhere—press conferences, talk shows, business lunches—trying to get their message out to Alaskans: open up the process. Allow companies other than the oil producers to bid on building the line. Trust Palin and her administration. They'd make it happen.

Unlike the experience they had when they were struggling under the leadership of Frank Murkowski, they now felt buoyed by the process. This, finally, was their chance to take Alaska back, and they had a governor who not only agreed but had the public behind her, and they liked her. They could work with her, as could many in the legislature. Palin brought fresh air with her to Juneau. Six-year-old Piper wandered the halls of the Capitol, charming legislators.

Palin got along with the Democrats particularly well. She might have gotten along with them better than any governor in decades, even better than Tony Knowles. She kept her conservative social beliefs out of the office and never once called the Alaska media "lamestream." Reporters called her Sarah. Editorials in papers large and small across the state praised her. Even the pro-industry Republicans, who didn't trust her, nonetheless showed respect. The oil industry, after all, was on the run. The FBI had kept their cards close, and no one knew yet what was going to be revealed when the indictments came down. That gave Palin leverage.

AGIA was a completely different approach to getting a natural gas pipeline. In all of the more than thirty years of talking about a line, this had never been tried before. The gist of the proposal was simple. The gas line act listed a set of what the administration called "must haves" for the state. There was hardly any talk of gas taxes in the legislation, nothing about what the state was going to have to give up, but rather what the state needed to get from the project. And mostly, what the state needed to get was what the three major oil companies didn't want to give—a reasonable opportunity for independent companies to put gas in the line at a fair rate. The authors of the legislation believed the Big Three—Conoco, BP, and Exxon—had controlled North Slope oil for decades by charging smaller companies too much to run oil down the pipeline. To them, the beauty of AGIA was that this project, unlike the trans-Alaska oil pipeline, would do away with control by a few big players. The operator of an open-access gas pipeline would have no reason to inflate transportation costs or lie to the state about them. An independent operator would treat all gas sellers the same. Its books would be open. The state would have access to information that it didn't have about the oil line. In the eyes of many, AGIA was a brilliant, albeit risky move. In the eyes of others—especially the Big Three—it was philosophically anathema, and a money loser to boot.

Palin often visited the war room when the details were being hashed out on AGIA. Rumor had it (and still does) that she's vague on details, that she only saw what she wanted to see and only heard what she wanted to hear. That might be true with some things, but those in the room writing this tricky piece of legislation recall that she was in the mix on this plan.

Rutherford said that she wouldn't support Palin in a presidential run, but she thought she was a great governor. "So many things convinced me of that. I was surprised and impressed," she said. "I worked for a lot of governors, but she was very, very involved."[6] Palin was so involved that other commissioners complained to the gas line team that they didn't get equal time with her, that she was "all oil and gas all the time."

Still, even amid meetings about tariffs, roll-in rates, and federal energy regulations, her Blackberry would buzz and she would multitask. Those in her inner circle—Frank Bailey, her director of boards and commissions; Ivy Fry, a close aide; Kris Perry, her Anchorage office director; or Meghan Stapleton, her press secretary—would pass on a piece of important information, like a talk show host saying negative things about the governor and the gas line, or a legislator making an off-the-cuff remark about her lack of accessibility. Or maybe a blogger had said something bad about her hair. It could be anything. Any hint of criticism would get her riled up and keep her eyes glued to the Blackberry.

This tendency only got worse after Palin left to run for vice president and came back. But Rutherford remembers from the beginning telling the governor and her advisers, some having never worked in government before, to avoid sending emails they didn't want the public to get their hands on. It's not how you do things, she told them. She advised them and Palin to ignore the criticism, since focusing on it could become disruptive. Palin would look at her and smile, or try to defend herself from criticism by objecting, "It's just not true!" Rutherford would say, "Governor, but some people believe it to be."

Palin's response: "But it's not true!"

Rutherford would tell her, "Good people can have different versions of reality."

Palin's response: "But it's not true!"

The governor didn't understand that people could go to the same talk, hear the same facts, and come out with different conclusions. More distracting yet, Palin always felt the need to respond. Sometimes she did it on the airwaves. Anchorage deejays Bob and Mark were a favorite outlet. But mostly she kept the responses in-house, often limiting them to her inner circle. Galvin remembered how, early on, his email address showed up on one of the numerous threads that ran throughout the day. "It was some snotty email," he said. "Something that Ivy had said about a legislator, and then Palin responded. They went back and forth. I finally went to the governor and said, 'Governor, you can't send emails like this. What happens if, in a month from now, Ivy leaves disgruntled and she's in the private sector and she releases these emails?'

"Right then, Ivy [Fry] comes into the room, and the governor said, 'Ivy, would you ever do anything like that?' And Ivy said, 'Of course I would never do anything like that!'"[7]

Galvin wouldn't confirm it, but one email exchange apparently involved a Fairbanks legislator, Jay Ramras, who was rumored to be dating a younger woman. In response to a public complaint made by Ramras that Palin didn't spend more time with him and his Republican cohorts, the governor emailed, "Doesn't he know why? I have two teenaged daughters, and everyone knows gotta keep the young 'uns away from the likes of Jay." It was the kind of email exchange that drove Galvin and Rutherford nuts.

In Palin's vice presidential acceptance speech before the Republican National Convention in September 2008, she paid homage to those who live and work in small towns. "We grow good people in our small towns, with honesty and sincerity and dignity," she quoted another writer as saying. That may be true. There are good and righteous people in small towns who are also concerned about who's saying what about you. No more so than in a small town in a small-time state like Alaska, where everybody talks about everybody else incessantly, and when they do so, it feels like a betrayal. To Palin, the whole state was her friend, and those criticisms stung, no matter who they were coming from.

Trying to explain Palin, Galvin said that "she's not impressed really with anything, and to a certain extent this applies to her own status. And for that reason, everything remains small and nothing takes on a sense of gravity. So, there's no perception of the relative importance of things." She didn't understand, Galvin said, that there are certain things a governor just doesn't do. A governor doesn't send out snotty emails about elected officials, nor do those in her inner circle. A governor doesn't call those who disagree with her "haters" (as Palin and her staff had taken to doing), or "evil" or "little pricks" or "dumb asses" or "greedy spenders," or write with glee about someone "ripping" an enemy "a new one" on a radio program, or gloat about how little a public official was able to raise for his charity such as the Special Olympics.[8] A governor does not allow her inner circle to be overwhelmed with cultish adoration or become preoccupied with incessant talk about evil enemies.

For all of that, however, Galvin said Palin did have an extraordinary talent for absorbing relatively complex policies and making quick sound bites out of them, which cut to the heart of anything she was opposing. "She's very instinctual that way," Galvin said. "She was just so good at the politics of it. I was, frankly, amazed at how good she was." But she was ruthless with her adversaries. Everyone who worked with her knew that if you got on her bad side—if you said anything bad about her, or worse yet, tried to humiliate her, which was the ultimate betrayal—you wouldn't ever get back on her good side. And a governor in Alaska, no matter how beloved, is going to face criticism. Her adversaries began to multiply.

This was the process for getting a natural gas pipeline going in Alaska under Palin' s leadership: First the Gas Line Act had to be voted in. After that battle was won, the administration would put together something that resembled a request for proposals from any company that wanted to build the line. The companies that applied, and agreed to the state's "must haves" and other terms of the act, would then, upon legislative approval, receive a state license and seek the necessary approvals and permits to build the line. As an incentive, the state offered the company that received the license up to $500 million in subsidies. The Palin administration rolled out the act in March 2007, and initially it looked like the political fight would be colossal. Executives from the Big Three flew into Juneau to deliver their best arguments against allowing an independent company—anyone but them—to build the line.

As the particulars of the gas line legislation were being worked out, a college student from Colorado started a blog, Draft Sarah Palin for Vice President. Adam Brickley could not have guessed what impact his suggestion would have on the future of Alaska.

CHAPTER 13

Hopefully Slow Gas Will
Begin to Pass . . . Quickly

February 2007 in America began with a woman, Senator Hillary Clinton, as the presumptive Democratic nominee for president. This had never happened before. In the Republican Party, Senator John McCain from Arizona announced he was in the race, but former New York City mayor Rudi Giuliani was considered the favored candidate. On February 10 a relatively unknown black man from Chicago, Barack Obama, stood outside on a frigid day in Springfield, Illinois, to announce his intention to challenge Clinton in the Democratic primary. In Springfield by mid-February the bright sunshine hints at spring.

In Alaska spring remains a long way off even in March. In the state's largest city, the Anchorage Fur Rendezvous Festival is just wrapping up. The winter carnival traces its roots back to a time when trappers came to town from the Alaska hinterland to sell their spoils. Now, though, it's an excuse to drum up business and to party. There's a Ferris wheel and helicopter rides and Eskimo blanket tosses. Pamplona meets Alaska in an event known as the Running of the Reindeer. The Iditarod Trail Sled Dog Race is set to begin. Men and woman will step onto the runners of sleds powered by dogs and ride 1,000 miles through some of Alaska's wildest, coldest landscape to Nome. It is a big deal in Alaska, the start of the beginning of the end of winter.

By March in Alaska, the sun sits high in the sky again, shining bright but cold, like a Hollywood ingénue. But at least the sun is back, not

hiding below the southern horizon down toward those other, more so-
phisticated lands. Alaskans know that spring is still a world away but see
reminders that it will be back one day. Sometimes keeping the faith during the long, dark winters is hard. Sometimes Alaskans can start believing that the purgatory spent among the dark winter spirits is fitting
retribution for something, sins committed in a past life, perhaps. But
then March hits and the sun chases those spirits away and the sins are
wiped clean. Alaskans, at long last, feel forgiven.

In Alaska this March, there is good news. Oil prices have risen to $66
a barrel. Americans are driving more than ever, pushing U.S. consump-
tion up by more than 500,000 barrels a day over a year earlier.[1] Prices
are further buoyed by concerns about the political situation in Iran, as
British sailors operating in the Persian Gulf were seized by the Islamist
government. Rising oil prices will help offset the losses the Alaska government expected because of falling oil production. North Slope oil production is now down to around 730,000 barrels a day, about
three-quarters of the 1 million barrels produced seven years earlier. But
because of rising oil prices and the tax hike passed eight months earlier,
the oil companies are pumping tens of millions of dollars of additional
revenue into state coffers.

Nobody knew for sure how much more tax revenue the state would
collect after the legislature passed the 22.5 percent tax on oil net profits.
The taxation formula was complex, and the oil companies could apply
for credits on some of their development and work on the Slope. Still,
there was a sense of optimism in Alaska that the state would share in any
profits to be made off spiraling global oil prices. The higher the oil price,
the more money Alaska would collect in taxes, and prices were rising.

The state's past fiscal problems suddenly solved by the vagaries of the
global energy markets, newly elected Governor Sarah Palin introduced
her plan to push construction on the natural gas pipeline, the project
that helped sink Frank Murkowski's administration. Like her predecessor,
Palin was now pinning her governorship on a thirty-year-old dream to
tap the state's massive natural gas fields and ship the gas south via a multibillion-dollar pipeline to produce heat and electricity in the Lower 48. As
in the past, supporters were touting the gas line as a bonanza for Alaska.

As the largest private energy project in U.S. history, they said, the gas line would draw thousands of welders, pipe fitters, and other workers north, much as the trans-Alaska oil pipeline had done in the 1970s.

Rising fuel and utility bills in many parts of the country were making the project increasingly feasible. Climate change hadn't hurt either. Discussions of how to reduce American CO_2 emissions were under way. Producing electricity with clean gas instead of dirty coal was looking attractive. All of these things were good for the Palin administration as it prepared to roll out a pipeline proposal with a snappy name, something that would roll off the tongue and permeate the consciousness of a state full of pipeline-weary citizens and lawmakers: AGIA, the Alaska Gasline Inducement Act.

Palin loved it. Pat Galvin, the state's revenue commissioner, thought the name sounded like a venereal disease, but he held his objections.[2] AGIA was complex, and most Alaskans didn't really know what the legislation meant for the state. But they trusted their new governor, whose approval ratings were in the stratosphere. State Democrats were particularly smitten with AGIA. One of them, former *Anchorage Daily News* columnist turned state legislator Mike Doogan, wrote a song in its honor, sung by a booming tenor to the tune of "I've Just Met a Girl Named Maria" from *West Side Story*:

> *AGIA, I've just read a bill named AGIA,*
> *And hopefully slow gas will begin to pass . . . quickly,*
> *AGIA, I've just read a bill named AGIA,*
> *And suddenly the route to all that gasline loot is freeeee.*[3]

Republican lawmakers adopted a more skeptical stance toward AGIA and Palin. She called herself a Republican, but her approach to the oil companies seemed very un-Republican. The Palin administration had essentially written up a list of demands for any company that wanted to build a gas pipeline in the state. In exchange for going along with the state plan, a pipeline builder would get up to $500 million in subsidies to pursue the project. This was to ensure that independent companies, without the resources that the major oil companies had, could apply. But there was little talk of gas taxes as part of the deal nor any talk of locking them in for some period of time, as the big oil companies had always wanted when pipeline discussions had come up in the past.

Offering the half-billion-dollar subsidy was sort of like throwing a dollar bill on the table as far as the oil companies were concerned. This was pocket change. BP alone had worldwide profits of more than $22 billion in 2006. Five hundred million dollars was not considered much of an incentive, given that the state could raise taxes to recoup that amount at any time. Unlike Murkowski, who proposed locking in tax rates for decades, the Palin administration refused to budge on taxes.

Palin was trying to break the hold three major oil companies had on Alaska's undeveloped gas. Their refusal to pump the natural gas to market had long been a contentious issue in the state. A former Democrat candidate for governor, Eric Croft, had gone as far as floating an amendment to the state constitution to allow Alaska to put a tax on the gas while it was still in the ground. Making them pay to sit on the gas, he argued, would encourage the oil companies to start building a pipeline. The industry fought hard against the amendment and it failed.

Opponents of Palin's scheme wondered what kind of legal mess she was moving the state toward. If an independent company built the pipeline, it would set the price for moving gas. Yet the big three oil companies would still hold the lease rights to the gas. What if they decided the price was too high, and they didn't want to pump gas into the pipeline? A legal battle to try to force them to ship gas could take years and in the meantime tie up the reserves. Indeed, Exxon was still in the courts fighting over how much it should pay in damages from the 1989 oil spill outside of Valdez.

This might have been the reason other governors had chosen a less confrontational approach and tried to negotiate a deal with industry. But Palin loved the game, and a new game required a new strategy. She and her advisers believed they held the upper hand, and they were going all in. Eventually the oil companies would bend to the potential for profit. Until that happened, this was a game of chicken, and Palin thrived on the notion that she would win in the end. This pipeline was, in her words, "God's will."[4]

And at least one of her gas team advisers thought the same. Tom Irwin sent her religiously infused emails. "I really praise God for you," he wrote once. Another time, he said, "We are part of God's plan."

Palin wrote to Irwin, "God's got all this in control as we give it up to Him!" And then she said this to her lieutenant governor: "Pray for wisdom for us, for the team . . . And may God's will be done with His resources."[5]

His will was to get those resources out of the ground, and no oil company could stop that.

If winter in Alaska is a long sleep with the cold spirits, then springtime is the trill of the earth's alarm clock. Snowmelt rushes in culverts and down the streets. The sky rings with the songs of birds stalking their mates by screaming holy hell at them. Smells come back. As the snowpack thins under the bright sun that stays longer and longer in the sky every day, objects emerge from the sea of white: bikes and garden tools, tin cans and plastic bags galore, footballs and tennis rackets, old shirts and jeans, kitchen wares. It's as if an alternate universe exists beneath the snow, one that sucks objects out of sight, finds them lacking, and pushes them back up again. Community groups organize doggie doo cleanup parties on the public trails. Kids in shorts jump on trampolines and chase one another across the slushy puddles.

Spring in Alaska is appropriately called "breakup," named for what the ice does in the big rivers, the Yukon, the Kuskokwim, the Tanana, and others. Since 1917, the town of Nenana in Alaska's Interior has held a lottery in which people guess the exact time the ice will move 100 feet to prove that it is indeed breaking up. Twenty-two people placed bets on 3:47 P.M. April 27, 2007. Each won a $13,785 share of that year's $303,272 pot.

Breakup. Good-bye cold, cold winter. Alaska is done with you. Winter makes Alaskans mean and snarly. Winter is part of the reason why alcoholism is such a problem, why sexual abuse runs rampant. Winter keeps Alaskans trapped in their houses, keeps them pale and hunched over, starved for Vitamin D and sometimes company. Winter freezes the fingers and toes off some Alaskans, turns their noses black with frostbite, and crusts their beards with ice. Winter is the reason why businesses fail, why the state is married to oil. Winter is a bad relationship. By April, Alaskans trust that it is finally going to end (many even convince themselves once and for all), and set out to wash that winter right out of their hair. Some Alaskans—the cabin dwellers, who haven't bathed for months—do so, literally.

In spring 2007, the state was preparing for a big breakup. Just like the year before, committee hearings in the state Capitol went on seemingly forever as lawmakers, lobbyists, and oilmen hashed out the latest proposal to usher in a new future for Alaska. Executives from the Big Three testified against AGIA. They droned on and on about "fiscal certainty" and how the administration was overreaching. What they were saying boiled down to this: They held the legal rights to tap the gas, and they would decide how the project moved ahead—not Sarah Palin and those rebels from the Magnificent Seven.

They were really saying, "We're more powerful than you are, Alaska. We'll fight you on this. Just wait and see. Your oil is running out, and soon all you'll have left is natural gas. Do you really want to take a risk by alienating those who have given you everything? Alaska, think of that dividend you collect every year. Remember that you don't pay state sales tax or income tax. Think about the subsidies available to start your crazy businesses that always fail. Think about your nicely groomed ski trails. Think about your lodges and your fishing streams and your snowmobiles and your four-wheelers and your airplanes and your boats and those never-ending summer days, when you get weeks off from your cushy jobs to play in this vast land, this Neverland Alaska. If we're not here, you won't have any of this. Alaska, if we're not here, the state will clear out and those who remain will have nothing. Think Appalachia with seven months of winter. That's you, without us."

AGIA might have sounded like the name of a Russian car or a venereal disease, but to the Palin administration, Democrats, and others it was more like the acronym for a missile launched at the hearts of those who assumed the state should do whatever the big oil companies wanted. AGIA was a declaration of war, a reckless war some thought, over the future of Alaska, and no one could have launched this battle but a Republican governor elected to lead at a time in Alaska history when anti-oil sentiment had reached new heights. Like so many of Palin's accomplishments, her success closely tracked the events and circumstances developing around her. She was either the smartest politician in the country or the luckiest.

Until the morning of May 4, 2007, a couple of weeks before the Alaska legislature was scheduled to adjourn, Sarah Palin's proposed gas pipeline legislation still looked like a long shot. Lawmakers seemed inclined to put off a vote on it. But on that Friday, everything changed. The U.S. Department of Justice announced it had arrested three lawmakers: Pete Kott, Vic Kohring, and Bruce Weyhrauch. They faced a host of corruption charges, including extortion and bribery, mail and wire fraud. All stemmed from their relationship with Bill Allen and his sidekick Rick Smith. The general theme was that the three had accepted bribes and favors from VECO in return for using their votes and influence to keep oil taxes low in 2006. Assistant Attorney General Alice Fisher said, "The public servants indicted today conspired to perform official acts in exchange for monetary and other financial gain to the detriment of Alaska, its economy, and its citizenry."

A few days later, Allen and Smith entered the federal courthouse in Anchorage and pleaded guilty to corruption charges. They admitted to illegally funneling more than $400,000 to legislators. Former Senate president Ben Stevens—Uncle Ted's son—was identified in court filings as someone who allegedly took more than $240,000 in phony consulting fees from VECO. Court documents for the first time suggested the FBI had been watching in 2006 as madness unfolded in the Baranof Hotel's Suite 604—Bill Allen's Animal House. Federal officials hinted that more indictments were coming. Lawmakers who had visited the Animal House or had any interactions with Allen were suddenly worried. Even if they didn't take any bribes, the things that happened in the Animal House could prove embarrassing. The good old boy atmosphere there might have been fine a few decades earlier, but it was now the early twenty-first century. There was no easy way for a lawmaker to explain to constituents why he paid a visit to the Animal House, and many—Republicans and some Democrats—had visited.

In the end, 10 percent of the legislators who had served during the 2006 oil tax battle would come under investigation. A host of lobbyists, staffers, and others associated with the lawmakers would also get caught in the spotlight of Polar Pen, including Jim Clark, who had been Frank Murkowksi's chief of staff. Clark eventually pleaded guilty to taking nearly $70,000 in illegal polling and consulting fees from VECO to support Murkowski's failed reelection campaign; Murkowski himself was never charged. And like some of the others charged or implicated in the VECO scandal, Clark saw his corruption conviction tossed out. An investigation of the government agents and prosecutors themselves would show that they had cut corners. With those discoveries, Polar Pen would implode. But all of that was a still a long way off. In May 2007, the stars were aligning, spring breakup was over, and Sarah Palin was about to prove blessed with impeccable timing yet again. AGIA would become one in a string of events that transpired during her short time as governor to help boost her toward a date with destiny.

After the indictments were announced, Palin said that unlike Murkowski's pipeline effort, AGIA was founded on trust, transparency, and openness. "That's what AGIA is all about, so there's a world of difference between today and a week ago," she said.[6] A day later, Palin was again talking about AGIA and the indictments, though it was hard for Alaskans to follow what she was saying, as was sometimes the case. "You know, it takes two to tango," Palin said. "Yesterday it was the Legislature who was under fire. But those who were exerting their powers will also have to be held accountable. And I think Alaskans will be very disappointed if they learn that the same people are still exerting power as the Legislature discusses AGIA."[7]

Bill Allen, VECO, and Big Oil were all poison, and anybody who had associated with them was tainted. It had become politically incorrect to question Palin's grand plan to take on the oil industry. "Nobody wanted to touch AGIA with a 10-foot pole," then revenue commissioner Pat Galvin recalled.[8] By mid-May, the Alaska legislature had approved the bill pretty well intact, which was nearly unheard of. Only one lawmaker voted against it, Republican state Representative Ralph Samuels. He confessed to a reporter later that he knew voting against AGIA would probably kill his political career, but he thought it was the right thing to do. Nobody else stood up. Palin was on a roll, and she wasn't done. Because of the alleged corruption surrounding Murkowski's petroleum profits tax bill passed the previous year, she told lawmakers she would be calling them back in the fall of 2007 to review it and consider increasing oil taxes. So, the pipeline and the oil taxes were both back on the table.

Along the way, an *Anchorage Daily News* reporter asked Palin what she thought of a blog championing her for vice president in 2008. "Oh come on," Palin responded, "I got enough to worry about here in Alaska for the next four years."[9] But there was more to this story than just some blogger making things up.

On June 18, 2007, 437 days before she was tapped by John McCain as his running mate, Palin met with the top editors from the *Weekly Standard,* who had arrived in Alaska's capital city on a cruise sponsored by the conservative political magazine. They had disembarked from their ship and strolled over to the governor's mansion to meet her. As she served halibut cheeks, Sarah Palin told the conservative heavyweights who had washed up at her door—William Kristol, Michael Gerson, and Fred Barnes—that she was in the process of finally, at long last, getting a gas line for Alaska and the country. It would be the biggest private construction project in U.S. history, she said. She explained how she had to take on Big Oil to make it happen, and how she was winning. The pitch made an impression. President George W. Bush's popularity was falling and Republicans had suffered a defeat in the 2006 midterm elections. The GOP was floundering. Palin seemed like a breath of fresh Alaska air— conservative, Republican, attractive, tough, and not in the pocket of corporate America. Sitting in the governor's mansion in Juneau, where the mountains seem to climb straight into the sky and primordial glaciers lurk just beyond, Palin could not have seemed anything like the Republicans the *Weekly Standard* editors knew in the Beltway. Palin was then at the height of her power. The visiting eastern Republicans, the ones who had struggled for decades to create an image of what the Republican Party was, must have felt amazed. Here she was, wish fulfillment in the flesh. Palin took the editors on a helicopter ride back into the mountains to visit a gold mine. They saw the beauty of Alaska, and a governor who was tough on industry but was no greenie. They were wowed. Barnes noted that Palin was not only strong but pretty. Michael Gerson called her "a mix between Annie Oakley and Joan of Arc."

A few weeks later, Barnes wrote a piece in the *Weekly Standard* entitled "The Most Popular Governor." He recounted Palin's rise from Republican outcast to the "GOP's newest star." In Alaska, he said, she was cleaning up government and taking on Big Oil. Meantime, every chance he got, Kristol extolled Palin's virtues. A year later, confident that his lobbying had worked, Kristol predicted on *Fox News Sunday* that "McCain's going to put Sarah Palin, the governor of Alaska, on the ticket."

The boys from the *Weekly Standard* weren't the only ones Palin welcomed north that summer. After their ship sailed, another cruised into the Juneau harbor. Another gang of prominent national conservatives walked down the plank and headed to the governor's mansion. Palin this time laid out a spread of salmon for writers and editors from the *National Review* magazine. Among others, the guests included Rich Lowry, the magazine's editor, former federal judge Robert Bork, former U.N. ambassador John Bolton, and Dick Morris, the former Clinton aide turned conservative political consultant and commentator.[10] Palin told them about her pipe dream and how the Lower 48 would soon be awash in natural gas. Biggest private construction project in U.S. history, she repeated again. She explained how she had to arm-wrestle Big Oil and uproot corruption that had reached the highest levels of state government. A senior editor described Palin as "a former beauty-pageant contestant, and a real honey, too. Am I allowed to say that? Probably not, but too bad." After she joined McCain on the 2008 ticket, Morris according to *The New Yorker*, wrote, "I will always remember taking her aside and telling her that she might one day be tapped to be Vice-President, given her record and the shortage of female political talent in the Republican Party. She will make one hell of a candidate, and hats off to McCain for picking her."[11]

CHAPTER 14

Exxon, Don't Let the Door
Hit You in the Stern

On the morning of July 30, 2007, a parade of government Suburbans drove south out of Anchorage along the Seward Highway on that stretch of two-lane road squeezed between the cliffs of the Chugach Mountains and the silty, tidal waters of Turnagain Arm. They were headed for Girdwood—Girdweird to some, that hippy ski town forty minutes from Anchorage. The Suburbans pulled up to what had been Ted Stevens's cabin, but was now more of a shabby chalet. Bill Allen and some of his oil roughnecks had added a second story and fixed the place up seven years earlier, but it wasn't exactly palatial. Search warrants in hand, FBI agents called a locksmith to open the door and spent the rest of the day and into the night combing the inside and outside of the house. They carried out trash bags full of evidence. They studied the second-floor deck that Dave Anderson, Allen's nephew, and his crew built. They took measurements and made notes. In some ways, they looked to the watching media more like building inspectors than agents pursuing a criminal investigation.

The FBI search on the home of the then second-oldest sitting senator was the turning point in both Stevens's career and the political corruption investigation. Stevens had served nearly four decades in the U.S. Senate. He'd once been third in line to the presidency. To Alaskans, he seemed politically invincible. At age 83, Stevens still donned his famous Hulk tie when he planned to do battle on the Senate floor. Until his house was raided, it seemed the only thing that could end his Alaska political career was old age. The thought that he would someday depart the scene terrified Alaskans. What would happen when the state lost his seniority in the Senate? With oil production on the decline and the natural gas pipeline still uncertain, Stevens was more important than ever to Alaska, a state in which about a third of all jobs can be traced to federal funding.

And now it wasn't his age that was the issue; the question was whether he would be indicted for allowing a grade school dropout to remodel and expand his 1,200 square foot cabin. Special agent Mary Beth Kepner, who headed up Polar Pen, believed Stevens failed to pay for all of the renovations on his cabin. Bill Allen, on whom the entire investigation depended, told Kepner he'd worked on Stevens's home as a favor to his friend, but Allen's accounts varied some. At times he said Stevens knew he was getting a special deal by having VECO take on the project. Still, Stevens paid various subcontractors and other parties. There was no doubt, though, that VECO was heavily involved in the remodel, and there weren't invoices for all of the work. Kepner knew that much, but she struggled with what Allen got in return for assisting his friend with the house project. At one point in the investigation, she even asked a reporter from *Alaska Dispatch*, "What do you think the quid-pro-quo was?"[1] It was a strange question coming from a special agent who had already searched the home of one of America's most powerful politicians. In the end, the feds would decide they didn't have enough evidence to prove Allen bribed Stevens. Instead, they would charge the senator with failing to disclose some $250,000 in "gifts," including the house renovation, on his disclosure forms, as required of U.S. senators.

Five days after the FBI ransacked Stevens's house, Alaskans shaken to the core, Governor Sarah Palin called for a special fall legislative session. She was about to propose a big hike in oil taxes. The tax structure the Alaska legislature passed in 2006 had come under a cloud of corruption, she said, and new state estimates showed that the tax was bringing in less revenue than expected. Though numbers compiled later would prove this lower estimate to be wrong, Palin went ahead and proposed lifting the tax from 22.5 percent of oil company net profits to 25 percent. As with AGIA, Palin and her administration came up with a catchy name for their new tax proposal. They spent some time writing down ideas until one morning revenue commissioner Pat Galvin's wife awoke and said, "I've got it." Thus was born Alaska's Clear and Equitable Share—ACES.[2]

The idea that Alaska wanted to raise taxes on crude for a second straight year outraged Conoco Phillips, BP, and Exxon. But there was little they could do. Their longtime supporter—Bill Allen—had ratted out lawmakers and even Ted Stevens. Now they were paying the price for passively condoning his wheeling and dealing on their behalf. The oil companies were never charged with any crimes, but their names were very much associated with the "corrupt bastards" who were supposedly running the legislature. If this wasn't enough of a problem, Palin planned to call the special legislative session in fall 2007. With the corruption trials beginning, there was no way the oil companies were going to persuade the legislature to resist raising taxes. There were too many Alaskans who saw this as a chance for revenge. They would back Palin on this one.

In September 2007, Pete Kott, the state representative who had been recorded by the FBI saying, "I sold my soul to the devil," went on trial in Anchorage. Kott had pleaded not guilty to accepting some $9,000 in bribes and favors from Bill Allen and Rick Smith in return for pulling strings in the legislature on behalf of Murkowski's oil tax bill. The federal judge in the case was Bill Allen's neighbor, the same one who'd complained about noise at Allen's house and had presided over Joe "Millionaire" Boehm's sex case involving Bambi Tyree, the ringleader who allegedly slept with Allen when she was fifteen years old.

At the start of Kott's trial, the prosecutors and defense team met in Judge John Sedwick's chambers. The prosecutors were a team made up of lawyers from the U.S. Attorney's office in Alaska and the U.S. Justice Department's public integrity section in Washington, D.C. They asked the judge that Tyree's relationship with Allen be kept out of the trial. Prosecutor Jim Goeke said a reference to Tyree might have shown up in some recordings that were provided to Kott's lawyer as part of the discovery of evidence. Specifically, he said, there might "be a line of inquiry concerning Mr. Allen's relationship with Tyree, and the government would posit that it has no relevance to this case whatsoever."[3]

Goeke had been involved in the Boehm case as a federal prosecutor, and he knew about Tyree's alleged relationship with Allen when she was a young teenager. His partner in the trial, assistant U.S. Attorney Joe Bottini, spoke to her himself about Tyree having sex with Bill Allen. They both knew Tyree alleged that Allen had asked her to sign a affidavit claiming they never had sex. They both knew Allen got Lisa Moore, the oilman's former prostitute, out of town to avoid having her testify in another case. They knew what such revelations could do to the jury in the Kott case. Allen was the government's chief witness. If Allen was painted as a sex offender, his character could be tarnished in the eyes of the jury. There were also concerns that if the connection between Tyree and Allen came out in the trial, the VECO executive might not testify at all or, worse, stop cooperating with the government. Goeke kept nearly all of what he knew from Kott's lawyers.

The defense team didn't know what to think of Goeke's request to keep Tyree out of the trial. Although her name rang a bell, Kott's lead lawyer couldn't think of a reason why he'd need to bring her up during the trial. Judge Sedwick either didn't remember Tyree or didn't see a reason to explain to Kott's lawyer who the young woman was and why her name might be important. Sedwick granted the prosecutors' request. "The fact that he's a philanderer isn't something that one usually gets into in a criminal felony trial unless for some reason that's relevant," Sedwick said. "I don't see how it's relevant."[4] Later an appeals court, disagreeing with Sedwick, found it very relevant.

When Alaskans weren't talking about Sarah Palin, her cronies among the state House Democrats, and their battle with Big Oil, they were talking about Kott's trial. It was good theater. The FBI played dozens of videos and audio clips in which Kott talked to Bill Allen about his "using and abusing them," with Allen saying, "I own your ass." The scenes from the Animal House at the Baranof Hotel were now public, and constituents knew what went on far away from most of them in Juneau, the isolated and rainy state capital, with no roads connecting it to the rest of Alaska. When Allen took the witness stand, it was the first time Alaskans got a good look at the political kingmaker, and it wasn't pretty. He was hard of hearing and could barely understand the questions. He stuttered and got words confused, the result of his motorcycle crash years earlier. He was a man who had lived the rich history of oil in Alaska, but the world he described wasn't nearly as glamorous as anyone would have expected. He was a doddering grandfather and an uneducated uncle. He didn't seem to have special powers or any special gift of persuasion. And yet Alaskan politicians did his bidding. Alaskans sold their state to this man, in some cases for just a few thousand dollars. It was hard to believe, but the video clips told the story. News stations and websites played scenes from the Animal House through the fall of 2007; low-lit footage of Bill Allen, lawmakers, lobbyists, and a few other guys drinking, swearing, and cussing, with Allen doing all he could—using and abusing them, promising jobs, money, twisting arms—to get tax legislation passed that would please the oil industry.

A jury found Pete Kott guilty by the end of September. He was later sentenced to six years in federal prison. At the sentencing prosecutor Nicholas Marsh commented that "what we saw here . . . was an unusual and extraordinary, outrageous, egregious pattern of self-serving conduct." Kott's conviction was a big win for the public integrity section, but prosecutors had their eyes on a far bigger prize to come later. For Palin, the conviction was more ammunition to use against the oil companies. "Given the implications of this verdict on the passage of last year's [2006 oil tax] legislation, I am more committed than ever to seeking a fair, untainted solution to our petroleum tax system," she said.[5]

After Kott's conviction, Vic Kohring went on trial. He declared he was innocent but admitted he was dumb for hanging around Bill Allen. Once again Alaskans watched the video clips from the Animal House and heard the conversations that seemed to show Kohring offering to help Allen influence the Murkowski oil tax bill. Alaskans watched as Kohring appeared to pledge his allegiance to Allen in exchange for some hundred dollar bills to tuck inside plastic Easter eggs for his daughter. Alaskans listened to the lawmaker's obsequiousness, his eagerness to do VECO's bidding. By this point, Alaskans had pretty much forgotten that the oil tax ended up passing at a higher rate than Allen wanted. Instead of 20 percent, it was approved at 22.5 percent. Depending on the price of oil, that increase was worth potentially billions annually more than the previous tax structure.

In fall 2007 oil was soaring to $90 a barrel. Palin, along with some lawmakers, thought they could raise more tax revenue from the oil companies. Was this fair? How did it fit with Alaska's low-tax ideology? Would the oil companies pull out? Some Alaskans were uneasy, but Palin convinced them that the state deserved it. The oil companies were getting rich off the backs of Alaskans, and Alaska was finally going to get what was owed to it.

Kohring's trial was still going on when legislators met in mid-October for a thirty-day special session to debate Palin's tax proposal, ACES. Just as had happened during the debate over AGIA, the federal corruption investigation shaped the outcome. On November 2, 2007, Kohring was found guilty on corruption charges. The verdict came two weeks before lawmakers were scheduled to adjourn. Any reservations legislators had about increasing oil taxes for a second year in row were all but drowned out by the reactions from constituents who'd watched the tapes while the words "clear and equitable share" hung in the air. Given that and the guessing game going on in Juneau over who would be arrested next for being too chummy with Bill Allen, Palin had plenty of basis to argue that her oil tax legislation would help restore public faith in state government. "The healing that has been needed, I believe, in state government can start with this trust being built," she said.

Palin had initially proposed a tax hike projected to generate about $650 million a year more than the state was generating in tax revenue at $95 a barrel oil. But then Democrats and a few Palin-supported Republicans got hold of her bill and added what amounted to a huge windfall tax. By the time the vote came on the final legislation, ACES was expected to raise taxes on the oil companies by about $2.4 billion annually at $95 a barrel, and as the price of oil rose, so would the state's take.[6] The Senate passed ACES in a 14–5 vote. The state House accepted the final version by a 26–13 margin. The tax increase under Murkowski was now officially the second largest in state history.

In her first year as governor, Sarah Palin had made more headway on oil and gas than Frank Murkowski ever did. In addition to the big new oil tax, she also managed to get lawmakers to sign off on AGIA with its complex framework for gas line construction and a $500 million subsidy to spawn competition. Palin was as efficient a governor as the state had ever seen, at least on oil and gas policy. She fostered a close relationship with Democrats built on a heavy dose of skepticism about the state's lifeblood industry. And they believed they had the upper hand. The companies could threaten to reduce their investment and spend money elsewhere—or even leave the state—but the politicians were confident it was only a bluff. The voters wanted the companies that supported Bill Allen to pay. It was ironic that ACES, with its huge new taxes, likely never would have passed had it not been for Bill Allen and his Republican friends in the Capitol.

State representative Mike Hawker, one of the Republicans who voted against ACES, summed up the mood at the time, telling an Associated Press reporter, "We have a guilt-by-association political environment in this building right now. It's been exploited by factions, as opposed to parties. Folks who voted against this bill did so because they are fundamental believers in a conservative economic philosophy. Those folks felt constrained."[7]

In December, just after her oil tax victory, Sarah Palin struck a pose for *Vogue,* the fashion magazine, intending to sweeten Alaska's image, she said. In that same month, Palin dismissed speculation she might leave Juneau for higher office before her term expired in 2010. "My role as governor is where I can be most helpful right now unless something drastic happens, and I don't anticipate that right now," she told *Anchorage Daily News* reporter Tom Kizzia.[8]

By February 2008, Palin was in Washington, D.C., to attend the National Governors Association conference. There she met Senator John McCain for the first time. She then flew to Los Angeles for a *Newsweek* conference also featuring Governor Janet Napolitano of Arizona. They were part of the magazine's Women and Power issue. Just days after she returned to Alaska, she announced that she was seven months pregnant. It was a shock, since she didn't look pregnant. In April, Palin's water broke in Dallas. She was there for the Republican Governors Association's energy conference. She gave a speech, got on a plane, and flew back to Alaska. It made little sense, but she acted so nonchalantly that in the end most Alaskans shrugged it off as more good luck for their governor. Palin seemed, after all, dipped in good luck.

As summer began, Palin called the legislators back for another special session. This time she wanted them to grant TransCanada Corporation, a Canadian company that builds pipelines, the gas line license and the $500 million subsidy to pursue plans for constructing the 1,700-mile natural gas pipeline from the Alaska Arctic to Alberta, Canada, where other lines would transport the gas to American markets. TransCanada was one of five companies that entered the state competition, and the only one that met the conditions, those must-haves outlined in AGIA.

By the time the legislature started considering TransCanada's plan in June 2008, opposition to AGIA had begun to solidify. First, the oilies had begun to organize. Second, a separate pipeline proposal was supposedly in the works—Denali, a joint venture of BP and Conoco Phillips, the other two big oil players in Alaska. They were going to look at building a pipeline independent of the state or its $500 million. BP and Conoco said they would put $600 million of their own money into gearing up to construct the line. Some questioned whether BP and Conoco were grandstanding to kill the TransCanada proposal, with no intention of developing their natural gas holdings until the state granted favorable terms on gas production taxes. At the Petroleum Club in Anchorage, you could elbow up to the bar and listen to employees from Big Oil joking around about Denali, calling it a $600 million PR blitz to wear down the Palin administration and its AGIA dreams. To those wary of decades of dashed gas line dreams and false promises, Doug Suttles, president of BP's Alaska operation, gave this official line at a press conference, "Watch, just watch."

"We are all watching carefully," Palin responded, "but we won't sit by and wait either."[9]

Only one giant pipeline was needed, and Palin had set the stage so that only the Canadian proposal would be considered. Her strategy was complex and fraught with potential pitfalls, the most obvious being the fact that the success of any project hinged on a pledge from the oil companies to ship gas through the pipeline. TransCanada builds and operates pipelines but doesn't own any Alaska gas. It was unlikely to secure financing to build anything, let alone a multibillion-dollar pipeline, without some commitment from the leaseholders of the gas that they would use the line.

"The wrinkle in the pavement here is who tells who what to do when," Bill Gwozd, vice president of gas services for Ziff Energy Group, told a *Newsweek* reporter as the debate began in Juneau in June 2008. "Oil producers don't appreciate somebody trying to force them to do something." But the forty-four-year-old governor of Alaska didn't really care. She embodied a growing anti-oil sentiment among Alaskans frustrated by the industry, and she enjoyed some of the highest approval ratings of any governor in the country. Palin may have not commanded an army capable of seizing the people's oil fields as Venezuela's Hugo Chávez did, but she talked a tough game. She once scolded Exxon for not showing enough interest in the natural gas pipe dream. "The sentiment shared by a lot of Alaskans," she told reporters at a news conference, "is that Exxon, 'Don't let the door hit you in the stern on the way out if you choose not to participate in progressing development of Alaska's resources.'" Exxon, it is worth noting, had by 2008 invested more than $20 billion in developing Alaska resources.[10]

The Alliance, a group of businesses that support the Alaska oil industry, got creative in trying to derail the governor's AGIA plan. They came up with lyrics sung to the tune of "How Do You Solve a Problem Like Maria?" from *The Sound of Music*. A group of well-dressed industry types sang, in public forum, the following words:

> *How do you solve a problem like AGIA?*
> *How do you tell the truth from all the hype?*
> *To keep our gas on track, you judge the deeds, the facts,*
> *Mere words won't build a pipe from Prudhoe Bay.*
> *The fiscal terms aren't there, our gas will go nowhere,*
> *The project's doomed without them anyway.*
> *How do you solve a problem like AGIA?*[11]

No catchy song, however, was going to be enough to kill AGIA. Especially given there was a little sweetener for Alaskans in another bill that was to be voted on during the special session. With oil hovering at about

$140 a barrel, the state and the oil companies were raking in the cash. Alaska could be looking at a surplus of billions of dollars, depending on how much discipline the legislature showed and how Palin used her red pen. There was so much extra revenue from oil taxes and royalties, in fact, that Palin proposed that each Alaskan, in addition to getting a yearly dividend check, receive another $1,200 to offset the rising costs of heating and fuel. Each Alaskan that year received $3,269 on top of the $600 some received from President Bush's federal tax rebate program. Come fall, most Alaskans—man, woman, and child—had received nearly $4,000 in government handouts.

This didn't sit well with everyone, however. Was Palin trying to buy support, some wondered? Meanwhile, a whisper campaign was developing that her administration was in chaos and she was using her office to carry out personal vendettas against her enemies. And there were rumblings that her husband, Todd—the "First Dude"—sat in on policy meetings and made decisions on judicial appointments.

One of the Palins' enemies was Alaska state trooper Mike Wooten, a former brother-in-law who had gone through a nasty divorce and custody battle with Sarah's sister. The Palins and Sarah's parents, the Heaths, talked about Wooten obsessively. To the Palin clan, he was enemy number one. They wrote to the judge involved in the divorce continually, claiming Wooten had committed crimes both as a trooper and as a family member. He once tasered his son, they said. He shot a moose illegally. He had been spotted drinking beer in his squad car, they said. He had threatened Chuck Heath and the whole Palin family. Chuck and Todd Palin seemed obsessed with Wooten, even going so far as to hire a private detective to watch him. They were the men in the family, trying to protect the women. Todd, part Alaska Native, was raised in the fishing town of Dillingham. When he moved to Wasilla to play basketball during his last year in high school, he was the heartthrob of Wasilla High. Sarah knew she had to have him. "It was her competitive streak coming out," Chuck said. Todd found a family in the Heaths. He became their "dream" son-in-law.

In 2007, the conversations in the Heath household often revolved around Wooten, so much so that Sarah's mother, Sally, took to leaving the room when the trooper's name came up. "I just can't listen to it any-more," she said when a reporter was visiting at her home. Sarah Palin told Todd much the same, asking the First Dude to stop bringing up Wooten.[12] Todd continued his fixation, however, carrying on "hundreds of conversations and communications about Trooper Wooten over the last several years with my family, with friends, with colleagues, and with just about everyone I could—including government officials," as he re-called later in a sworn statement to a legislative investigator.[13]

Within the Palin clan, conspiracy theories abounded about why he wasn't fired or put in jail, or why he was allowed to see his son at all. The judge, the conspiracy went, was a friend of Wooten's troopers and wanted to see the family crumble; Wooten had the other troopers in his pocket; and the union was behind it all. Once Sarah got into office, Todd got to work letting everyone with any power in state government know about Wooten's crimes.

The person who had the most power over this situation was Palin's public safety commissioner, Walt Monegan. He was part Alaska Native and grew up in the village of Nyac. It was a gold mining community with a population of fifty-four people and a one-room schoolhouse. Monegan left to join the U.S. Marine Corps. After completing his mili-tary service, he became an Anchorage patrol officer in 1974 and rose through the ranks to become chief of police from 2001 to 2006. Mone-gan was soft-spoken, articulate, and popular throughout the state. As someone who'd grown up in rural Alaska, he had a particular concern for the domestic violence and sexual abuse problems there. Many thought it rather odd when Sarah unceremoniously fired him in July 2008 without an initial explanation.

The first explanation came a few weeks after the firing in a blog writ-ten by Andrew Halcro, the independent gubernatorial candidate who had challenged Palin two years earlier. Halcro broke the story that Palin fired Monegan because the commissioner wouldn't fire Wooten. Such a claim from any other blogger in the state might not have gotten much at-tention. But Halcro, a former legislator, was respected. His reporting was usually accurate. He had been hounding the administration for months, perhaps at times unfairly, but his sources were reliable, and nobody could question his intelligence. This was the backdrop for what would become a midsummer bomb. It mushroomed into Troopergate, a tawdry family feud that ended up being front-page news all across the country.

After riding so high so long, Sarah Palin now faced her first real problem as governor. Troopergate was hanging over her administration. The Alaska Legislative Council launched an investigation into the matter. The council—made up of senators and representatives, which at the time included eight Republicans and four Democrats—agreed to retain an independent investigator assigned to look into the matter. It was an investigation that Palin at first welcomed. She promised to cooperate and make her staff available for any questions the investigators might have.

Meanwhile, the state's business went on. The rivers swelled with fishermen from places like Iowa and Kentucky. The hostels and trails swarmed with backpacking students from Turkey and France. Climbers donned their crampons, took out their ice axes, and stared hard at the hard mountain, Denali, the highest peak in North America. Softball games lasted until all hours of the night. Bears ate berries on the mountainsides, and moose walked nonchalantly into backyard gardens to put the vegetables out of their growing pains. Toward the end of July, legislators were once again in the state capital, still debating over whether or not to grant a license to build a gas pipeline to a company that had no gas to ship and no clear timeline for construction. And then something happened to push the process along. Another gift for Palin at precisely the right time. These gifts almost began to seem eerie.

Ted Stevens was up for reelection in 2008 and, as in years past, faced no serious challengers in the GOP primary. Still, Alaskans wondered about his ties to Bill Allen and the FBI raid on his house a year earlier. Stevens had refused to talk about the investigation, leaving reporters and bloggers tripping over themselves trying to figure out what would happen next. The answer came swiftly at the end of July. The eighty-four-year-old senator from Alaska was indicted. Although most experts and some media pundits wondered why the government would trouble itself over campaign disclosures, the national media went crazy over a "corrupt" Republican

politician accused of accepting gifts from an oil tycoon. That it was a ranking member of the U.S. Senate, a Republican, only made the story better.
Palin again saw an opportunity and pounced. "News such as this rocks the
foundation of our state . . . It is my hope our legislators do not let this dis-
tressing news distract them from their critical work in the current special
session," she said. "The state Senate is poised to make history this week, as
it considers approving a license for TransCanada to move forward with an
Alaska gas pipeline. This long delayed project is finally on the verge of pro-
ceeding. It is critical not only to our state's economic future, but could also
help alleviate the energy crisis that is currently devastating our nation."[14]

Three days later, on July 31, 2008, Ted Stevens—flanked by two
lawyers, his wife, and his daughter—appeared in front of a federal judge
in Washington, D.C., where the charges had been filed. The feds claimed
he accepted gifts from VECO, most of them related to his cabin's remodel, and failed to report them on his Senate finance disclosure forms.
All told, Stevens had paid $160,000 for the remodel. But the FBI said he
got $250,000 worth of work and other unreported gifts. Prosecutors of-
fered Stevens a deal: plead guilty to one felony count, and they'd waive
any jail time. Stevens turned the plea down.[15] He was up for reelection.
The state primary was on August 26, which he'd easily win, and there
were only ninety-eight days before the November general election. He
was facing Anchorage mayor Mark Begich in the general, a young and
popular Democratic politician. Stevens's lawyers asked for a speedy trial.

The Alaska House voted 23–16 and the Senate 14–5 to give the AGIA license and $500 million to TransCanada. At a press conference, celebrat-
ing the victory, Sarah Palin was careful to say that this was only a "first
step" and that there was a "heck of a lot of more work to do." In fact, she
said, that there was "harder work from henceforth to make sure it happens." Palin signed the legislation and then flew to Arizona later that day.

Two days later, in the early hours of August 29, the networks began announcing that Republican presidential contender John McCain had chosen
as his running mate an attractive governor hailing from the Last Frontier.

CHAPTER 15

Crude Awakening

Sarah Palin arrived in the governor's office ready to fight corruption and advocate for transparent government, and she had a great relationship with the media. In the fall of 2008, it took the arrival of the Outside press corps in Alaska to discover that Palin had some flaws. For one, her administration was full of high school friends making significantly more money than they could have earned in the private sector. Alaskans didn't find out that Palin had attended five colleges until after she was tapped by John McCain. They learned from Outside sources about her upbringing in the Assembly of God, where churchgoers sometimes speak in tongues and pray with exorcists from Africa. They found out that she was charging the state to live at home in Wasilla and commute to her office in Anchorage, as well as to take her daughters along on state business, sometimes staying in expensive hotels on the state's dime.

Pro-family groups were surprised to hear that Palin was supposed to be a conservative cultural warrior. As governor, she didn't talk much about abortion and she vetoed a bill that would have barred the state from providing benefits to same-sex couples. Alaska reporters who had previously called her by her first name and were generally glowing in their coverage of her administration were surprised to find that they were part of the "lamestream media" responsible for many of the ills that befell the country. Those who hadn't felt the sting of her jabs before were surprised at how harsh they could be. Her commissioners and many of the legislators who supported her found out how eager she was to take credit for everything that had happened in the state while she was governor. The

Corrupt Bastards Club was surprised to learn that it was she, and not the Justice Department, who brought them down.

Old-fashioned Republicans wondered how she could frame herself as a low-tax, small-government fiscal conservative while championing billions of dollars in new taxes on the state's largest industry, signing two of the biggest state budgets in history, and growing government by leaps. And if all of that weren't enough to make them wonder if she was a RINO—Republican in name only—there was the fact she had done more than any governor since Jay Hammond to transfer wealth from business, which earned it, to her fellow Alaskans, who collected it for nothing other than living in an oil-rich state. Democrats, with whom she had so famously gotten along, were surprised to learn how much she despised Democrats. Everyone was surprised to learn that she was such a big fan of President Ronald Reagan, and that she was so beautiful.

Alaskans had known Palin was attractive, but the woman who appeared on their TV sets during the 2008 presidential election campaign was stunning. She had all of the natural parts to her before she joined John McCain on the campaign trail, but never in such relief. It was almost as if Republican operatives had snatched Palin, put her in a room, and made a virtual version of her (one who would come back to haunt). Had she been like this all along, Alaskans wondered. Had she just taken advantage of a mood in the state in order to become governor and, from there, seek national attention? Did she merely use Alaska's establishment Republicans and good old boys as scapegoats, riffing off their demise to catapult herself into a whole new realm? Was she who she said she was?

One thing Alaskans learned for certain was just how willing Sarah Palin was to give up their state in favor of her larger aspirations. For nearly three months in the fall of 2008, it seemed nobody was running the state. Alaska reporters with questions on issues facing the state had them answered by the McCain-Palin campaign, if they were answered at all. Palin's commissioners couldn't get in touch with her. The McCain campaign dispatched "advisers" to the Last Frontier to help the Alaska Department of Law handle the Troopergate affair and other ethics complaints, and they seemed to have taken over the state attorney general's office.

(At one point, when tensions were particularly high, the real Alaska attorney general decided to take a vacation in Kansas.) There was a showdown between the Alaska Legislative Council and the Palin administration—and thus the McCain campaign—over the investigation into Troopergate and the roles that Palin, her husband, and her administration played in pursuing Alaska state trooper Mike Wooten and pressuring his boss, public safety commissioner Walt Monegan, to fire him. The Legislative Council, a bipartisan committee of state lawmakers, had appointed a special investigator to look into the matter.

The relatively benign investigation, however, turned into a hot-button issue in the presidential race. Palin, who had told Alaskans to "hold me accountable," dismissed all attempts to do so by claiming the probe had become political now that she was a vice presidential candidate. Her lawyer and McCain operatives said the Legislative Council's investigation couldn't be trusted. In a tricky legal move, Palin decided the only way to take the investigation out of the lawmakers' committee, which was now being called a partisan "circus" even though the committee consisted of eight Republicans and four Democrats, was to file an ethics complaint against herself. By so doing, she placed the matter before the state's three-member Personnel Board. The board's members serve at the pleasure of the governor, and board rules mandate investigations remain confidential until completed. The Legislative Council, however, refused to stop its investigation. This meant there were two inquiries into Troopergate under way, which helped set up a colossal fight between the McCain-Palin campaign and the state of Alaska. All of this over a public safety commissioner who lost his job and a former brother-in-law who shot an illegal moose and allegedly told Palin's father, in the heat of an acrimonious divorce, that he was going to "eat a f'ing lead bullet."

As the McCain-Palin campaign peaked, a few people from the Alaska office, with the help of Palin's former press secretary, held press briefings in an office surrounded by old strip malls on Northern Lights Boulevard in Anchorage. Dressed in suits and ties, they put on serious faces and pronounced themselves the "Palin truth squad." They tried to convince the press that Walt Monegan had been a rogue commissioner, a bad one who wasn't doing his job. They also assembled elaborate charts and graphs that attempted to show how partisan politics were playing out in the Legislative Council's Troopergate investigation. One flow chart came to be dubbed the "The French Connection" because it had the name and photograph of Alaska state congressman Hollis French at the top. A former state prosecutor and a Democrat, French was overseeing the legislative investigation. Ironically, French had been a huge champion of Palin's battles with Big Oil, but now he was just another liberal threatening the governor in his relentless pursuit to get to the bottom of Troopergate. Beneath French, the chart showed other liberals who were part of the bipartisan Legislative Council, with arrows pointing to the center of the chart at a picture of Democrat presidential candidate Barack Obama. Somehow an investigation that had started in July with Palin's blessing had by September turned into an Obama campaign setup.

Democrat supporters of the Palin investigation accused the McCain campaign of playing "Karl Rove-style politics" in Alaska. The few traditional political supporters Palin had left in Alaska accused the Obama campaign of spreading lies about their governor. Alaska's political baggage got aired across the country. Every Alaskan had an opinion, and this time it wasn't about oil taxes or politicians taking bribes from Bill Allen. This was presidential politics unfolding in a far, dark corner of America. Dueling protests took place in front of Alaska government buildings. Bloggers blogged ferociously. Invectives were traded, threats of violence shared. At one point, more than a thousand people gathered in a downtown Anchorage park to call for, among other things, the attorney general's resignation. He had sided with Palin's attempt to torpedo the Legislative Council's investigation by having the Personnel Board take it over. Signs at the rally read, "Thou Shalt Not Lie"; "I can see corruption from my house," a mockery of Palin's recent statement to a national reporter that "you can actually see Russia" from Alaska; and "Dude, where's my governor?" The latter referenced Troopergate revelations that showed Todd Palin, the "First Dude," appeared to have spent a goodly amount of time manipulating the levers of power for his wife the governor.

Former Republican governor Wally Hickel, an old-school Republican and onetime member of the Alaska Independence Party, felt compelled to speak out. Hickel had been disappointed when Palin turned her back on his idea for a state-owned natural gas pipeline in favor of AGIA. Yet after Palin joined McCain, Hickel cooled down and initially supported her campaign for vice president. Later he would come to regret that. "My hopes were dashed," he wrote in a 2009 editorial. "Palin became the spokesperson for the divisive voices in American politics."[1] First it was the Alaska Democrats who felt the sting of Palin's words. Then it was the state's pro-choice, pro-industry Republicans. Finally the venom she spewed on the national campaign trail—which her spokeswoman amplified in bizarre ways in Alaska—was enough to make Hickel independents feel that they too were under attack. That was bad. A new narrative began to emerge, one that painted Sarah Palin as an opportunist using Alaska for her own gain. Her poll numbers back home began to show it. Once she held an approval rating of over 80 percent in Alaska. In late September 2008, her numbers had dropped into the 60s and were falling by the day.[2] By the end of 2010 Sarah Palin was viewed favorably by only 33 percent of state residents, according to a Public Policy Polling survey which found that 58 percent of state residents opposed her. And her polling numbers have continued to decline.[3]

Sarah Palin's vice presidential run, Troopergate, and the onslaught of international attention on Alaska in fall 2008 overshadowed a historic event that might have held momentous import under other circumstances. A man who helped achieve statehood in 1959, served in the Alaska legislature, and then represented the young state in the U.S. Senate for forty years went on trial in Washington, D.C., on charges of corruption. For Ted Stevens it was a personal nightmare. Even his detractors agreed that he had done so much good for his adopted home.

When Stevens entered the Senate in 1968, Alaska was a backwater. The state's two largest cities, Anchorage and Fairbanks, didn't get a direct road link—the George Parks Highway—until 1971. Most rural villages lacked water, sewer, telephones, TV, often even electricity or an airport. Stevens helped modernize the state, bringing electricity, health care, and even subsidized air service to rural inhabitants. Many Alaskans revered him.

He was almost eighty-five years old when he went on trial, and he had no shortage of critics Outside. He'd been relentless in his pursuit of federal funding—pork-barrel dollars as his detractors called it—for his home state. Gruff, at times rude, Stevens was sardonically called "Uncle Ted" after federal spending to his home state doubled during his stint as Senate Appropriations Committee chairman. His chairmanship had ended a few years earlier, but Stevens found plenty of other ways to keep the money flowing north, much to the dismay of some of his colleagues. Senator John McCain had railed against Stevens through the years, especially over Alaska's Bridge to Nowhere. His running mate, Sarah Palin, had been for the bridge during her governor's run, and then was against it.

As he was facing trial, Ted Stevens was up for reelection against Democrat Mark Begich, the young mayor of Anchorage and son of Nick Begich, an Alaska congressman who was killed in a plane crash thirty-six years earlier. Whether Stevens could win another six-year term depended largely on what would happen in a federal courthouse in Washington, D.C. Stevens had wanted a jury of his peers—Alaskans—but the feds had successfully argued the alleged crime—failing to report "gifts" of more than $250,000 on his Senate disclose statements—had occurred in D.C. Stevens's trial unfolded as Sarah Palin bounced around the country campaigning for the McCain-Palin ticket in the fall of 2008.

Bill Allen, meanwhile, continued cooperating with the feds and remained free—so free that after selling VECO a year earlier, he and his children purchased a twin-engine jet. Allen, then seventy-two, was allowed to fly around the country in it. Life as a convicted felon wasn't so bad for Allen. He and other VECO owners and executives had pocketed $146 million on the sale of the company. Allen's son, Mark Allen, owned a horse that would go on to win the Kentucky Derby. And if all went well, Bill Allen's cooperation with the Polar Pen investigation would greatly limit the amount of time he would eventually spend in prison.

Allen's greatest challenge was keeping a lid on his past. The alleged relationships with teenage girls posed a threat to his credibility as a government witness. By the time Ted Stevens went on trial, Alaska media had already discovered his connection to Bambi Tyree. And then there was the proverbial other woman, Paula Roberds, who had come forward to claim she'd been Allen's prostitute starting when she was a teenager.

In the weeks before Stevens's trial, Roberds, a hotel housekeeper, now twenty-four, sat down with an *Alaska Dispatch* reporter and detailed her relationship with Allen. Roberds said she was fifteen when she first took to the streets, and based on photographs she provided of herself at the time, she looked it. One night in 1999 on a street corner in midtown Anchorage, she said, a white Land Rover pulled up alongside her. "I remember he rolled his window down and asked me if I wanted a ride. I jumped in," Roberds recalled. "He asked me if I was a cop. I said 'no.'" Thus began what she claimed was a two and a half year sexual relationship with Bill Allen, who at the time was in his early sixties. Soon after they met in 1999, Roberds alleged Allen became her main client, spending "more money on me than anyone else." And, she said, he was never mean to her. He was, she said, the best trick she ever had. The sex happened at Allen's home, at a storage lot where he kept a camper, and in hotels, she said. Over time, she learned that Allen was a wealthy and powerful man. In mid-2000, Roberds moved to the Seattle area with a boyfriend, but she continued to see Allen. He paid for her to fly to Anchorage and put her up at the Hilton Hotel. "Every trip I came up here [Anchorage] on, I charged him $2,000," she said, "and on top of that, he would give me spending money." Sometimes other girls joined Roberds and Allen for sex, she said, but mostly it was just the two of them. Roberds began to believe Allen considered her something of a girlfriend. She reckoned the businessman had paid her more than $20,000. In 2001, however, the couple abruptly stopped seeing each other. "One of the times he picked me up from the Hilton . . . and he asked me, 'Is this all about the money, or do we have a relationship going on?'" Roberds said. "After I told him, 'It's all about the money,' he got pretty upset and that's how things went sour." Bill Allen, a successful, competitive, and fearless businessman in America's oil province, was apparently dumbstruck that Roberds rejected his feelings for her.[4]

Unlike Bambi Tyree, whom Allen had allegedly paid to stay quiet, Paula Roberds never got any hush money. When she saw Allen's photograph in

a newspaper identifying him as the linchpin for the Alaska corruption
cases, she decided she wanted to pursue charges and possibly a civil suit;
she wanted to make money. Roberds sounded believable, despite her mo-
tivations, and told her story to Anchorage police as well as reporters. By
the time the Stevens trial opened, the senator's lawyers knew about
Roberds. FBI special agent Mary Beth Kepner, who was heading up the
Polar Pen investigation, dismissed her as irrelevant. When asked about
the woman's allegations, she described Roberds as someone involved in
past run-ins with the law.[5] But a local police detective interviewed
Roberds and opened a file. Allen was again under investigation for sexually abusing a minor. Kepner kept Allen updated on any impending articles about the sex allegations that she heard about through her source
relationship with at least one reporter. And when news stories did appear
implicating the oilman, "Allen would become unglued," she later said.[6]
No doubt if Kepner told Allen about what Roberds was saying to reporters, he probably became unglued, as did the team of federal prosecutors taking on Ted Stevens.

Roberds was just one more unexpected brushfire prosecutors had to
put out. They hadn't planned to prepare a case against Ted Stevens on
such short notice. They still had thousands of pages of documents and
hundreds of hours of surveillance tapes to go through, and a new player
to integrate into the team. Brenda Morris had been brought in as the
lead prosecutor to supplant the young Nick Marsh, who had helped
manage much of the case in Alaska. Although new to the case, Morris did
have a few things going for her: She knew how to get under a defendant's
skin, and she was an African American trying a fat cat Republican senator in Washington, D.C.

Even before the Stevens trial began, the Alaska corruption investigation
had changed the political landscape of the nation by helping propel Sarah
Palin into the governor's office and helping her win victories against Big
Oil. Those victories, in turn, raised her profile and landed her next to
John McCain. The story was different for Stevens. Before he was charged,
he was well on his way to winning reelection yet again. Some Alaskans
might have believed the state was on the way to having a natural gas

pipeline constructed thanks to Palin's AGIA plan, but Stevens was more dependable for the economy than any pipe dream. Many voters understood the importance of the federal dollars flowing north, and they wanted the pork Stevens brought home to keep coming. The best way to ensure that was to keep Stevens in the Senate.

The list of character witnesses for the defense included some of the most powerful figures in the nation's capital: Senator Orrin Hatch, the Utah Republican, and Senator Daniel Inouye, Stevens's longtime Democrat friend from Hawaii; former secretary of state Colin Powell; and a whole cast of Alaska characters, including a sled dog trainer and the president of an Alaska Native corporation. Bambi Tyree's name was also on the list. The local cop who was investigating Allen on sex crimes was on the list too. One of Tyree's ex-boyfriends who supposedly knew about her connection to Allen was also there. Stevens was represented by the firm of Williams & Connolly, led by Brendan Sullivan—one of the country's premier white-collar defense layers. His past clients included Oliver North during the Iran-Contra scandal and the lacrosse players from Duke University during a high-profile rape case, which ultimately was dismissed because of an overzealous local prosecutor and the victim's questionable story.

In mid-September 2008, one of the first witnesses in Stevens's trial was supposed to be former VECO employee Rocky Williams, who helped manage the remodeling of the senator's house. The prosecution flew him from Alaska to Washington to prepare him for trial. The defense also planned to call him as a witness. But that would never happen; prosecutors would make sure of it. Had Williams taken the stand, the jury might have learned some things that boosted the senator's case. Earlier in 2008, when a reporter interviewed Williams, the ex-VECO worker said the more than $130,000 that Stevens had told media at the time that he'd paid for the remodeling of his house should have covered all of the costs. If the costs were inflated, Williams said, it was "because VECO was holding it up." "Uncle Bill had to get involved," Williams said, and he added stuff to the project that Ted and Catherine Stevens didn't ask for or even know about. Williams recounted a conversation he had with Stevens in which Uncle Ted and others insisted that everything should be done above board. It was part of a larger conversation during which everyone involved in the project was present, including Stevens, Allen, and Allen's nephew, Dave Anderson. Williams told the guys, "Look, Bill is already a lobbyist. He's already under scrutiny. So it's (the house renovation) got to be straight. It's got to be clean." Everyone agreed. Williams recalled that he wanted to tell what he knew to a federal grand jury, but he didn't believe prosecutors wanted these details to come out. He concluded they were just hearing what they wanted to hear and goading him on to say things that weren't really true. Or not the whole truth anyway.[7]

When prosecutors met with Williams just days before the trial, they were disappointed again. "After a final preparatory session, which included a mock cross-examination, prosecutors decided Williams was not a witness the prosecution wanted to use," Chad Joy, an FBI agent involved in Polar Pen, later told U.S. District Court Judge Emmet Sullivan, who presided over the Stevens trial. Joy was FBI agent Mary Beth Kepner's partner on Polar Pen. During the Stevens trial, he grew frustrated by what he alleged as ethical missteps by the FBI and federal prosecutors. After the trial, Joy would send Judge Sullivan a formal complaint against Kepner and several prosecutors involved in Polar Pen. The allegations ran the gamut, everything from Kepner being too cozy with Allen—wearing a skirt for him when he testified against Stevens, visiting him in his D.C. hotel room alone. Joy claimed that she often dined with another cooperating witness, accepted gifts from him, and told him sensitive details about the case. He also alleged that one of their sources got Kepner's husband a job, and that she was too open with the media. But most damning for the case was Joy's claim that prosecutors withheld information favorable to the defense, redacted information they shouldn't have, and sent Rocky Williams back to Alaska as a ploy to keep him from the defense. The prosecutors told Stevens's attorneys that Williams was sick.[8] Williams was indeed suffering from liver failure, but the real problem was that the prosecution team didn't like what he was telling them. So, according to Joy's complaint, they "came up with a great plan." Claiming to be concerned about his health, they shipped him back to Alaska without telling the defense they were doing so. Once Williams was gone, he was too sick to fly back to Washington, D.C. Joy claimed he advised the prosecutors multiple times that they should tell the defense team and judge the truth, but they ignored him. Williams died a couple months after the trial ended.[9]

The Stevens trial started in the fourth week of September, around the same time Sarah Palin's now infamous Katie Couric interviews were airing. As images of Palin flooded the airwaves—as she talked confusingly about Putin rearing his head and stumbled over questions about the financial crisis, John McCain's record as a maverick, and the books and magazines she had or had not read—Stevens, a highly educated and successful U.S. senator, sat with a scowl on his face, listening to what oil and construction workers did or didn't do to his cabin. Brenda Morris, the lead prosecutor, strutted around the courtroom. She embraced the jury with her eyes as she laid out Stevens's alleged crimes.

He'd accepted more than $250,000 in illegal gifts, she said; most of them from Bill Allen. They included not only the renovation of Uncle Ted's chalet but also a $6,000 generator, some furniture, a massage chair worth almost $2,700, a permanently attached professional gas grill, a multidrawer tool cabinet complete with tools, a sweetheart deal for a new Land Rover for Stevens's daughter, and a sled dog. Morris told the jury Stevens used VECO as his personal handyman. "If the defendant needed an electrician, he contacted VECO. If the defendant needed a plumber, he contacted VECO," she said. "We reach for the Yellow Pages, he reached for VECO."[10] All of these services, she added, should have been reported on Stevens's disclosure forms, but he somehow overlooked that obligation as a senator. Uncle Ted was corrupt, she told the jury.

Stevens, Morris pointed out to the jury, was a career politician. "You do not survive politics in this town for that long without being very, very smart; very, very deliberate; very forceful and, at the same time, knowing how to fly under the radar," she said, with a knowing look.[11]

Brendan Sullivan, Stevens's attorney, countered that Uncle Ted was known as the Senate workhorse, and he didn't have time to mess with all the details related to his remodel; his wife, Catherine, took care of them. And no matter what, Sullivan told the jury, Stevens paid every bill that was sent to him and asked for others. Sullivan blamed Bill Allen for allowing costs to escalate without telling Stevens what the expenses would be or even showing him all the bills. Sullivan blamed Allen for foisting furniture on the elderly Stevens, for basically taking over his house. "He didn't want these things. He didn't ask for these things. He never once hid anything," Sullivan said.

Eventually Bill Allen took the stand to testify against his onetime best friend. Allen looked like a kindly grandfather. His personal story came off as that irresistible combination of the great American success married to the fatal America tragedy. He talked about his childhood as a migrant fruit picker. He explained how he dropped out of school to help the family. He talked about how he fell in love with the oil business after he got his first job with El Paso Gas when he was fifteen. He described coming to Alaska as a young welder and rising to own one of the largest and most lucrative companies in the state. He explained a 2001 motorcycle accident and how that still affected his speech. He said his words didn't always come out right, and he couldn't hear real well, hence the earphones that he wore. He spoke glowingly of Stevens and their relationship. He loved Stevens, he said, and loved Alaska. He only wanted to help build the state. He was an earnest, salt of the earth kind of person. If he wanted to ingratiate himself to one of the most important men in the country by bestowing gifts on him, who could blame him? But as a senator, wasn't it Stevens's ethical duty to refuse such gifts?

Emails offered as evidence by prosecutors showed that Uncle Ted knew that he wasn't getting billed for all of the work on cabin. However, he continually asked Allen for the bills. Allen ignored him, he told the jury, because "I really didn't want to" send him the bills. Why? "Because I wanted to help Ted."

Why, he was asked.

"'Cause I like him," Allen said softly and a little regretfully.

Gone was the foul-mouthed kingpin of Alaska politics Allen had once been. In his stead was a generous old man with a speech impediment who just wanted to help a friend. When a note was read to the jury, a note that Stevens wrote to Allen about making sure that Allen billed him for everything, Allen's explanation as to why it meant nothing seemed completely plausible. The note said: "Dear Bill. Thanks for all the work on the chalet. You owe me a bill—remember Torricelli, my friend. Friendship is one thing—compliance with these ethics rules entirely different. I asked Bob (Persons) to talk to you about this so don't get P.O.'d at him—it just has to be done right." Robert Torricelli was a New Jersey senator who had gotten in trouble and dropped out of his reelection race when it became public that he didn't report campaign contributions. Bob Persons was the friend of the two who was helping watch over the remodel. Allen testified on the stand that Persons explained at the time that the senator was just covering "his ass." When Allen looked at the jury, a little ashamed, and said, "Maybe I shouldn't have said 'ass.'" Jurors chuckled along approvingly.[12]

Sullivan vigorously questioned Allen about his statement. Sullivan wanted to know exactly when Persons said it, and exactly when Allen recounted the conversation to the feds. Allen at times acted confused, as if he couldn't understand the questions, and in the end just said that Persons had said it. "'Hell, don't worry about those invoices. Ted's just covering his ass.' That's exactly what he said," Allen testified. The words came in soft vowels and soft tones. This was the accent picked up in New Mexico and the state's gas fields. These were the words of a kindly, blue-collar grandfather made good from the sweat of his brow, the kind of man who spoiled his grandchildren while dreaming of sending them to college to make sure that their hands never had to be calloused like his. He was a kindly old man who didn't like to offend the ladies with profanity. After that, any defense that Stevens offered that he had wanted to pay the bills if Allen had just sent them was countered by the words that hung in the courtroom: "Ted's just covering his ass."

According to Chad Joy, the whistleblower FBI agent, his partner Mary Beth Kepner wore a skirt on that day as a "present/surprise" for Allen. Kepner did not normally wear skirts, Joy said after the trial in his whistleblower complaint to the judge.

Ted Stevens's lawyers decided not to introduce the sex allegations against Allen or question him or FBI agents on whether those charges had played a role in his decision to cooperate with the feds. Exactly why may never be known. The lawyers declined to comment on their trial strategy, but it is possible they decided Allen's alleged proclivity for young girls would have wounded Stevens as much as Allen. It was possible that the idea of Stevens being friends for years with an oilman who had allegedly carried on sexually with underage girls—including one who claimed Allen bought her silence—could taint the senator himself in the eyes of the jury. Besides, the prosecutors appeared to be in trouble with their case, and the groundwork was already being laid for an appeal should the jury find Stevens guilty.

Judge Emmet Sullivan was losing patience with the prosecution. First, he found out about the prosecutor's sending Rocky Williams back to Alaska. Then it turned out that some time sheets supposedly indicating how much time Allen's nephew, Dave Anderson—the self-declared foreman on the remodeling project—worked on Stevens's house were inflated. Anderson had been in Portland, Oregon, working on another project and tacked that time onto Stevens's bill.

"It's very troubling that the government would utilize records the government knows were false," Judge Sullivan said. "And there's just no excuse for that whatsoever," he admonished prosecutor Nicholas Marsh. "All along the government knew that was a lie. Why did you do it? I want an answer."

"We didn't see the case that way," Marsh said. He claimed the billing information wouldn't have made much difference. "We looked at this in a different light."[13]

Judge Sullivan threatened the prosecution he would reveal to the jury that they deliberately withheld information from the defense. In the end, however, he just told the jury to ignore the time sheets. Likewise, he told them to ignore anything related to a car on which Allen supposedly helped Stevens get a sweetheart deal. Further, under Sullivan's orders, the prosecution was forced to release more records. Within those records was one nugget for the defense: an old interview in which Allen told an FBI agent that if Stevens had been billed for the work, he would have paid the invoices. Judge Sullivan was again infuriated. Stevens's lawyers called for a mistrial. The judge again admonished the prosecution but allowed the trial to continue.

During the trial, it was also revealed that the FBI had recorded conversations between Bill Allen and Ted Stevens in 2006, while Allen was secretly cooperating with the feds. In a conversation from October 18, 2006, Stevens and Allen spoke about the potential investigations; at that point, Stevens knew already the FBI had served search warrants and was honing in on VECO. He told Allen that the oilman needed to "get a mental attitude that these guys can't really hurt us. You know, they're not going shoot us. It's not Iraq. What the hell? The worst that can be done, the worst that can happen to us is we round up a bunch of legal fees and, and might lose and we might have to pay a fine, might have to serve a little time in jail. I hope to Christ it never gets to that, but I don't think it will. I'm developing the attitude that I don't think I did anything wrong, so I'm going to go right through my life and keep doing what I think is right."[14]

In the same conversation, Allen and Stevens talked about their friendship. Stevens again told Allen to remain strong and that they should keep a distance now that the feds had turned up the heat.

At one point, Allen said, "I'm sorry this whole thing is happening, though, to you." And then he said, "Hey Ted, uh, I love you, you know."

"Bill, I consider you to be one of my best friends," Stevens said back. Then he talked about how they were both on the same cover of a magazine in the 1980s. "We've been together that long, you know. We've been working together for years for this state. These bastards are not going to stop us working for this state and doing what we think is right," he said.[15]

Back in Anchorage that October, a continent away from D.C., one Troopergate investigation was complete and the Alaska Legislative Council was meeting to discuss the findings before releasing them to the public. News of this event drew a throng of reporters from around the world to the hallways of the Alaska legislature's offices in Anchorage. Brits mingled with the Japanese rubbing shoulders with bloggers from Alaska in the same building where the FBI served search warrants in 2006 to kick off the Polar Pen probe that had put Stevens on trial. It was the same building across from the Pioneer Bar, where the history of the town was chronicled in pictures on the walls: Earthquake-shattered town, boom town, bust town, and now a town deeply divided by presidential politics. Sarah Palin supporters stood outside, wielding signs that read, "I love you Sarah" and "My Pal Palin." Inside, the Alaska Legislative Council was greeted by reporters yelling questions. But perhaps most disconcerting was the group of demonstrators wearing clown noses and carrying balloons in the shape of kangaroos. They yelled, "Welcome to the circus!" as the council shuffled into a conference room and closed the doors.

Indeed, Alaska had become a circus, a place full of funhouse mirrors. Palin had been in the public eye for less than two months, but already everything was distorted and misshapen. The national economy was sliding into an unprecedented financial crisis, but John McCain's relationship with the Keating Five had become a footnote. The talk was dying down about Obama's relationship with indicted Chicago slumlord Tony Rezko. In Washington, Uncle Ted was battling potential prison time for corruption. And what news were Alaskans and other Americans awaiting with bated breath? News on whether state legislators believed Sarah or Todd, or both of them, pressured a public safety commissioner to fire a trooper who tasered his son to allegedly show the kid what it felt like, illegally shot a moose because his wife couldn't bring herself to do it, and allegedly threatened his father-in-law, Sarah's dad, with an "f'ing" bullet. Morning became afternoon that day at the legislative building. Some reporters sneaked out to grab a beer at the Pioneer. Others stayed on station and drank diet Dr. Pepper, just about the only selection in the vending machine. A few napped in the hallway. The legislators finally emerged into public view at about 4:00 PM. "Governor Palin knowingly permitted a situation to continue where impermissible pressure was placed on several subordinates in order to advance a personal agenda, to wit: to get Trooper Michael Wooten fired," they announced. The governor, they said, let her husband use the governor's office and its resources, "including access to state employees, to continue to contact subordinate state employees in an effort to find some way to get Trooper Wooten fired. . . . She had the authority and power to require Mr. Palin to cease contacting subordinates, but she failed to act."[16] The Palin camp reacted loudly and angrily, a response that was to become her trademark. Palin's lawyer, Thomas Van Flein, said the "partisan nature of this investigation in-

eluctably compelled [the special investigator] and Sen. French to never-
theless smear the Governor by innuendo, and by presenting incorrect
representations of what the law is."[17]

Palin spoke the next day. Three local reporters were allowed to ask her
one question each during a conference call. Palin was traveling to
Philadelphia to drop the ceremonial first puck at the Flyers' hockey
opener. It was one of the few times she had spoken to the Alaska media
since being tapped as the GOP vice presidential candidate.

The conference lasted about five minutes. She opened it up by saying,
"Well, I'm very, very pleased to be cleared of any legal wrongdoing . . .
any hint of any kind of unethical activity there." In response, *Anchorage
Daily News* reporter Lisa Demer said, "Governor, finding number one
on the report was that you abused your power by violating state law. Do
you think you did anything wrong at all in this Troopergate case?"

"Not at all, and I'll tell you, I think that you're always going to ruffle
feathers as you do what you believe is in the best interest of the people
whom you are serving," Palin said. "In this case I knew that I had to have
the right people in the right position at the right time in this cabinet to
best serve Alaskans, and Walt Monegan was not the right person at the
right time to meet the goals that we had set out in our administration. So
no, not having done anything wrong, and again very much appreciating
being cleared of any legal wrongdoing or unethical activity at all."[18]

"Have you read the whole report?" Demer asked. Palin didn't respond.

Reporters were confused. Palin had always been good at putting a positive spin on things, but this was something new and different. Palin was
claiming the report that had implicated her in misdeeds had instead
cleared her.

Obama was ahead in the polls, and some in the McCain camp were
looking to spread the blame for their candidate's falling numbers. Palin
had not helped her cause by criticizing McCain's choice to pull out of
Michigan or fumbling her interviews. Some in the Republican Party elite
were beginning to call her a cancer. Chris Buckley, the son of the late
William Buckley Jr., the conservative idol and founder of the *National
Review,* said, "The thought of Sarah Palin as president gives me acid re-
flux." His father, he added, "would have been appalled."[19]

Palin's seeming disconnect on the Troopergate decision raised questions about whether there was something really wrong with her. Her
campaign adviser suggested that she get off the Atkins diet. Others whispered thoughts about postpartum syndrome, or the long Alaska winters. Perhaps, they wondered, this is what so many hours of darkness do
to one's brain.

But the intellectual elite couldn't stop Palin from drawing big crowds
as she dashed around the country lambasting the first black man to run
in the general election for president as a guy who "palled around with
terrorists." Everywhere she went, in small towns in upstate New York,
Pennsylvania, South Carolina, New Hampshire, Maine, people turned
out in droves. Everywhere she went, she found a variant of Wasilla, or
some sort of redux of Alaska Republican Party picnic people—folks who
wore camouflage pants and plaid hunting jackets with National Rifle Association hats on their heads. They carried signs that read, "Christians
for Palin," and "Pro-life for Palin" and "Obama Bin Lyin'." She told one
crowd in Maine, "I feel like I'm at home. I see the Carhartts and the steel-
toed boots . . . and the NRA hats." The crowd roared and chanted her
name: "Sarah! Sarah! Sarah!"[20]

CHAPTER 16

Breakup

As Sarah Palin was making a name for herself in the Lower 48, cracks in her leadership were starting to show in the Alaska hinterland. The governor's rural affairs adviser resigned in mid-October 2008, about the time the last barges of the year traveled up the Yukon and Kuskokwim rivers to deliver fuel to help rural Alaskans survive the winter. If Anchorage is a world away from D.C., rural Alaska is a world away from Anchorage, and a galaxy away from the rest of country. This is a place past the end of the road, far past it. The villages of rural Alaska are off the grid. Ted Stevens's money helped many but didn't reach all of them. Some don't have running water, and the so-called honey bucket serves as a toilet. There are no doc-in-the-box clinics if you get sick or injured. No cinemas, no shopping malls, no waterslides or parks or much of anything. Life is hard and many people are underemployed and rely on subsistence— hunting and fishing—to feed their families.

Freeze-up, the icing over of the rivers, came early to western Alaska in the fall of 2008, and barges couldn't get through to some villages. With fuel prices skyrocketing, a few villages couldn't afford the fuel that the barges brought, and the boats turned away. Fuel prices in America were high, but they hit the stratosphere in rural Alaska. Home heating fuel was nearly $10 a gallon in some places. This, coupled with a bad fishing season, had some Alaska Natives worried they might not survive the winter. How would they keep warm? How could they afford to fuel their snowmachines to hunt for food? Milk in Bethel, a major rural hub in western Alaska, was nearly $10 a gallon, a can of soup about $3. Rural residents called for the state to declare a fuel emergency, but there was no one in state government to help them. Governor Palin was off running for vice president and had time to answer only three questions from Alaska reporters. For many other things, she had no time.

The Alaska Native community, normally not quick to criticize the state's leaders, began to turn on Palin while she was still on the campaign trail. Myron Naneng, president of the Bethel-based Association of Village Council Presidents, asked one reporter, "From her house, is she able to see the Native community and the issues we have to deal with?"[1] The president of the Alaska Federation of Natives took umbrage at Palin's dismissal of Walt Monegan and the subsequent defamation of his character by the McCain-Palin campaign and their supporters: "I cannot allow a fellow Alaska Native to have his reputation tarnished and used as a political football," Julie Kitka wrote in an editorial.[2]

Back in Washington, D.C., former secretary of state Colin Powell took the witness stand to say good things about Ted Stevens during his trial. "He was someone whose word you could rely on," said Powell. "As we say in the infantry, this is a guy you take on a long patrol." Susan Covich, Stevens's daughter, also testified, talking about her experiences while staying at her father's house when Stevens wasn't there. She said Allen used the place so often that when she went to Girdwood, she began to stay at a hotel. The few times she showed up when Allen was at the residence, she found the bedroom doors closed and the atmosphere generally "creepy." One time, when she planned to stay the night, she pulled up and noticed, "There were lights on, cars in the parking lot. It just got too creepy, so I just drove on."[3]

Catherine Stevens testified that she was the one who handled the bills and that no, she didn't want many of the "gifts" that seemed to magically appear in the cabin. The metal stairs that had been attached to the house hung out at an odd angle that could be dangerous for kids. She thought the gas grill a fire hazard. A big black couch deposited in the house by Bill Allen's crew was ugly and had cigarette burns on it. But she couldn't exactly explain why she didn't ask Allen to take the stuff away. Just as Joe

"Millionaire" Boehm couldn't explain how the teenagers had taken over his house, neither could Catherine say how Bill Allen had taken over the Stevens's cabin. "Once he hit his head in 2001, it was almost impossible to have a conversation with him," she said.[4] It was the best explanation she could provide.

Then there was the matter of the wraparound deck installed in 2002 after the initial renovations had been completed. Why hadn't Catherine Stevens paid for that? Where did she think that labor came from? She said that she once asked her husband's Senate staff about why they didn't get a bill, but then she forgot about it. This led to the revelation that Stevens's staffers were helping pay the couple's personal bills—bills, as it turned out, that included charges at Saks Fifth Avenue, Nordstrom, and Neiman Marcus. Referring to a Stevens aide who maintained the couple's checkbooks, prosecutor Brenda Morris quipped, "She was your human ATM."[5]

Finally it was Ted Stevens's turn to tell his version of what happened, his chance to explain how the investigation into the remodeling of his house had been blown out of proportion, time for him to note that he did pay for many costs, and to make clear he would have paid more had he known there were outstanding bills. Uncle Ted was a former prosecutor who back in the 1950s gained some fame for supposedly helping to bust down doors in Fairbanks, brandishing a pistol beside police on raids. He had answers for the questions put to him, but he wasn't anything like the folksy grandfather Bill Allen had been on the stand. Uncle Ted was in one of his moods. Some on the jury found him an arrogant patriarch. Where Allen was the naive former oilman and son of fruit pickers, Ted Stevens was the Harvard law school grad who'd gone to Washington, D.C., in 1968 and never left. Stevens said he was busy in the Senate and did not keep track of all the details during the remodel. Allen seemed to just bring stuff to the house and never sent bills. "You were the lion of the Senate, and you didn't know how to stop a man from putting unwanted things in your home?" Morris, the prosecutor, snapped back at Stevens.[6]

Morris asked if Stevens remembered the furniture in the home, like the black leather couch and other items Allen had brought to the house.

The stuff "with the cigarette burns," Morris asked, "it remains there?" Stevens said yes. She then produced an email that Stevens had sent to Allen about the furniture, asking if it was okay for him to give it to "Ben and Elizabeth," Stevens's son and daughter-in-law, who were looking for a larger house. "Is the old stuff we had still in the warehouse?" he asked Allen in the email.

"You're trying to regift the furniture that's so hideous to your son, isn't that correct?" she asked Stevens. Was this the same Ben Stevens who had received $243,000 in consulting fees from VECO, Morris asked; the same son who made $715,000 from the Special Winter Olympics? Ted Stevens insisted he paid all bills sent to him. He believed that the $160,000 he'd spent had covered the remodel, the generator, and the porch. But Morris wouldn't let up. He lost his temper a few times and called her "Ms." He insisted on being fuzzy about details, insisted that his work kept him too busy to worry about the minutiae, insisted his wife paid the bills. "That's all there is to it," Stevens said, which were the words that wrapped up his defense before closing arguments.[7]

It was around this time in October that Sarah Palin went "rogue." She had been in this situation before when she was an oil and gas commissioner working with the good old boys—Governor Frank Murkowski and Alaska GOP chairman Randy Ruedrich. Now she was again working for someone who was destined to lose. She knew what to do. Stories began to appear revealing Palin had broken free of her McCain handlers and was walking to the back of the campaign plane to talk to reporters. A few times she stopped to answer questions on the rope line at political rallies, which sent the campaign into panic mode. She began to criticize the McCain campaign, saying it wasn't attacking Obama hard enough. She said she didn't like the way the campaign was relying on robo calls produced by the Republican National Committee. She called the calls irritatingly "old" and "conventional." When it was revealed the hockey mom and her family had amassed a new $150,000 wardrobe, she was, once again, quick to blame the RNC for thrusting the clothing upon her.

Pundits began wondering if she was trying to protect her reputation for a future political run. They praised her "independence" and how she was finally coming into her own. Headlines began appearing that described her as the new face of the Republican Party—or perhaps a new party, a GOP spinoff. Pundits suggested her supporters were made up of those who felt betrayed by the old, irritatingly conventional GOP. A few wondered even before the 2008 vote if she would be back to make a presidential run in 2012.

On October 27, 2008, a twelve-member jury convicted Ted Stevens on all seven counts of failing to report gifts on his Senate disclosure forms. Uncle Ted stood stone faced while the verdict was read. Outside the courthouse, he told reporters that he was innocent and needed to return to Alaska to fight for reelection in nine days. The Alaska GOP softened the battlefront by sending an email to Alaskans proclaiming Stevens innocent and blaming an "overzealous" federal government for his convictions. Stevens and his attorneys charged that the verdict was the result of prosecutorial misconduct before and during the trial. They would soon file motions to overturn the verdict.

As Palin raced across the nation in a last-ditch effort to pick up votes, Stevens was on his way back home. At Ted Stevens Anchorage International Airport, the senator was greeted by a group of burly guys on Harley Davidson motorcycles. They escorted him to a rally, where supporters cheered him on. They wore T-shirts and waved signs that read, "F*#@ the Feds, Vote for Ted." He got up to the podium, looking tired, worn, and heartbroken, and told the crowd that it was good to be home, in "the land that I love," he said. It was a land, he vowed, he would continue fighting for.

While the state Republican Party urged Alaskans to vote for Uncle Ted, Palin sent out a press release calling for him to resign from the Senate. "Even if elected on Tuesday," Palin said, "Senator Stevens should step aside to allow a special election to give Alaskans a real choice of who will serve them in Congress." This reinforced her reformer reputation among Lower 48 voters, but it didn't help her in Alaska. This single act of crossing Ted Stevens irrevocably sealed her fate with many in Alaska's GOP, not to mention some independents and Democrats. It was seen as yet another example of her willingness to betray Alaska for her own greater political gain.

Winter creeps across Alaska until one day everything is white. The sun sinks lower on the horizon every day, and the gloom of winter descends. Some remember the promise they made the winter before that it would be their last in Alaska, but by then it's too late to escape. Where summer beneath the midnight sun is all frenzied activity, winter is a stasis, a settling in that seeps into you. By November, these languid winter spirits are almost old friends that you can't bear to leave. And even if you could fight their power and move on, where would you go? To some suburb in the Lower 48 where lawns are shaved and people go to work in pleated khakis and tucked shirts? Could you survive in the big city? Or in a lonesome countryside surrounded by flat and forlorn farms? No Big Oil or big fights with those oil companies. No wolves or bears or moose or sled dog races or whale blubber or melting glaciers or mountains to climb and die on. No place to help grow and shape with a narrative that is still fresh and new and in the making. Could you live in a place where you would be simply a number among hundreds of thousands, a place where most of the harsh edges of life have been sanded off, a place whose story has been told and retold? A place that offers no more big adventures, no more undiscovered lands, no more undiscovered selves?

The beginning of the long winter touches Alaskans. The tourists and summer fishermen are gone, and Alaskans settle in for six months of darkness and cold. They depend on each other to get through it. They are forgiving. So no matter what had come before, no matter what partisan divisiveness she had spawned, hearts swelled all across the state when Sarah Palin's plane touched down at Ted Stevens Anchorage International Airport on November 4—Election Day. She arrived early in the morning and headed to Wasilla, where she voted in the same building she attended as a schoolgirl, sat in as councilwoman, and spent so many years in as mayor discussing ordinances, property taxes, and cats in trees. She spoke briefly to reporters, waved good-bye, and headed back to the Lower 48 to stand by John McCain to greet a sad crowd and a brighter sun in Arizona.

That night at a convention center in downtown Anchorage, Alaskans gathered to see who won. "Election Central," as they call it, is a place where results for state and Alaska congressional races are put up on an overhead projector as Republicans and Democrats mingle with their candidates. There was a bar roped off in the corner. Extra tables had been set up for the international reporters who were still in Alaska covering Palin. Even Al Jazeera had reserved space. Palin and McCain would lose, of course, everyone knew. The polls were clear on that. The real news was that Ted Stevens was down only a few thousand votes to Mark Begich, the Democrat opponent who was nearly half his age. Even though Stevens had been found guilty and faced possible prison time, many Alaskans still wanted him as their senator. The election turned out to be close, but Stevens never made up the early margin. About two weeks after Election Day, he conceded the race to Begich, who had won by fewer than 4,000 votes.

That same month in 2008, Ted Stevens delivered his final speech on the Senate floor before returning home. It was like listening to a history of Alaska. Stevens had been in all of the big battles that shaped and formed the state—even before Alaska was a state. Those who listened to him in the Senate forgot for a while about the criticism he'd faced over earmarks and federal spending, about the oilman who'd remodeled his house, about Stevens's convictions. Some of the senators had tears in their eyes:

> When I came to the Senate, Alaska had been a state for less than a decade. We were then more of an impoverished territory than a full-fledged state. The commitments made by the federal government on our statehood act were unfulfilled, and, Mr. President, some are still unfulfilled. Alaska had not received the land and resources it had been promised. Poverty and illness reigned supreme in rural regions of our state. And I remember so well when Senator Kennedy and I went to the Arctic

and examined some of those villages. It was just disaster. Our fisheries were in peril, primarily from the intrusion of foreign vessels that were anchored just a few miles offshore 12 months out of the year. Many people doubted whether Alaska had what it took to be a successful state, and they asked whether Alaska was still Seward's folly. Mr. President, we proved that those doubters were wrong. Working with one another as Alaskans and with great friends here in the Senate, Alaskans took control of our own destiny.

In 1958, as legislative counsel for the Department of Interior, I worked on Alaska's Statehood Act. Section 4 of that act committed Congress to settle Alaskan Native land claims. In 1971, Congress did enact the Alaska Native Claims Settlement Act, settling aboriginal claims in our state. Native corporations, established at my request, to manage $1 billion paid for our state and federal government and the 44-million-acre land settlement are now driving forces in the Alaska economy. In 1973, after a dramatic tie-breaking vote by the vice president of this chamber, an amendment which closed the courts of this country to further delay by extreme environmentalists, the president signed into law the Trans-Alaska Pipeline Authorization Act. That act dramatically improved America's energy security and secured the economic future of Alaska. In 1976, Congress passed what became known as the Magnuson-Stevens Act to fight foreign fishing fleets which endangered America's fisheries. Because of that act, America's fisheries today are the most productive and the best managed in the world.

Working within the framework of these basic laws, Alaskans have labored in the appropriations and administrative process to make statehood a reality. Where there was nothing but tundra and forest, today there are now airports, roads, ports, water, and sewer systems, hospitals, clinics, communications networks, research labs, and much, much more. Mr. President, Alaska was not Seward's folly and is no longer an impoverished territory. Alaska is a great state and essential contributor to our nation's energy security and national defense. I'm proud to have had a role in this transformation . . .

My motto has been here, "To hell with politics. Just do what's right for Alaska." And I tried every day to live up to those words.

It's fun to be governor of Alaska when oil prices are high, state coffers are full, and the state's rainy day savings account is yielding huge dividends to residents. The people love you and tell you so often. And politics is easy when the bad guys are clear and distinct, or better yet, on trial or awaiting trial—when the FBI is searching offices, indicting corrupt bastards and your enemies are going to prison. Sarah Palin had lived as that governor for almost two years, but when she came home from the presidential campaign, oil prices were down—in December, they hovered at about $40 a barrel—the public was still bruised over how she let McCain's campaign infiltrate the state, and her old foil—the oil-dependent good old boys—had gone the way of yesterday. Even the Alaska Permanent Fund was suffering, its value dropping from a high of more than $40 billion in 2007 to $26 billion in early 2009.

The day before the general election, the state Personnel Board's investigator released its findings on Troopergate. Unlike the Alaska Legislative Council's probe, which found Palin had misused her power, the Personnel Board questioned her behavior but cleared her of violating state ethics laws. It was good news for the governor, though by then it had little effect on people's conclusions about Troopergate. Much of America had already divided cleanly on their views of Sarah Palin. The same was true in Alaska.

Palin had enemies now. It was a new world for her. The media that had once been so easy on her had turned, and there were those "pathetic" Alaska bloggers nipping at her heels. Palin lashed out at them like a moose surrounded by snarling wolves. If this was some sort of strategy, it might have worked in a bigger state. But in the confines of Alaska, those reporters and bloggers were her constituents and some, even her supporters. Every time she attacked them for criticizing or mocking something she did—as when she went to pardon a turkey before Thanksgiving 2008 and then stood talking to a TV camera about the brutal nature of politics as a bird in the background was fed into a shredder—Alaskans were pulling back from the woman almost all of them once loved. It didn't help that she'd started accepting speaking engagements Outside while dodging reporters in the state, or fought to keep secret emails that she wrote on state time, or refused to accept stimulus funds under the guise of fiscal responsibility, or set up a political action committee to raise funds that many suspected would go to boost her national credibility, and her future political career.

Every time a question was raised about the governor's actions or behaviors, she or someone in her administration fought back, which only perpetuated the conflict. Palin had the First Dude and aides around to spur her on. But she also had a larger national base now too. New groups of bloggers around the country began to sprout up to defend their heroine against her attackers. Soon it became the war of the bloggers, with Palin or one of her staffers sometimes entering the mix to turn up the heat.

Marty Rutherford, Palin's deputy commissioner at the Department of Natural Resources, worried about the governor's attitude after she came home to Alaska. Rutherford knew all too well how important it would be for Palin to put her head down, get her mind straight, and go to work for Alaska. She needed to see through her new—and increasingly controversial—oil and gas policies. Her first term as governor depended on it. Rutherford knew that if Palin's support continued to slide, so would likely the support for those policies on which she and others had worked so hard. Rutherford and others in the administration knew the long history of Alaska and oil, how powerful the companies were, how persuasive they could be. She understood that the big initiatives that they had all worked so hard to put in place—ACES and AGIA—could be undone with the stroke of a pen. She understood well, too, the role a popular governor had played in achieving success on those initiatives.

But Sarah Palin seemed bored with those battles, and she was distracted by the noise still reverberating around her failed run as vice president. In January, she had a softball of an opportunity to win back support in the state. Nick Tucker, who lived in the remote Yupik Eskimo village of Emmonak in far western Alaska, wrote to a regional newspaper about the trouble he and his fellow villagers were having getting enough to eat and stay warm. "My family of ten, with a household of six adults and four minors, is one of the causalities of our current high costs of heating fuel and gasoline that are devastating families and households here in Emmonak of 847 residents," said Tucker, a community leader and Vietnam War veteran, in his letter to the editor. "I am 63 and my wife is 54. For the first time, beginning December 2008, I am forced to decide between buying heating fuel or groceries . . . Couple of weeks ago, our 8-year-old son had to go to bed hungry . . . We are several months behind on our city water and sewer bills."[8]

Emmonak was one of the villages in western Alaska that couldn't get fuel in October, when Palin was on the campaign trail, because of the early freeze-up. Problems were compounded when the region was hit by a harsh cold snap. Tucker wrote about putting out a call on the radio to his neighbors and being deluged with stories of hunger and cold. He ended his letter with a plea for help from the Alaska community and state government. It didn't take long after this appeared in the tiny regional paper for the plight of Emmonak to make news all across the world—mainly because Palin failed to respond quickly.

The storyline became simple: Sarah Palin lets Alaska Native villagers starve and shiver. On the presidential campaign trail she had said, over and over again, that under her, the state had put away billions in savings. And yet she couldn't feed the residents of her own state? As the governor dug in her heals, seemingly unwilling to visit the area to find out exactly how bad the situation was, donations from all over the world began to be shipped into Emmonak and other western Alaska villages. Finally, more than a month after the letter was sent, Palin decided to visit some of the villages. She was flown by evangelist Franklin Graham, whose group, Samaritan's Purse, planned a 44,000-pound food drop. Palin herself brought cookies. The cookies, plus the arrival of an evangelist in an area where the Native population had been scarred by missionaries over the past hundred years, didn't sit well with many.

Nick Tucker caught up with Palin while she was visiting one of the villages. She nodded her head when, tears in his voice, he told her that he and his people needed her help. "This is just temporary help," he said, referring to the food drop-off. "The Native people are a very strong people, and this is probably the only time they cried out for help. They're hungry . . . You know that all the oil money and everything else came out of our land." He begged her for help. "Don't forget us," he pleaded. She said she wouldn't.

Suddenly being governor was no fun at all. There were too many problems. Alaska Natives were hungry. They lacked an economic future. With Stevens gone, what little money had been coming in to boost Native communities was threatened. Oil prices were sliding. The bloggers were after her. The Democrats were after her. The pro-industry Republicans were after her. She had so much to offer the rest of the country, and yet she was trapped in the frozen North. Anytime she tried to break out to give an interview to let the world know that she was still alive, she would face new criticism or someone would file an ethics complaint against her. And instead of working to change the laws so that she and governors after her wouldn't be dogged by such complaints, she wrote scathing emails and in some cases press releases about those who filed the complaints, which just made things worse.

And things kept going downhill. In March, Citgo—an oil company owned by socialist Venezuela—announced it would send millions of dollars in free heating fuel to Alaska Native villages. This was nothing new. For years Citgo had been giving millions of dollars of fuel to impoverished areas all across the country, including in Alaska. But this time, the fact that America-bashing Hugo Chavez had to give fuel to Sarah Palin's Alaska, the nation's biggest oil province, with billions of dollars in the bank, made the headlines particularly embarrassing. As Palin continued to lash out against the slightest criticism, the criticism then intensified, and so the drama went on for months.

In early 2009, Ted Stevens was enmeshed in a battle to clear his name. Judge Emmett Sullivan, who had presided over Stevens's trial, had lost patience with federal prosecutors over their handling of the case. The Justice Department took the unusual step of assigning new prosecutors to the case, who found boxes of documents that had never been disclosed to the defense.

Most damning, prosecutors had withheld an April 2008 interview they had with Allen. In the interview, they asked him about the note that Stevens's lawyers had questioned Allen so vigorously about during the trial, the note where Stevens told Allen, "You owe me a bill—remember Torricelli, my friend. Friendship is one thing—compliance with these

ethics rules entirely different." When the note was brought up during
the trial, Allen had said that Bob Persons, their mutual friend, had told
him to disregard Stevens's request. "Ted's just covering his ass," Persons
told Allen, according to the oilman's testimony. But the prosecutors
failed to share with the defense an interview they had with Allen six
months before the trial. Four prosecutors and one FBI agent brought
Allen in and grilled him about Stevens's note. He told them that yes, he
remembered getting it, and no, he hadn't talked to Persons about the
note. It appeared Allen had fabricated the most important piece of testimony in the trial. And, it appeared, that the prosecution spurred him
on to do so.

Judge Sullivan was outraged when the new prosecution team informed him of what it had found. "In nearly 25 years on the bench, I've
never seen anything approaching the mishandling and misconduct that
I've seen in this case," the judge later said. U.S. Attorney General Eric
Holder asked the judge to toss out the convictions against Stevens. The
judge did so, and also launched an investigation into suspicions of prosecutorial misconduct that, as of this writing, have not been released.

Bill Allen would eventually be fined $750,000 and sentenced to three
years in a Southern California federal prison, a reduced sentence for helping the government with Polar Pen. By mid-2011, the feds seemed unlikely to charge him for sex crimes stemming from his relationship with
Bambi Tyree, Paula Roberds, or any other women he allegedly slept with
as girls. Anchorage police detectives, teamed with a prosecutor from the
U.S. Justice Department's Child Exploitation and Obscenity Section,
had hoped to see Allen charged for sex crimes with minors. But in mid-
2010, the Justice Department inexplicably dropped the case, despite the
recommendation from the federal prosecutor and his supervisor. Holder,
though vague on details, said at a Senate hearing in March 2011 that the
Justice Department's "decisions were made only on the basis of the facts,
the law, and the principles that we have to apply." Allen has maintained
his innocence.

In the wake of the botched Stevens case and the revelation that prosecutors had failed to turn over evidence, former Alaska state representatives Pete Kott and Vic Kohring were released from prison pending the

appeal of their convictions. A federal appeals court later tossed their convictions, ruling that prosecutors should have, among other things, shared information about Tyree and sex allegations against Bill Allen. "Such evidence could have been used, at a minimum, on cross-examination to impeach Allen's testimony," the appellate judges wrote in their decision to toss Kott's conviction. They also wrote that such acts would have given Allen an incentive to cooperate in the first place. In August 2011, federal prosecutors were gearing up to retry Kohring and Kott again, but by then their crimes seemed like they belonged to another age.

Ted Stevens would live another seventeen months after his convictions were tossed, knowing in his heart that had he not been railroaded by federal prosecutors and agents he would likely still have been fighting for Alaska's future. Old age wouldn't kill Uncle Ted. It would be the foggy mountains of southwestern Alaska. On August 9, 2010, he boarded a floatplane at a lodge for a quick flight to a nearby river to fish for salmon. The plane crashed along the way. On September 26, prosecutor Nick Marsh went down in his basement in his home in Tacoma Park. His wife found him later that day with a rope around his neck.

Sarah Palin might have had a second life in Alaska had she wanted it, had she put her head down, stopped fighting, and gotten to work. Second lives litter the forty-ninth state like broken dreams, and Alaska is the land of broken dreams. The gold miners left many behind. So too did the late Senator Bob Bartlett, who long ago warned against dependence on Outside corporations. The delegates to the state constitutional convention saw many of their dreams die. They had high hopes when they wrote about this country called Alaska, when they thought that they were passing down "a state that will be glorious in her achievements, a homeland filled with opportunities for living." This would be a land, they wrote, "where you can worship and pray, a country where ambitions will be bright and real, an Alaska that will grow with you as you grow. We trust you; you are our future. We ask you to take tomorrow and dream; we know that you will see visions we do not see."

The dreams pretty much all died, but then a lot of them began a second run. Bush rat governor Jay Hammond and ex-governor Wally

Hickel both matured into senior statesmen, their mishaps and failures mostly forgotten in their later years. They became allies in their fight to resist oil's power over the state. Ted Stevens was moving on with his life before he died, many Alaskans believing he was a victim of a federal witch hunt. Even former governor Frank Murkowski was already on the way back, his past sins all but forgotten.

Sarah Palin could have had a rebirth too, but she chose to go in another direction.

Maybe she just didn't like the odds in Alaska. Annual oil production was hovering at about 700,000 barrels—down from more than 2 million two decades earlier. The owners of the trans-Alaska oil pipeline were starting to worry there wouldn't be enough oil flowing in the line to operate it in years to come. As for the state's natural gas pipe dream, it was becoming increasingly uncertain whether Alaska would land the next boom project. Another source of natural gas, shale gas, was being heralded in the Lower 48. Some were speculating that it could provide enough energy to power the United States for more than 100 years. Many of the same oil companies that hit it rich in Alaska were making big investments in shale. Maybe the country didn't need Alaska's natural gas yet. Maybe the oil companies were beginning to lose interest in Alaska. Lawmakers were starting to think maybe Palin's AGIA gas pipeline was a mistake. There were even lawmakers who wanted to lower oil taxes to entice the industry to increase oil development and production. The issue of corruption appeared to be fading fast in the rearview mirror, and the oilies were beginning to see the cracks in her armor and support. They once again began to descend upon Juneau.

So when Sarah Palin quit, it wasn't completely unexpected. Some close to her had seen it coming. Since her return from the vice presidential campaign trail, she simply wasn't happy, nor much involved in the workings of the state. Some described her as detached. Others said she seemed sad and angry. Her decision to quit was probably sewn up when it was announced that she was going to be writing a book and some began to speculate she had landed a multimillion-dollar advance. How could Alaska compete with that, with its impoverished Native population, its penny-ante corruption scandals, its declining oil production, and its uncertain future? There were, after all, fans Outside who adored her and said they needed her to do for the rest of the country what she had done for Alaska.

Palin picked the day before the Fourth of July 2009 in the backyard of her house in Wasilla to announce it was all over. Lake Lucille was behind her. A few members of her cabinet stood dutifully nearby. And in this setting Sarah Palin said good-bye to the children of Alaska. She didn't blink.

EPILOGUE

In early August 2010, Ted Stevens and a group of friends headed out on a floatplane from a southwestern Alaska lodge for some silver salmon fishing on the Nushagak River. The lodge was owned by GCI, one of Alaska's dominant telecommunications companies, where Stevens had been a frequent visitor over the years, as were other dignitaries, lobbyists, and politicians. Among those visiting the lodge that summer was former NASA chief Sean O'Keefe. Stevens and eight others were aboard the de Havilland Otter for the short flight to the Nushagak. Above a stretch of lush green hills and tundra, clouds dancing over the mountaintops, licking the glacial tarns, the airplane was a red humming speck floating over the land of the lost. Perhaps the humming soothed the pilot, luring him into another time and place just long enough for the mountain to open its mouth and breathe in. Nobody is sure what happened, but the plane skidded hard, ripping a hole through alder-packed brush on the mountainside—ripping a hole through the heart of Alaska.

Five people died on impact, including the former senator. Another four passengers, including O'Keefe and his son, survived the crash. Badly banged up, they spent long hours trying to keep awake, trapped in the plane among the bodies and chilled by the rain, waiting for rescuers. Their plight and the deaths of the other passengers were eclipsed by the loss of Stevens. Alaskans were left in shock, in part because they'd lost former governor Wally Hickel a few months earlier. To call this a passing of an era is an understatement. In those immediate days, the state felt like it was now on its own.

The next week, a motorcycle procession led the way to an Anchorage church. People gathered along the roadside, waved signs, and threw flowers at the Harleys accompanying the hearse. The sun came out seemingly for the first time all summer on the day of Ted Stevens's funeral. About 3,000 showed up for the memorial. Twenty-three current and former U.S. senators attended. Senior officers from all the branches of the military were represented. A dozen or so foreign dignitaries sat in the pews. Four of Alaska's living former governors were there: Bill Sheffield, Tony Knowles, and Frank Murkowski. Sarah Palin sat in the pew with Todd. Governor Sean Parnell, in whose hands she left the state when she resigned, was an honorary pallbearer. The applause was loud when Vice President Joe Biden told the crowd gathered in the church, "No state has ever had a more fierce defender of that state's way of life than Ted Stevens."

Alaskans may have felt conflicted about the charges against Stevens, but did it really matter anymore? The feds had cut corners, the former senator's criminal convictions had been tossed, and his overwhelming legacy in the state overshadowed any implied wrongdoing on his part. That might not have excused Stevens from getting cozy with Bill Allen and allowing the oil contractor to renovate his cabin, but a fair number of Alaskans were angrier at the Justice Department than at their beloved former senator. Stevens had proved his worth long ago. He'd lost his Senate seat but had prevailed in his fight against the feds. Uncle Ted wasn't a quitter.

On the contrary, the eighty-six-year-old was still very much involved in Alaska and its future. Stevens's latest cause was advocating for the state's long-sought natural gas project. He'd deemed Sarah Palin's pipeline plan—AGIA—a failure, saying the markets for Alaska natural gas had dried up in the Lower 48, in large part due to new shale gas developments across the country. He was now calling for the state to invest in a project that would export liquefied natural gas on tankers to Asia. For her part, Palin had nothing to say on Twitter or Facebook about the pipeline or any of the other policies she'd started while governor. She never weighed in on Alaska politics, despite the growing resistance to her oil tax hike and AGIA pipe dream. She had other priorities in 2010, among them filming a new cable TV show—*Sarah Palin's Alaska*.

When Palin abruptly resigned as governor in July 2009, she said she no longer could be an effective leader. The state was spending "millions of dollars" (it turned out to be closer to a half million) to knock down bogus ethics complaints against her, bloggers were attacking her baby son, Trig, and a "full-court press" had judged her unfairly. Palin promised that her resignation was for the best for Alaska and America. "All I can ask is that you trust me with this decision, and know that it is no more politics as usual," she'd said. Perhaps anywhere in the country people would frown on a governor who walked out on them for no reason other than she possessed a thin skin and hubristic ambitions her state role couldn't fulfill. But to Alaskans, quitting is something you don't do.

You can get away with a lot in this state. You can fall off barstools, have affairs, suffer from drug problems, forget to brush your hair, wear anything you want, live in any kind of structure you desire, and still have friends and family, still command purpose, still pursue a livelihood. You don't need a degree to be respected, nor do you need money or connections.

But you cannot quit the state and still be a respectable Alaskan. You have to stick in there with the rest of us, no matter how icy the road, cold the temperature, tall the mountain, rough the sea, no matter how miserable it is. And often it is indeed miserable. But then something happens: the rescuers arrive, the seas calm and a whale pod arrives, the bear runs away, an old man wearing a wolf hat pedals by on a bicycle with moose antlers duct-taped on the handlebars and places a ten-pound silver salmon in your hands. You stop to help a villager, who has never seen stoplights, cross a road. The whirl you see in the far distance is a sled dog musher, gliding across the snow, chasing the song of the northern lights into a great white unknown. The clouds clear. The mountains emerge. The sea sparkles. The tundra erupts with life, and you fight on.

Since quitting, Palin has penned a best-selling memoir, landed a gig with Fox News, and promoted SarahPAC, her political action committee. She has made millions and now is a national celebrity/political pundit— a figurehead in the evolving tea party movement. And she did all of this while hardly showing her face in Alaska. Word had it that she didn't even go the grocery store anymore. Nor did she comment on state issues. Now, in the wake of Ted Stevens's death, Alaskans were about to get a sense of how Palin's role outside office might shape their state.

In the chilly, rainy summer of 2010, talk in political circles was about a new kid on the tundra—Joe Miller, a Fairbanks lawyer. A graduate of Yale law school and West Point and a Gulf War veteran, Miller was challenging Senator Lisa Murkowski, daughter of Palin foe Frank Murkowski, in the Republican primary. Miller and Sarah Palin were ideological friends, and she was backing him. Perhaps this would be Palin's legacy to Alaskans—to get Joe Miller, a tea party candidate originally from Kansas who embodied the antigovernment sentiment sweeping parts of the country, elected as Alaska's senator.

In some ways Miller seemed to be a throwback, believing Alaska could and should support itself without help from the feds. He advocated the state taking over federal lands and developing the resources. He even suggested mining in Denali National Park and Preserve, home to North America's tallest peak. Entitlements and earmarks were crushing the nation and Alaskans needed to do their part, he said. The sentiment struck a chord with survivalists and weekend warrior types, fitting into the growing tea party movement that Palin now championed. The ties between Miller and the ex-governor stretched back at least to early 2008. At the time, the two teamed to try to unseat Palin's longtime foe Randy Ruedrich, the chairman of the Alaska GOP, during the party's annual convention. Miller, then a part-time lawyer for the Fairbanks North Star borough, would wait for his coworkers to head out for lunch, then log on to their government computers and vote in an online poll set up to get rid of Ruedrich.

There was something different about Miller—something hinting of cabals, secret groups, and militant causes, perhaps, lurking just below the surface. At the state GOP convention, Miller appeared trailing a security detail—men with sunglasses, earpieces, and semimilitary bearing. When the pope came to Alaska in 1981, he had bodyguards. A few presidents have passed through Alaska over the years, also with security. But you'd never find either of the Murkowskis, Ted Stevens, Wally Hickel, or even Sarah Palin—while she was governor, at least—with bodyguards.

In 2008 Miller was not running for office. Yet somehow it had come to him, perhaps transmitted on one of those mysterious frequencies received only by a chosen few, that there was a GOP plot to kill him and Palin, according to reporter Jill Burke of *Alaska Dispatch,* who later, through emails and interviews with former coworkers, detailed some of the more bizarre manifestations of Miller's paranoia. He feared someone might tamper with his tires, causing him to have a car wreck. At his office, Miller asked his coworkers to lock doors. He requested security cameras. And he thought up an escape route—from what, nobody knew—in case the main office door became compromised.[1] Despite the precautions and illegal use of computers, however, Joe Miller and Sarah Palin failed to oust Randy Ruedrich in 2008. And Ruedrich didn't quit.

Two years later, Miller saw a chance to attack the old guard again, this time running for the Republican U.S. Senate nomination against Lisa Murkowski. In 2010 he somehow got himself together—for a while at least—and screwing the screw back into the part of him that allowed him to function, campaigned hard and effectively. It was an improbable race. Murkowski was the ranking member on the Senate Energy and Natural Resources Committee and enjoyed the respect of her colleagues. She had big business Republicans and moderates behind her. Her campaign war chest was overflowing, and if she ran into trouble, she had her biggest weapon of all: Ted Stevens, whose heavy hand and statewide popularity she relied on.

Around the time of Stevens's death, however, the polls began to defy the pundits who'd decided Miller's campaign was doomed. Nor could Lisa Murkowski believe her own party would reject her for someone running on cutting federal funding and earmarks to Alaska. The polling, she assumed, was a blip, an aberration. Also, she was still mourning the loss of her good friend and mentor. With Ted Stevens's enthusiastic support, she would have almost certainly been assured of a win. But he was gone.

A week after Stevens's funeral, political junkies throughout Alaska and beyond were riveted by the primary night results. The numbers coming out of the elections division showed Joe Miller beating incumbent Lisa Murkowski. On Twitter, Sarah Palin posted, "Keeping fingers crossed, powder dry, prayers upward." If Miller won, would Palin be vindicated? Would the promise she made to keep working for Alaskans be kept? Lisa Murkowski didn't think so. "I think she's out for her own self-interest. I don't think she's out for Alaska's interest," she told reporters that night.[2] To Palin, Miller, and their tribe, that sounded a lot like the old, arrogant GOP. The counting continued after the primary election, but Murkowski didn't gain enough ground. Miller captured 51 percent of the vote compared to Murkowski's 49 percent. As a writer observed in the 1970s when George Wallace ran up surprise wins in several presidential primaries, "The galoots were loose!"

Miller's Democratic opponent in the general election was Sitka mayor Scott McAdams. A virtual unknown, McAdams turned out to be a better politician than anybody expected. He wasn't as smart and quick on his feet as Miller, but he stood a sliver of a chance at winning, had Murkowski decided to go quietly. But as summer started turning into fall, Murkowski shook herself awake, as if from a long slumber, and started exploring ways to stay in the race, even if it meant risking defying her own Republican Party. There was talk that the Libertarian Senate candidate might step aside for Murkowski in the general election. This would have allowed her name to be listed on the ballot for November's general election.

But more than three weeks after the primary election, Murkowski chose a riskier path—a write-in campaign that would require Alaskans to spell, pretty much to the letter, her name when they headed to the voting booths in November. It seemed a nearly impossible feat, and pundits proclaimed there was no way, with a name like Murkowski, that she could win. The only candidate ever to win a U.S. Senate election as a write-in candidate was Strom Thurmond of South Carolina, in 1954. But despite the odds, something in Murkowski took hold. In the early fall of 2010, venturing into uncharted waters, she seemed to be transformed overnight. As it turned out, she found she wasn't really the arch conservative she thought she must be to win Alaska's heart. In fact, she discovered, she was a sensible, moderate Republican who loved her state in much the way Ted Stevens had loved it. She believed that neither Miller nor McAdams could do as much for Alaska as she could. And she would fight her heart out trying to prove it.

As national interest in her write-in campaign grew, she gave a figurative finger to those in the U.S. Senate and the National Republican Senatorial Committee who were calling for her to step down for the sake of the party, and to give Miller, the GOP nominee, his chance. She campaigned ferociously across the state. "It's liberating," she later recalled. "One of the many things I learned is that you've got to be who you are."[3] And who knew that Lisa Murkowski sang while her rail-thin body turned supple and swayed? "Fill in the oval," the song went, "write her on the line. Mur-kow-ski. Ski!" Spelling bee commercials flooded the airwaves. School kids got creative and drew posters of a mooing cow on skis to help voters remember how to spell her Polish name. She barreled into Ted Stevens's old stomping grounds. Up north into Barrow, down the Arctic coastline into Nome, and down farther to Bethel. "To hell with politics," Murkowski told crowds over and over. "Let's do what's right for Alaska."

Joe Miller wasn't swaying or singing. Local reporters had dug deep into his background, and the cracks were starting to show. The man railing against entitlements had, among other things, taken federal farm subsidies and received benefits from a state health care program for low-income families. Most damning, though, was the 2008 episode in which Miller secretly used coworkers' computers, while employed as a part-time attorney for the Fairbanks North Star borough, in his quest to unseat Alaska GOP chairman Randy Ruedrich. Wasn't Miller using government computers to conduct party business on government time? Wasn't he doing much of what Sarah Palin had accused Ruedrich of doing when they both were commissioners at the Alaska Oil and Gas Conservation Commission seven years earlier? Who knew? Sarah Palin wouldn't comment.

It took a lawsuit, spearheaded by the online news site *Alaska Dispatch*, to get the borough to release records detailing Miller's transgressions. And when the media sued, Miller lashed out. At a press conference, he declared he was drawing "a line in the sand" and would answer no more questions about his background. True to his word, after a Miller town hall meeting, when *Alaska Dispatch* executive editor Tony Hopfinger—one of the authors of this book—asked him whether he'd been reprimanded for his conduct while working at Fairbanks borough, Miller's wannabe Secret Service security guards—the owner of an army surplus store with ties to the militia and two active-duty soldiers—put Hopfinger in handcuffs until the local police arrived, rolled their eyes, and took off the handcuffs immediately. Miller's guards claimed Hopfinger was trespassing, even though the event was held at a public school and attended by other reporters. The campaign quickly went into spin mode, sending out a press release titled, "Liberal Blogger 'Loses It' at Town Hall Meeting." The incident came during the 2010 midterm elections, with Sarah Palin supporting a number of tea party candidates nationwide, some who were clashing with reporters who were questioning their experience and background. Hopfinger was not a liberal or a blogger, and it was Miller who had lost it. As Anchorage police spokesperson Dave Parker put it, Hopfinger was "no danger to the public. Tony is not known for his ground-fighting style."[4] The bizarre incident was photographed by other journalists and whipped round the world. The next day, Scott McAdams and his staff posed for a photo in handcuffs. For Halloween, Murkowski took her young nephews trick or treating, dressed as security guards.

Those last few weeks of Miller's run were a disaster, the tea party candidate imploding under the weight of paranoia and hypocrisy before Alaskans' eyes. Murkowski and her supporters had the upper hand, and when election night rolled around, she was ahead of him. The vote counting continued for weeks after the election as Miller and his lawyers pored over each ballot, hoping to find misspellings of her name. In the end, Murkowski beat Miller by just over 10,000 votes, and he finally conceded the race to her, with minimal graciousness, on New Year's Eve.

It is now late June 2011, the weekend before the summer solstice, the midnight sun shining in all of the dark corners of the state. Winter is a world away. It's almost a year since Ted Stevens died. Sarah Palin has bought a home in Arizona. Recently news outlets all across the country spent thousands of dollars to send reporters to Juneau to dive into the more than 24,000 pages of emails that promised to tell the narrative of Sarah Palin's tenure as Alaska's governor.

They were digging for dirt. They were digging for signs of the evil, conniving woman they had led the public to believe she was. What they found instead was what nearly any Alaskan could have told them: a small-town major with big dreams for her state, convinced they would come true just by being articulated. Someone who seemed to pay more attention to personalities than to action. Someone whose internal chatter, it seemed, was etched in sound bites, without any kind of real ideological or practical discipline. Someone who was given responsibility without being ready for it. What they found in those massive stacks of paper was a slice of Alaska.

Bill Allen, the oilman who tarnished Stevens and helped propel Palin in Alaska politics, is due to be released from a halfway house later in 2011. Oil prices are again above $100. The Alaska Permanent Fund, that rainy-day savings account seeded with oil money that pays dividends to residents, is worth more than $39 billion. The state is running an estimated surplus of more than $3 billion, reaping the benefits of high oil prices and the tax hike Palin championed while governor. Her former lieutenant governor, Sean Parnell, is now at the helm. He's worried about Alaska's oil patch and whether the companies will invest in new projects, so much that he advocates lowering oil taxes. Once again, oil executives are descending on Juneau with their charts and graphs. Once again, hours upon hours are spent sitting on committee hearings, listening to the oilies go on and on about profit margins, the costs of doing business in Alaska. Once again, they're subtly communicating that Alaskans are nothing without them. Meantime, a battle wages over proposed offshore oil development in Alaska's Arctic—one of the last big prospects for crude—and what it may or may not do to the environment.

And the natural gas pipeline, that fabled project supposed to deliver the next boom, seems all but dead. Under Palin's pipeline policy, the state continues to subsidize a Canadian company to explore the possibility, even though Big Oil appears to have little interest in it. BP and Conoco Phillips, which had teamed up to pursue a competing gas pipeline project, called it quits in May 2011.

And so uncertainty over future oil and gas development lingers, as it has for years now. What will replace it and how will Alaska survive? The question hangs over the state like an approaching whiteout. The answer, some believe in 2011, is in the melting Arctic and new technology. Climate change is opening up the Far North and spawning big dreams in Alaska again, from building icebreakers and ports to serve increasing Arctic shipping traffic to mining precious rare earth metals to encouraging oil fracking on the North Slope.

But maybe Alaska doesn't need another boom right now. Maybe it doesn't deserve it quite yet. The lessons from the booms and busts, political scandals and opportunists, are clearer now. Alaska has been maturing. Old guard leaders like Ted Stevens and Wally Hickel are gone, and so is Sarah Palin. With them they've taken big dreams and big dependency. The corruption has been exposed and internalized. The oil curse that haunts Alaska and other oil provinces is better understood.

A generation of Alaskans has lived through it all. They are no longer children trying to fulfill the promise of their founding fathers. They are adults upon whom great responsibility is thrust. And if they have learned anything, if they've woken up some from that long, crude slumber, perhaps it's that dreams die, reality sets in, and that riches and power ultimately are earned through the necessary and tedious steps of building a state—a state that, after all it's been through, just may be ready to realize its full potential and the richness of the promise. Or not. We'll see.

NOTES

PROLOGUE

1. U.S. Justice Department, indictment against Peter Kott and Bruce Weyhrauch, May 3, 2007; conversations between Kott, Bill Allen, Rick Smith, and Bob McManus, FBI surveillance video, May 7, 2006.

CHAPTER 1

1. E. L. "Bob" Bartlett, "Meeting the Challenge" (speech to the Alaska Constitutional Convention, November 8, 1955).

2. Vic Fischer, "Alaska's Constitution," in G. W. Kimura, ed., *Alaska at 50: The Past, Present, and Next Fifty Years of Alaska Statehood* (Fairbanks: University of Alaska Press, 2009), 152–153.

3. Thomas A. Rickard, *Through the Yukon and Alaska* (San Francisco: Mining and Scientific Press, 1909).

4. Alaska Humanities Forum, *Governing Alaska: The Constitutional Convention*, Alaska History and Cultural Studies Curriculum Project, 2003–2006.

5. Resolution by the members of the Alaska Constitutional Convention, February 5, 1956.

6. Richard J. H. Johnston, "Alaska Sets Up Statehood Drive," *New York Times*, October 14, 1956.

7. Kyle Hopkins, "Palin Era Begins at Inauguration: Governor Sworn In, Goes to Work Today on Natural Gas Pipeline," *Anchorage Daily News,* December 5, 2006.

8. Jack Roderick, *Crude Dreams: A Personal History of Oil and Politics in Alaska* (Fairbanks: Epicenter, 1997), 213.

9. John M. Sweet, *Discovery at Prudhoe Bay* (Blaine, WA: Hancock House, 2008), 202.

10. Sweet, *Discovery,* 207.

11. "Alaska Strikes It Rich," *U.S. News & World Report,* December 9, 1968, 50.

12. Roderick, *Crude Dreams,* 225.

13. Jack Roderick, interview by Amanda Coyne, 2010.

14. Lawrence E. Davies, "$900 Million Is Bid for Oil Leases in Alaska," *New York Times*, September 11, 1969.

15. Doug O'Harra, "Death of the Bard," *Anchorage Daily News,* July 15, 1990.

16. Davies, "$900 Million."

17. Marie Drake, "Alaska's Flag," a poem written in 1935 and adopted as Alaska's state song in 1959.

18. Roderick, *Crude Dreams,* 279–280.

19. Davies, "$900 Million Is Bid."

20. Kay Fanning with Katherine Field Stephen, *Kay Fanning's Alaska Story* (Kenmore, WA: Epicenter, 2006), 128.

21. Hopkins, "Palin Era."

CHAPTER 2

1. David Whitney, "Formative Years: Stevens's Life Wasn't Easy Growing Up in the Depression with a Divided Family," *Anchorage Daily News,* August 6, 1994.

2. Bill Allen and Ted Stevens, telephone call monitored by FBI surveillance, October 18, 2006.

3. Whitney, "Formative Years."

4. Ibid.

5. David Whitney, "The Road North: Needing Work, Stevens Borrows $600, Answers Call to Alaska," *Anchorage Daily News,* August 9, 1994.

6. Donald Craig Mitchell, *Take My Land, Take My Life: The Story of Congress's Historic Settlement of Alaska Native Land Claims, 1960–1971* (Fairbanks: University of Alaska Press, 2001), 222.

7. Whitney, "Road North."

8. Ted Stevens, interview by Maclyn P. Burg, Dwight D. Eisenhower Library, October 6, 1977.

9. Clause-M. Naske, *Bob Bartlett of Alaska* (Fairbanks: University of Alaska Press, 1979), 201–228.

10. Clause-M. Naske, *Ernest Gruening: Alaska's Greatest Governor* (Fairbanks: University of Alaska Press, 2004), 1–24.

11. James A. Wickersham diary [05], January 1 to May 15, 1903, Alaska State Library.

12. Naske, *Bob Bartlett of Alaska,* 40–49.

13. Ibid., 223.

14. Naske, *Ernest Gruening,* 215–216.

15. Michael Carey, "Stevens's Rise to Political Power Started Out Slowly," *Anchorage Daily News,* September 4, 2007.

16. Herman E. Slotnick, "The 1964 Election in Alaska," *Western Political Quarterly* 18, no. 2 (1965): 439–442.

17. Mitchell, *Take My Land,* 235.

18. "Bob Bartlett," *Anchorage Daily Times,* December 12, 1968.

19. Gregg Erickson, "Ranking Alaska's Governors," *Anchorage Daily News*, September 15, 2008.

20. Malcolm B. Roberts, *The Wit and Wisdom of Wally Hickel* (Anchorage: Searchers, 1994), 44.

21. Mitchell, *Take My Land,* 235.

22. Ibid., 237–238.

23. Ibid., 238–242.

24. Jack Roderick, interview by Amanda Coyne, 2010.

25. "Alaska: Rush for Riches on the Great Pipeline," *Time,* June 2, 1975.

26. Michael Rogers, "The Dark Side of the Earth: Alaska Faces the Facts: Nothing, Not Even Black Gold, Comes for Free," *Rolling Stone,* May 1975.

27. Dermot Cole, *Amazing Pipeline Stories* (Fairbanks: Epicenter, 1997).

28. Rogers, "Dark Side," 128–130.

29. Ibid.

30. Joe McGinniss, *Going to Extremes* (1980; Kenmore, WA: Epicenter, 2010), 221.

31. Jack Roderick, interview by Amanda Coyne, 2010.

32. Barb Mee, *Senator Ted and Mee* (Anchorage: BAM, 2010), 51.

CHAPTER 3

1. Lewis Lapham, "Alaska: Politicians and Natives, Money and Oil," *Harper's,* May 1970.

2. Malcolm Roberts, interview by Amanda Coyne, February 2011.

3. Sam Howe Verhove, "To Alaska's Big Dreamers, No Bridge Is Too Far," *Los Angeles Times,* August 7, 2006.

4. George Bryson, "Sometimes a Great Notion," *Anchorage Daily News,* December 17, 1989.

5. Mike Gravel Papers, University of Alaska, Alaska and Polar Regions Collections, Elmer E. Rasmuson Library.

6. Bryson, "Sometimes a Great Notion."

7. Darcy Denton Davies, *Alaska State Funded Agricultural Projects and Policy: Have They Been a Success?* (University of Alaska, Agricultural and Forestry Experiment Station, May 2007).

8. Ginny Fay, "A History of Alaska's Mega Projects," *EcoSystems: Economic and Ecological Research,* June 2003.

9. John Strohmeyer, *Extreme Conditions: Big Oil and the Transformation of Alaska* (Anchorage: Cascade, 1997), 101.

10. Strohmeyer, *Extreme Conditions,* 101.

11. Tom Kizzia, "A Tale of Two Terminals," *Anchorage Daily News,* November 17, 1989.

12. Fay, "History of Alaska's Mega Projects."

13. Ibid.

14. Neil Davis, *Energy/Alaska* (Fairbanks: University of Alaska Press, 1984).

15. Jay Hammond, *Tales of Alaska's Bush Rat Governor* (Fairbanks: Epicenter, 1994), 265.

16. Malcolm B. Roberts, ed., *The Wit and Wisdom of Wally Hickel* (Anchorage: Searchers, 1994), 43.

17. Hammond, *Tales of Alaska's Bush Rat Governor,* 254.

18. Matthew Berman, *Changing Alaska's Oil and Gas Production Taxes: Issues and Consequences* (University of Alaska, Institute of Social and Economic Research, April 2006).

19. Alaska Legislative Council, Oil and Gas Hearings before the House and Senate Finance Committee, February 19–20, 1968.

20. Chuck Logsdon, interview by Amanda Coyne, May 2011.

CHAPTER 4

1. Addie Chancellor, letter to U.S. District Court Judge John W. Sedwick, September 14, 2009.

2. Ibid.

3. Marilu Waybourn, *Homesteads to Boomtown: A Pictorial History of Farmington, New Mexico, and Surrounding Areas* (Virginia Beach: Donning, 2001), 13.

4. Bill Allen, testimony given at the federal corruption trial of Pete Kott in Anchorage, Alaska, September 12, 2007.

5. "The Lost Frontier: A North Slope Gusher Brings a 'Pointy Shoe' Invasion," *Seattle Times,* September 24, 1989.

6. Harold Heinz, interview by Amanda Coyne, February 2011.

7. Richard Mauer, "VECO Chairman's Ties to Arco Go Back 15 Years," *Anchorage Daily News,* December 9, 1984.

8. *International Directory of Company Histories,* vol. 7 (New York: St. James, 1993).

9. Paul Laird, "Don't Mess with Bill," *Alaska Business Monthly,* November 1987.

10. James Love, "Oil Money in Alaska Politics," *Multinational Monitor* 5, no. 8 (1984).

11. Michael Carey, "Dankworth Much More Than a Stereotype," *Anchorage Daily News,* December 27, 2008.

12. Transcript, meeting of the Alaska Public Offices Commission with Bill Allen, John Kerrigan, Ed Dankworth, and Theda Pittman, March 1983.

13. Love, "Oil Money."

14. Richard Mauer, "Allen to Open a New Chapter in Powerful Alaska Career," *Anchorage Daily News*, November 21, 1989.

15. Marybeth Holleman, Oliver Scott Goldsmith, and Linda Leask, *Review of Social and Economic Conditions,* February 1988, May 1988, April 1989, June 1989.

16. Hal Spencer and Patti Epler, "Senate Stands Firm on Keeping Tax Cut for Oil Producers," *Anchorage Daily News*, April 16, 1987.

17. Patti Epler, "Declining Prices Put Pressure on Alaska Oil Drillers," *Anchorage Daily News*, February 9, 1986.

18. Spencer and Epler, "Senate Stands Firm."

19. Craig Medred, "Once Oil Hit the Water, the Cause Was Lost," *Anchorage Daily News*, September 17, 1989.

20. Hal Bernton, "VECO Reports $460 Million Spent on Spill," *Anchorage Daily News*, September 8, 1989.

21. David Postman, "Repeal of Oil Tax Break Gets New Life," *Anchorage Daily News*, April 20, 1989.

22. David Postman, "Senate Reverses on ELF, Cuts Oil Tax Break: Cowper Signs Bill," *Anchorage Daily News*, May 9, 1989.

23. Carey, "Dankworth Much More."

24. Doug O'Harra, "Death of the Bard," *Anchorage Daily News*, July 15, 1990.

CHAPTER 5

1. E. W. Piper, "Robertson's 'Green Troops' Prepare for the Long Haul," *Anchorage Daily News,* April 28, 1988.

2. David Postman, "Newcomers Rock GOP Convention: Abortion Opponents Want Candidates to Toe Party Line," *Anchorage Daily News*, March 30, 1990.

3. Chuck and Sally Heath, interview by Amanda Coyne, fall 2007.

4. Chuck and Sally Heath, interview by Amanda Coyne, August 2006.

5. Jim Holycross, interview by Amanda Coyne, September 2008.

6. Louise Potter, *Early Days in Wasilla* (reprint; Wasilla: Alaska Books, 2002), 85–98.

7. From a series of interviews with Amanda Coyne from 2006 to 2008.

8. Wasilla city councilman Nick Carney, resolution no. wr97-09, prepared for the Wasilla city council.

9. Walter J. Hickel, *Crisis in the Commons: The Alaska Solution* (Oakland, CA: Institute for Contemporary Studies/Institute of the North, 2002), 196.

10. David Postman, "Third Party Opens Way for Hickel-Coghill Team," *Anchorage Daily News,* September 21, 1990.

11. John McPhee, *Coming into the Country* (New York: Farrar, Straus & Giroux, 1976), 313.

12. Wally Hickel, interview by Tony Hopfinger, August 13, 2008.

13. From a series of interviews with Amanda Coyne from 2006 to 2008

14. "Candidates Answer the Questions," *Mat-Su Valley Frontiersman,* September 13, 1996.

15. Interview by Amanda Coyne, September 2008.

16. John C. Stein, "New Roads," *Mat-Su Valley Frontiersman,* February 12, 1997.

17. Editorial, *Mat-Su Valley Frontiersman,* March 7, 1997.

18. David Whitney, "Stevens Says He'll Run If State Pledges Support," *Anchorage Daily News,* January 21, 1988.

19. Paul Kane, "Palin's Small Alaska Town Secured Big Federal Funds," *Washington Post,* September 2, 2008.

20. Irl Stambaugh, interview by Amanda Coyne, September 2008.

CHAPTER 6

1. Jack Roderick, interview by Amanda Coyne, winter 2010.

2. Cliff Groh, "Live from the Ted Stevens Trial—Day Seven," alaskacorruption.blog spot.com, October 1, 2008.

3. Tony Hopfinger, "Bill & Ted's Excellent Adventure," *Anchorage Press,* January 2, 2008.

4. Dave Anderson, interviews by Tony Hopfinger and Amanda Coyne, October 2007–July 2009.

5. Rick Halford, interview by Tony Hopfinger, November 2007.

6. Anderson, interview by Tony Hopfinger, November 2007.

7. Clem Tillion, interview by Tony Hopfinger, August 2008.

8. Stephanie Martin and Alexandra Hill, *The Changing Economic Status of Alaska Natives, 1970–2007* (University of Alaska, Institute of Social and Economic Research, 2009).

9. Citizens Against Government Waste, *Congressional Pig Book,* 2003–2006.

10. State of Alaska, Division of Public Assistance, *How to Use Food Stamps.*

11. Jennifer LaFleur and Michael Grabell, "Villages Testify to Disparity in Benefits Alaska Native Corporations Provide," Pro Publica, March 17, 2001.

12. U.S. Senate Committee on Homeland Security and Government Affairs, Subcommittee on Contract Oversight, July 2009.

13. Richard Mauer, "Ben Stevens' Secret Fish Deal," *Anchorage Daily News,* September 18, 2005.

14. Liz Ruskin, "Stevens Irate over Suit Query," *Anchorage Daily News,* September 10, 2005.

15. Jill Burke and Craig Medred, "Ted Stevens' Alaska," *Alaska Dispatch,* August 10, 2010.

16. Richard Mauer, "Charity Work Paid Well for Ben Stevens," *Anchorage Daily News,* July 7, 2002.

17. Barb Mee, *Senator Ted and Mee* (Anchorage: BAM, 2010), 63.

18. Tony Hopfinger, "The Master Builders," *Anchorage Press,* August 14, 2003.

19. Joel Gay, "Stevens Calls Investments Ethical," *Anchorage Daily News,* December 20, 2003.

20. Liz Ruskin, "Defense Contractors Come to Hook a Senator, Fish," *Anchorage Daily News,* July 4, 2003.

21. Liz Ruskin, "Stevens Made a Million in Profit," *Anchorage Daily News,* June 15, 2005.

22. Brandon Loomis, "Power Ritual: Local Group Says Outsiders Decide River's Fate: Kenai River Classic Called a Venue for Influence Peddling," *Anchorage Daily News,* July 7, 2007.

23. Don Hunter, "Stevens Humbled by Honor: Senator Says Airport Memories Happy, Sad," *Anchorage Daily News,* July 10, 2000.

24. Hunter, "Stevens Humbled."

25. David Whitney, "Mr. Stevens Goes to Washington," *UCLA Magazine,* Winter 2000.

26. "Alaska's Economy: The Trend Is Disturbing," editorial, *Anchorage Daily News,* December 21, 1999.

CHAPTER 7

1. Dave Anderson, interview by Tony Hopfinger, November 2007.

2. Jo Thomas, "The Missing Chapter in the Bush Bio: A Modest Summer in Alaska," *New York Times*, October 21, 2000.

3. Tony Hopfinger, "Palin Got Help from Corrupt Oilman During Her First Run for State Office," *Alaska Dispatch*, September 4, 2008.

4. Kirsten Deacon and Dave Anderson, interviews by Amanda Coyne and Tony Hopfinger, 2007–2008.

5. Amanda Bohman, "Wasilla Mayor Shines at Forum," *Fairbanks Daily News-Miner*, August 7, 2002.

6. Lisa Demer, "BP Casts Anchorage Lawmaker Adrift," *Anchorage Daily News*, October 17, 1996.

7. Don Hunter and Ben Spiess, "Ulmer's Gun Hard to Hide," *Anchorage Daily News*, July 22, 2002.

8. Ben Spiess, "Ulmer Outlines Tax Plan," *Anchorage Daily News*, September 5, 2002.

9. Frank Murkowski, interview by Amanda Coyne, February 2011.

10. "Maverick Mom," editorial, *Anchorage Daily News*, January 30, 2006.

CHAPTER 8

1. Pat Forgey, "Federal Probe Has Critics Asking Why State Didn't Act First," *Juneau Empire*, July 1, 2007.

2. Jim Clark, interview by Amanda Coyne, November 2010.

3. Gavel to Gavel Archives, Confirmation Hearing: AK Oil and Gas Conservation Commission-Sarah H. Palin, Randy Ruedrich, February 26, 2003.

4. Jim Clark, interview by Amanda Coyne, November 2010.

5. Bridget Boehm and Terry Shurtleff, interview by Amanda Coyne, 2007.

6. Terry Shurtleff and Dennis Millhouse, interview by Amanda Coyne, 2007; Statement by Tina Arndt, January 12, 2007, and statement by Vince Blomfield, December 27, 2006, taken on behalf of attorneys representing Josef Boehm.

7. Liz Ruskin, "Senator's Campaign Gets VIP Help," *Anchorage Daily News*, September 6, 2003.

8. Sarah Palin, email, November 14, 2003.

9. Palin, email, November 14, 2003.

10. Jim Clark, interview by Amanda Coyne, November 2010.

11. Tom Kizzia, "Push for Private Prison Was Downfall," *Anchorage Daily News*, August 12, 2008.

12. Bob Bundy, interview by Tony Hopfinger, October 2007.

13. Statement by Vince Blomfield, December 27, 2006, taken on behalf of attorneys representing Josef Boehm.

14. Anchorage Police Department, incident report, January 2, 2008.

15. "Allen Teen Sex Inquiry Reopened," *Anchorage Daily News*, February 3, 2008; Anchorage Police Department, sexual abuse of a minor report, February 12, 2004; Lisa Moore, interview by Kevin Vandergriff, John Eckstein, and Frank Russo.

16. Bambi Tyree, interview by Frank Russo and John Eckstein, October 28, 2004.

17. Anchorage Police Department, sexual abuse of a minor report; Lisa Moore, interview by Kevin Vandergriff, John Eckstein, and Frank Russo, February 12, 2004.

18. Jill Burke, "Child Sex-Trafficker Wanted Bill Allen As Trial Witness," *Alaska Dispatch*, November 8, 2009.

19. Dave Anderson, interview by Tony Hopfinger, 2007–2008; Heather Resz, interview by Tony Hopfinger, 2008.

CHAPTER 9

1. Timothy Egan, "Built with Steel, Perhaps, but Greased with Pork," *New York Times*, April 10, 2004.

2. Egan, "Built with Steel."

3. "Senators Clash over 'Bridge to Nowhere,'" *Seattle Times*, October 21, 2005.

4. Scott Goldsmith, *How Vulnerable Is Alaska's Economy to Reduced Federal Spending?* (University of Alaska, Institute of Social and Economic Research, July 2008).

5. Goldsmith, *How Vulnerable Is Alaska's Economy?*

6. Michael Carey, "Tough Time for Ted," *Anchorage Daily News*, November 28, 2005.

7. Sean Cockerham, "Oil Industry's Good Fortune Fuels Calls for Higher Taxes," *Anchorage Daily News*, June 27, 2005.

8. Sarah Palin, "Odd Couple's Motivation Not Political," *Anchorage Daily News*, December 17, 2004.

9. Sean Cockerham, "Jet Plan Will Fly, Governor Declares," *Anchorage Daily News*, April 21, 2005.

10. Marty Rutherford, interview by Amanda Coyne, February 2011.

11. Tony Knowles, Pat Pourchot, and Marty Rutherford, interviews by Tony Hopfinger, 2008.

12. Daniel Johnston, interviews by Amanda Coyne, 2010–2011.

13. Jim Clark, interview by Amanda Coyne, 2010.

14. Marty Rutherford, interview by Amanda Coyne, February 2011.

15. Kay Cushman and Kristen Nelson, *Sarah Takes on Big Oil* (Anchorage: PNA Publishing, 2008), 35.

16. Don Hunter, "Gathering Supports 'Magnificent 7,'" *Anchorage Daily News*, October 29, 2005.

17. Tony Hopfinger, "Bill & Ted's Excellent Adventure," *Anchorage Press,* January 2, 2008.

18. Richard Mauer and Lisa Demer, "Key Players Contest FBI Whistle-blower Allegations," *Anchorage Daily News*, February 15, 2009.

19. Mary Beth Kepner, interview by Tony Hopfinger, 2008.

CHAPTER 10

1. FBI video surveillance tapes of Bill Allen and Rick Smith in Suite 604 at Baranof Hotel, March 4, 2006.

2. U.S. Justice Department, indictment against Peter Kott and Bruce Weyhrauch, May 3, 2007.

3. Matt Volz, "From Barroom Joke to Federal Warrants," Associated Press, July 30, 2008.

4. Fred Dyson, interview by Amanda Coyne, 2011.

5. Richard Richtmyer, "Analysts See Oil's Gain, Not Tax Pain," *Anchorage Daily News*, March 29, 2006.

6. Daniel Johnston, interview by Amanda Coyne, 2010.

7. Sarah Palin, "Oil, Gas Deal Should Show 'Maximum Benefit for All Alaskans,'" *Mat-Su Valley Frontiersman*, March 19, 2006.

8. FBI video surveillance of Vic Kohring, Bill Allen, and Rick Smith in Suite 604 at Baranof Hotel, Juneau, March 30, 2006.

9. Kyle Hopkins, "Convicted Lawmaker Spends Last Hours of Freedom on the Glenn," *Anchorage Daily News,* July 1, 2008.

10. FBI video surveillance of conversations between Pete Kott, Bill Allen, Rick Smith, and Bob McManus in Suite 604 at Baranof Hotel, May 7, 2006.

11. Matt Volz, "Gas Contract Gives Oil Firms Easy Out," Associated Press, May 12, 2006.

12. Sharon and Bob Benson, interview by Amanda Coyne, 2007.

13. Kyle Hopkins, "200 Rally to Voice Oil, Gas Concerns," *Anchorage Daily News,* May 6, 2006.

14. Jim Bowles and Bill Allen, FBI wiretapped phone call, June 6, 2006.

15. Pete Kott, Rick Smith, and Bill Allen, FBI wiretapped phone call, June 8, 2006.

16. FBI video surveillance of conversations between Pete Kott, Bill Allen, and Rick Smith in Suite 604 at Baranof Hotel, June 8, 2006.

CHAPTER 11

1. Tony Hopfinger and Michael Isikoff, "The Veep's Pipeline Push," *Newsweek*, August 23, 2008.

2. Brandon Loomis, "Bruins' Brush with Color," *Anchorage Daily News*, May 20, 2007.

3. David Dittman, interview by Amanda Coyne, Winter 2011.

4. Sarah Palin, interview by Amanda Coyne, August 2006.

5. Laura Mitchell Harris, "Campaign Heats Up," *Mat-Su Valley Frontiersman,* September 25, 1996.

6. Sarah Palin, interview by Amanda Coyne, August 2006.

7. Palin, interview by Amanda Coyne, August 2006.

8. Mary Pemberton, "Oil Officials Call 22.5% Rate the Nation's Highest," Associated Press, August 12, 2006.

9. Sheila Toomey, "Alaska Ear," *Anchorage Daily News*, August 27, 2006.

CHAPTER 12

1. Fred Dyson, interview by Amanda Coyne, 2011.

2. Telephone conversation between Bill Allen and Ted Stevens, FBI surveillance report, October 18, 2006.

3. Sarah Palin, *Going Rogue: An American Life* (New York: HarperCollins, 2009), 2–3.

4. Amanda Coyne, "What Does Andrew Halcro Want?" *Anchorage Press,* November 2006.

5. Frank Murkowski and Jim Clark, interview by Amanda Coyne, 2010–2011.

6. Marty Rutherford, interview by Amanda Coyne, February 2011.

7. Pat Galvin, interview by Amanda Coyne, 2011.

8. Palin administration emails, received by Bill Dedman, msnbc.com, and compiled by Crivella West, January 25, 2010.

CHAPTER 13

1. Nelson D. Schwartz, "Behind High Oil and Gas Prices," *Fortune,* March 30, 2007.

2. Pat Galvin, interview by Amanda Coyne, 2011.

3. Lyrics by Alaska state congressman Mike Doogan, March 2007.

4. Gene Johnson, "Palin: Iraq War 'a Task That Is from God,'" Associated Press, September 3, 2008.

5. Sarah Palin, emails to Tom Irwin, March 11, 2008; Sarah Palin to Sean Parnell, August 29, 2007; Tom Irwin to Sarah Palin, July 12, 2008.

6. Kay Cashman and Kirsten Nelson, *Sarah Takes On Big Oil* (Anchorage: PNA Publishing, 2008), 136.

7. Tom Kizzia and Sabra Ayers, "Kohring's State House Committee Post Pulled," *Anchorage Daily News*, May 5, 2007.

8. Pat Galvin, interview by Amanda Coyne, 2011.

9. Sabra Ayres, "100 Days in Charge Are Sweet for Palin," *Anchorage Daily News*, March 13, 2007.

10. Jane Mayer, "The Insiders: How John McCain Came to Pick Sarah Palin," *The New Yorker*, October 27, 2008

11. Mayer, "Insiders."

CHAPTER 14

1. Mary Beth Kepner, interview by Tony Hopfinger, 2008.

2. Pat Galvin, interview by Amanda Coyne, 2011.

3. "Motion to Dismiss or, in the Alternative, for Discovery." *United States v. Peter Kott,* September 24, 2009.

4. "Motion to Dismiss."

5. Sarah Palin, "Governor Palin Responds to Kott Verdicts," press release, September 2007.

6. Gregg Erickson, "Climate for Tax Hike Was Unexpected," *Anchorage Daily News*, December 2, 2007; Alaska Department of Revenue, *Oil and Gas Production Tax: State's Report to the Legislature,* January 18, 2011.

7. Steve Quinn, "Oil Industry Clout Pushed Back by Palin, Legislators," Associated Press, November 19, 2007.

8. "Palin Flies High As Reformer," *Anchorage Daily News*, December 27, 2007.

9. Tony Hopfinger, "Pipe Dreams," *Newsweek,* June 2, 2008.

10. Hopfinger, "Pipe Dreams."

11. Lyrics by Paul Laird. Sung at the joint meeting of the Alaska House Rules Standing Committee Subcommittee on AGIA and the Senate Special Committee on Energy, June 2, 2008.

12. Chuck and Sally Heath, interview by Amanda Coyne, fall 2007.

13. Bill White, "Todd Palin Campaigned Years to Get Trooper Fired," *Anchorage Daily News,* October 8, 2008.

14. Governor Sarah Palin, statement on the indictment of Senator Ted Stevens, July 29, 2008.

15. Jeffrey Toobin, "Casualties of Justice," *New Yorker,* January 3, 2011.

CHAPTER 15

1. Wally Hickel, "Alaskans Can Rise Above Petty Politics, Hateful Acts," *Anchorage Daily News*, September 27, 2009.

2. Ivan Moore Research, press release, September 23, 2008.

3. Public Policy Polling, December 28, 2010.

4. Tony Hopfinger, "Another Sexual Abuse Claim Threatens to Taint Star Witness in Stevens' Trial," *Alaska Dispatch,* September 17, 2008.

5. Mary Beth Kepner, interview by Tony Hopfinger, 2008.

6. Jill Burke, Tony Hopfinger, and Amanda Coyne, "Kott Alleges Prosecutorial Misconduct," *Alaska Dispatch,* September 25, 2009.

7. Rocky Williams, interview by Tony Hopfinger, April 2008.

8. Chad Joy, whistleblower affidavit filed in U.S. District Court, January 14, 2009.

9. Chad Joy, whistleblower affidavit.

10. Erika Bolstad and Richard Mauer, "Stevens Prosecutor: Veco a 'Handyman Service,'" *Anchorage Daily News,* September 25, 2008.

11. Matt Apuzzo and Tom Hays, "Stevens Blames Contractor in Gift-Giving Trial," Associated Press, September 25, 2008.

12. Paul Courson, "Senator's Request for Bill Mere Window-Dressing, Witness Says," CNN, October 1, 2008.

13. Richard Mauer and Erika Bolstad, "Judge Limits Evidence, Won't Halt Trial," *Anchorage Daily News,* October 8, 2008.

14. Telephone conversation between Bill Allen and Ted Stevens, FBI surveillance report, October 18, 2006.

15. Telephone conversation between Bill Allen and Ted Stevens.

16. Stephen Branchflower, *Report to the Legislative Council,* October 10, 2008.

17. Thomas Van Flein, statement in response to Branchflower report, October 10, 2008.

18. Lisa Demer, "Palin: Troopergate Report Cleared Her of Wrongdoing," *Anchorage Daily News,* October 11, 2008.

19. Sheryl Gay Stolberg, "Free to Be His Own Buckley," *New York Times*, October 17, 2008.

20. "Sarah Palin Rallies in Bangor," WABI TV (Bangor, Maine), October 16, 2008.

CHAPTER 16

1. Tom Kizzia, "Natives Claim Palin Neglects Issues," *Anchorage Daily News*, October 19, 2008.

2. Julie Kitka, commentary, *Anchorage Daily News*, September 27, 2008.

3. Cliff Groh, "Will the Lion Roar? Live from the Ted Stevens Trial, Day 15," alaskacorruption.blogspot.com, October 15, 2008.

4. Cliff Groh, "The Reckoning," alaskacorruption.blogspot.com, October 16, 2008.

5. Richard Mauer and Erika Bolstad, "Sen. Stevens Takes the Stand," *Anchorage Daily News*, October 17, 2008.

6. Brent Kendall, "Stevens Struggles in Cross-examination," *Wall Street Journal,* October 17, 2008.

7. Richard Mauer and Erika Bolstad, "Testimony Ends in Stevens Trial," *Anchorage Daily News*, October 20, 2008.

8. Nick Tucker, "A Village in Peril," *Alaska Dispatch,* January 14, 2009.

EPILOGUE

1. Jill Burke, "Joe Miller's Paranoid Attempt to Overthrow the Alaska Republican Party," *Alaska Dispatch,* October 31, 2010.

2. Sean Cockerham and Kyle Hopkins, "Miller on Verge of Toppling Murkowski," *Anchorage Daily News,* August 25, 2010.

3. Lisa Murkowski, interview by Amanda Coyne, April 2011.

4. William Yardley, "News Editor Detained by Security Guards for Alaska Senate Candidate," *New York Times,* October 18, 2010.

INDEX

Abortion, 62–63, 72, 73, 89, 103, 115, 183,
185, 219
Accountability
Kingdom Palin, 74
Palin, 221
ACES. *See* Alaska's Clear and Equitable
Share
AGIA. *See* Alaska Gasline Inducement Act
Agnew, Spiro, 27–28
AIP. *See* Alaska Independence Party
Alaska, 250
Arctic area, 36, 261 (*see also* Arctic
National Wildlife Refuge)
area of, xviii, 4, 11
attorney general office, 220–221, 222
conquest of, 26
constitution/constitutional convention,
xviii, 3, 4, 5, 6, 7, 8, 9, 10, 42, 45, 73,
165 (*See also* Palin, Sarah: and Alaska
constitution)
Department of Fish and Game, 166–167
Department of Law, 220
Department of Natural Resources (DNR),
137–138, 139, 140, 141, 187, 188
failed projects in, 40
governors in, 111, 244
House of Representatives, xiii, 22, 84,
162, 210, 217
legislative special sessions, 206, 207, 211,
217
modernization of, 223
Oil and Gas Conservation Commission,
114–115, 116, 118–122, 172, 177, 259
Personnel Board, 221, 222, 245
population, 29, 37, 93
Public Offices Commission (APOC), 113,
122, 155

Revenue Department, 188
rural areas, 86–87, 88, 107, 237–238,
243, 246–247
Senate Finance Committee, 54, 59
sovereignty of, 140
springtime in, 199
state budget, 15, 54, 55, 56, 105, 107,
136, 186, 220
statehood for, 3, 6, 11, 19–20, 27, 70,
223, 244
state income, 32, 41, 44
state song, 14–15
U.S. Attorney's office in, 207
winters in, 7–8, 199–200, 242 (*see also*
Temperatures)
Alaska, University of, 3, 4, 37, 38
Alaska Brooks mountain range, 25
Alaska Dispatch, 145, 206, 225, 257, 259
Alaska Federation of Natives, 238
Alaska Gasline Inducement Act (AGIA),
189–190, 193, 197, 200, 202–203,
210, 212, 213, 217, 246, 251, 254
Alaska Highway, 28
Alaska Independence Party (AIP), 6, 69–70
Alaska Legislative Council, 216, 221, 222,
233, 234
Alaska Natives, 25–27, 34, 36, 37, 61, 112,
246–248
Alaska Native Claims Settlement Act, 27,
87, 244
and Sarah Palin, 238
See also Corporations: Alaska Native
corporations
Alaska Permanent Fund, xvi, 42–43, 46, 93,
95, 101, 131, 186, 244, 261
Alaska Railroad, 92
Alaska Right to Life, 183

Alaska's Clear and Equitable Share (ACES), 207, 210, 211, 246
Alaska State Fair (2006), 182–183, 184
Alcoholism, 199
Allen, Bill, xiii–xv, xvii, xx, 3, 48, 49–55, 56–57, 70, 79, 84, 85, 86, 92, 94, 95, 99–100, 102–103, 113, 115, 134, 138, 142–145, 147–152, 154–156, 179–180, 201, 207, 211, 238, 261
   alleged sexual misconduct of, x, 124, 125, 127, 145, 181, 182, 208, 225, 226, 231–232, 249, 250
   and Ben Stevens, 150
   children of, 181
   downfall of, 176
   guilty plea for bribery, 49, 59, 201, 249
   and Jim Bowles, 162–163
   meeting with FBI agents (2006), 181–182
   motorcycle accident in 2001, 59, 230
   and natural gas pipeline, 142
   at Pete Kott's trial, 208–209
   and "Settlement Agreement and Release of all Claims" document, 144
   sisters of, 49–50
   and Ted Stevens, 81–82, 165, 182, 216, 229, 233 (see also Stevens, Ted: "Ted's cabin" remodeling)
   and Ted Stevens's trial, 230–233, 239, 240, 248–249
   See also VECO Corporation
Allen, Mark, 83, 224
Alliance, The (group), 213
Alternative energy, 55
Alyeska Pipeline Service Company, 29, 31, 138
Alyeska Ski Resort, 79
Anchorage, 7, 13–15, 24, 29, 37–38, 39, 100, 116, 124, 127–128, 168, 183, 221, 223, 243
   Anchorage Fur Rendezvous Festival, 195
   Hotel Captain Cook in, 24
   Kodiak Café in 180
   Pioneer Bar in, 184, 233
   population, 55
   ski center in, 89
   Ted Stevens Anchorage International Airport, 76, 92, 241, 242
Anchorage Daily News, 15, 52, 56, 59, 75, 88, 131, 177, 197, 203, 211, 235

"Voice of the Times" columns in, 102, 172
Anchorage Daily Times, 23, 59
Anchorage Nordic Ski Association, 88
Anderson, Bob, 11
Anderson, Dave, 79–80, 82–83, 84, 85, 99, 102, 127–128, 142, 205, 228, 232
   letter to Bill Allen's lawyer, 143–144
   and "Settlement Agreement and Release of all Claims" document, 144
Animal House at Baranof Hotel (Juneau), xiv, 144, 145, 147, 150, 154, 158–159, 164, 180, 201, 208, 209
Animals, 26, 37, 40, 67, 182. See also Bears; Caribou; Moose; Whales; Wolves
ANWR. See Arctic National Wildlife Refuge
APOC. See Alaska Public Offices Commission
ARCO. See Atlantic Richfield Company
Arctic Circle, 36
Arctic National Wildlife Refuge (ANWR), 86, 93, 101–102, 104, 108, 112, 130
Arrests, 201. See also Convictions (criminal)
Assembly of God church (Wasilla), 63, 66, 219
Atlantic Richfield Company (ARCO), 11–12, 25, 43, 51–52, 53, 62, 85, 94
Aurora borealis, 88

Bailey, Frank, 190
Bankruptcies, 53
Banks, 55, 94
Barbados, 100, 127, 149, 163
Barley, 38, 39–40
Barnes, Fred, 203–204
Barnes, Ramona, 84
Barrymore, Drew, 83
Bars, 29, 34, 55, 57, 63, 68, 74
Bartlett, Bob, 6–7, 15, 16, 20, 23, 109, 250
   health problems of, 21–22
   obituary for, 23
Bears, 28, 61, 83, 112, 166–167, 216
Beck, Larry Allan, 13–14, 59–60
Begich, Mark, 217, 224, 243
Begich, Nick, 224
Benson, Sharon and Don, 159–160
Bering Sea, 88
Bearing Strait, 24
Bethel, 237
Biden, Joe, 254

Big Oil. *See under* Oil
Binkley, John, 58, 109, 162, 167–168
Birds, 28, 37, 157
Blackwater, 87
Bloggers, 193, 245, 246, 248, 255, 260
Bodyguards, 256
Boehm, Josef, 116–118, 124, 126, 239
Bolton, John, 204
Bork, Robert, 204
Bottini, Joe, 125, 208
Bowles, Jim, 141, 162–163, 164
BP. *See* British Petroleum
Bribery, xvii, 59, 83, 145, 149, 151, 164,
    201, 207. *See also* Corruption
Brickley, Adam, 193
Bridge to Nowhere, 129–130, 224
British Petroleum (BP), xiv, 12, 15, 25, 43,
    51, 53, 90, 94, 106, 132, 133, 134,
    138, 142, 147, 153, 159, 166, 176,
    179, 190, 198, 207, 212
  and Conoco Phillips, 261
  work camp at Prudhoe Bay, 29–30
Buckalew, Seaborn, 10
Buckley, Chris and William, Jr., 235
Budgets. *See* Alaska: state budget
Bumpus, Charles, 66–67
Bundy, Bob, 124, 181
Burke, Jill, 257
Bush, George W., 101, 108, 203, 214
  Bush-Cheney 2000 election campaign, 59

Cambodia, 35
Campaign contributions, 53, 54–55, 69, 83,
    90, 100, 103, 113, 123, 149, 179, 231
Canada, 169–170, 187, 212, 261
Canneries, 5–6
Carey, Michael, 54, 59, 131
Caribou, 5, 28, 113
Carr, Jesse, 30
Carr-Gottstein Foods, 93
Carter, Jimmy, 132
Carter, Mary, 63–64
Chancellor, Addie, 49–50
Chaney, Dick, 59, 119, 165–166
Chávez, Hugo, 213, 248
Chennault, Claire Lee, 18
Christian Right, 63, 69, 72, 73, 103, 105.
    See also Religion; Republican Party:
    Christian Republicans
Chugach Mountains, 62, 182

Citgo, 248
Civil rights, 6, 20
Clark, Jim, 114, 116, 121, 135, 140, 163,
    188, 202
Class, xviii, 124
Climate change, 197, 262
Clinton, Bill, 108
Clinton, Hillary, 195
Coal mining, 70, 135
  coal bed methane development, 120, 121
Cocaine/crack cocaine, 28, 30, 117, 125. *See
    also* Drugs
Coghill, Jack, 10
Collective ownership, xvii, 8, 36, 45
Coming into the Country (McPhee), 70
Competitive advantage, 45, 46
Conoco Phillips, xiv, 53, 94, 132, 133, 134,
    138, 141, 142, 147, 159, 162, 176,
    190, 207, 212
  and BP, 261
Construction boom, xv
Construction unions, 30
Consultants, 44, 139, 157, 201, 204, 240
Convictions, criminal, xv, 29, 67, 209, 210,
    250, 254. *See also* Allen, Bill: guilty plea
    for bribery; Stevens, Ted:
    indictment/conviction of/tossed
    convictions
Cook Inlet, 38, 51, 79, 99, 116
Cordova Coal Party, 70
Corporations, 6, 54, 90, 250
  Alaska Native corporations, 27, 53, 76,
    87, 130, 227
  mergers/acquisitions, 93–94
Corrections Group North, 100
Corrupt Bastards Club, xiv, 149–150, 154,
    183, 207, 220
Corruption, xiv, xvi, xvii, xviii, 3, 9, 10, 15,
    49, 52, 118, 122, 125, 127, 162, 180,
    187, 203, 204, 205, 206, 210, 216,
    222, 226, 229, 251
  arrests concerning, 201 (*see also*
    Convictions, criminal)
  See also Bribery; Corrupt Bastards Club
Couric, Katie, 229
Covich, Susan, 238
Cowper, Steve, 56, 58
Credit card debt, 42, 154
"Cremation of Sam McGee, The" (poem),
    14, 60

Crime, 31, 57, 124, 214, 224. *See also*
    Convictions, criminal
Croft, Eric, 135, 198
Cronyism, xvii
Crosby, Ralph, 90
Culture wars, 183
Curry, Traci L., 177

Dairy farms, 38–39, 40
Dankworth, Ed, 54, 56–57, 58, 59, 83
Deacon, Kirsten, 142–143
Debates, 185
Delta Junction, 40
Demer, Lisa, 235
Democratic Party, 4, 6, 20, 26, 39, 47, 72,
    73, 93, 100, 115, 134, 152, 165, 176,
    197, 216, 220, 221, 248
Denali (The Alaska Gas Pipeline), 212
Denali National Park and Preserve, 38, 216,
    256
Development issues, 16, 20, 22, 24, 27, 31,
    35, 36, 39, 52, 55, 56, 68, 69, 86, 93,
    103, 105, 115, 118, 130, 131, 133,
    139, 165, 198, 213
Dividends. *See* Oil: oil dividend checks
Dixiecrats, 6, 61
DNR. *See* Alaska: Department of Natural
    Resources
Domestic violence, 215
Doogan, Mike, 197
Draft Sarah Palin for Vice President (blog),
    193
Drugs, 117, 123, 124, 126, 151, 173. *See
    also* Cocaine/crack cocaine
Dyson, Fred, 151–152, 179–180

EADS North America, 90
Eagle River, 183
Eagles, 28
Earmarks, 76, 77, 130, 131, 256, 257. *See
    also* Spending: federal spending in Alaska
Earthquakes, 13, 24
Economic growth, 75
Education, 108, 168, 186
Eggleston, Rick, 57–58
Ehrlichman, John, 29
Eisenhower, Dwight, 11, 19, 34
Elections, 103
    1984, 55
    1988, 61–62

2000, 59
2002, 104, 106, 109
2006, 141, 180, 187, 203
2008, 216, 217, 242–243, 256–260
2010, 260
2012, 241
    Wasilla mayoral elections, 67, 72, 77
    write-in campaigns, 258–259
Elmendorf Air Force Base in Anchorage, 89
Emails, 191, 199, 230, 241. *See also under*
    Palin, Sarah
Emmonak village, 246–247
Employment, federal, 92. *See also* Jobs
Endangered species, 35
Entitlements, 259. *See also* Subsidies
Environmental Defense Fund, 27
Environmental issues, 3, 27, 35, 36, 37, 57,
    108, 167
Eskimos. *See* Alaska Natives
Espionage, 12
Evergreen Resources, 120–121
Everybody Loves Whales (film), 83
Exxon Mobil/Exxon, xiv, 25, 43, 53, 57,
    132, 133, 134, 138, 142, 147, 159,
    176, 190, 207, 213. *See also* Oil: *Exxon
    Valdez* oil spill

Fagan, Dan, 169, 170, 184
Faiks, Jan, 56, 57
Fairbanks, 7–9, 19, 24, 29, 30, 31, 223
    North Star borough, 259, 260
Fairbanks Daily News-Miner, 37, 130
Family values, 103
FBI, xiv, xvi, xvii, 15, 48, 122–123, 126,
    127, 128, 143, 144–145, 148, 149,
    150, 152, 165, 180, 189, 201, 205,
    208, 216, 228, 245
    search warrants served by (2006), 182,
    183–184, 233
    See also Allen, Bill: meeting with FBI
    agents (2006); Polar Pen investigation
Fischer, Vic, 10, 39
Fish, Alice, 201
Fishing, 34, 57, 87, 88, 90, 131, 166, 237,
    243–244
    fish traps, 5–6
Fluoridation, 67, 68
Flying Tigers, 18
Food issues, 39–40, 57, 247, 248
Food stamps, 87

Fox News, 255
Fox News Sunday, 204
French, Hollis, 222, 235
Frontiersman newspaper, 67, 74
Fry, Ivy, 190, 191
Fund-raising, 90, 100, 119, 170. *See also*
    Campaign contributions

Gakona, 88
Galvin, Pat, 187, 188–189, 191, 192, 197,
    202
Gays, 89, 185, 219
GCI (General Communications
    Incorporated), 253
George Parks Highway, 29, 223
Gerson, Michael, 203–204
Girdwood, 79, 81, 144, 183, 205, 238
Giuliani, Rudi, 195
Goeke, Jim, 207–208
Gold mines, 108
Goldwater, Barry, 22
Good old boys, 72, 74, 75, 76, 103, 113,
    162, 176, 201, 240
Graham, Franklin, 247
Gravel, Mike, 23, 38
Green, Russell, 18
Gruening, Ernest, 6, 20–21, 22, 23
Guam, 87
Gulf Oil, 15
Guns, 61, 68, 72, 73, 74, 105, 107, 173,
    185
Gwozd, Bill, 213

Halcro, Andrew, 180, 185, 186, 215–216
Haldeman, H. R., 28–29
Halford, Rick, 83–84
Halliburton, 87
Hammond, Jay, 34–36, 38, 41, 42, 43, 47,
    66, 71, 104, 161, 220, 250
Hatch, Orrin, 227
Hawker, Mike, 211
Hazelwood, Joe, 57, 58
Health care, 87, 168, 170–171, 259
Heath, Chuck and Sally, 36, 64–66, 73, 74,
    174, 214–215, 234
Heating fuel, 237, 246, 247, 248
Heat wave, 116
Heimel, Steve, 169
Heinze, Harold, 51, 53, 56–57
Hercules C-130 cargo planes, 12

Hickel, Wally, 10, 23–25, 35, 43, 69,
    70–72, 104, 109, 161, 187, 222–223,
    250, 253
Holder, Eric, 249
Hollings, Fritz, 92
Homer, 91
Hood, Jerry, 109
Hopfinger, Tony, 259–260
Hotel Captain Cook (Anchorage), 24
Housing, 29, 30, 37, 55, 89
Humble Oil (Exxon), 25
Hunting, 237
Hurley, Katie, 10, 73
Hurricane Katrina, 130
Hyde, Leonard, 89–90

Idealism, xvii, 9
Iditarod Trail Sled Dog Race, 195
Infrastructure, 41, 43. *See also*
    Roads/highways
Inouye, Daniel, 92, 227
Iran, 41, 196
Iraq, 87
Irwin, Tom, 141, 187, 188, 199

Jackson, Henry "Scoop," 88
Japan, 25
Jenkins, Paul, 172–173
Jobs, 57, 92, 130, 168, 206. *See also*
    Unemployment
Johnston, Daniel, 139, 153
Joy, Chad, 145, 228–229, 231
Juneau, 7, 33–34, 45, 183. *See also* Animal
    House at Baranof Hotel (Juneau)

Keith, Toby, 116
Kelly, Thomas E., 15
Kenai River, 90, 91
Kennedy, Ted, 243
Kepner, Mary Beth, 145, 150, 181, 206, 226
    complaint against, 228–229, 231
Kerrigan, John, 138
Ketchikan, 104, 129
Kickbacks, 52
Kitka, Julie, 238
Kizzia, Tom, 211
Knowles, Tony, 69, 94–95, 99, 109, 138,
    150, 162, 180, 185, 186–187, 254
Kodiak Café (Anchorage), 180
Kodiak Island launch facility, 91

Kohring, Vic, 154–157, 201, 209, 210,
    249–250, 250–251
Kott, Pete, xiii, xiv, xv, 148–149, 150,
    158–159, 162, 163–164, 201,
    249–250, 250–251
    trial of, 207–209
Kristol, William, 203–204

Large, Bill, 172, 173–174, 175
Leasing. See Oil: oil leasing
Legislators, 44, 46
Leman, Loren, 105–106
Liberalism/liberals, 73, 106, 109, 170, 222
Libertarians, 68–69, 115, 258
Lobbying/lobbyists, xiv, 38, 53, 59, 76, 83,
    90, 100, 102, 105, 113, 149, 153, 158,
    180, 202, 209
Lockheed Martin, 87, 90
Logging, 104, 108
Logsdon, Chuck, 47
Longevity bonus, 112
Lotteries, 39, 199
Lowry, Rich, 204

McAdams, Scott, 258, 260
McCain, John, xix, 71, 92, 183, 195, 204,
    211, 217, 234, 240
McClatchy Company, 88
McManus, Bob, 159
McPhee, John, 70
Magnificent Seven, 141, 187, 188
Magnuson-Stevens Act, 244
Malls, 29, 37, 38, 55, 63
Marsh, Nicholas, 209, 226, 232
Marshall, Steve, 179
Matanuska Maid Dairy, 40
Matanuska Susitna Valley (Mat-Su Valley),
    62, 63, 72, 120, 171, 182
Mauer, Richard, 52
Media, 21, 52, 56, 66, 83, 90, 108, 121,
    122, 126, 135, 189, 205, 216, 224,
    227, 235, 245, 259
    "lamestream" media, 189, 219
    See also Television
Mexico and Its Heritage (Gruening), 20
Military bases, 89, 90
Miller, Joe, 256–260
Minerals, 5, 6, 7, 131, 262
Minimum wage, 108
Mitchell, Donald Craig, 23

Mitchell, John, 28
Monegan, Walt, 215, 221–222, 235, 238
Moore, Lisa, 124–125, 126, 208
Moore, Shannyn, 169
Moose, 28, 37, 64, 65, 83, 112, 113, 214,
    216, 234
Morris, Brenda, 226, 229, 239–240
Morris, Dick, 204
Mortgages, 55
"Most Popular Governor, The" (Barnes), 204
Mount McKinley (Denali National Park and
    Preserve), 166
Mulva, Jim, 147
Murkowski, Frank, xvii, 10, 95, 103–104,
    106, 107–109, 111–115, 119,
    131–132, 133–134, 160, 163, 167,
    180, 203, 240, 254
    and appointment for vacant senate seat,
        109–110
    downfall of, 118, 251
    and the Magnificent Seven, 141
    mistakes of, 115–116
    and natural gas pipeline, 112, 134, 135,
        136–137, 141, 158, 159, 161–162,
        164, 165, 176, 186
    purchase of jet airplane, 135–136, 162
    run for reelection, 161–162
    secret negotiations with oil companies,
        133–134, 136–137, 141, 142, 147,
        152, 158, 159
    wife of, 136
Murkowski, Lisa, 110, 111, 116, 119, 122,
    130, 176, 256, 257, 258, 260
Myers, Mark, 187

Naneng, Myron, 238
Napolitano, Janet, 211
National Bank of Alaska, 93–94
National Governors Association Conference
    (2008), 211
National Petroleum Reserve-Alaska, 86
National Review magazine, 204
National Rifle Association, 236
Natural gas, 10, 11, 12, 50, 118
    cost of building pipeline, 188
    export of liquefied natural gas, 254
    pipeline, xiv, xv, 32, 71, 94, 100–101,
        104, 108, 112, 130, 132–134, 147,
        157, 161, 167, 169–170, 183,
        186–187, 188, 217, 251 (see also Alaska

Gasline Inducement Act; Murkowski, Frank: and natural gas pipeline; Palin, Sarah: and natural gas pipeline)
pipeline route, 169–170, 186–187
prices, 94, 101, 132, 188
profits from, 133
See also Shale gas
Nenana, 199
Nepotism, 150
New Deal, 63
New Mexico, 49, 50
Newsweek, 211, 213
New Yorker, The, 204
New York Times, 9, 129
Nixon, Richard, 24, 27, 35, 61
North Sea, 52
North Slope, 5, 11, 12, 24, 25, 31, 51, 169, 187, 262. *See also* Prudhoe Bay
Nuclear Test Ban Treaty, 87

Obama, Barack, 195, 222, 235
Oil, 4–5, 9, 17, 69, 128, 131
Big Oil, 10, 13, 48, 52, 200, 203, 204, 212, 222, 226, 261 (*see also individual companies*)
collective ownership of, xvii
Deepwater Horizon oil spill (2010), 35
Exxon Valdez oil spill, 57–58, 59, 70, 83, 198
independent companies, 190, 197
offshore drilling, 35, 130, 261
boom, xix, 12, 13, 31, 65
dividend checks, xvi, 42, 46, 93, 101, 214
find on Kenai Peninsula and Cook Inlet, 11
fracking, 262
leasing, 6, 10, 13–15, 138
pipeline, 25–26, 27–32, 41, 44, 61, 64, 65, 70, 133, 137, 138, 190, 244, 250
prices, 32, 34, 38, 41, 53, 55, 58, 93, 101, 105, 107, 129, 152, 175, 196, 209, 210, 214, 244, 245, 261
production, 32, 42, 45, 46, 47, 75, 93, 107, 118, 133, 196
spills, 35, 166 (*see also* Oil: *Exxon Valdez* oil spill)
profits from, 44, 45, 47, 152, 154, 196, 198
Prudhoe Bay oil field, xv, xvi, xix, 11–15, 25, 37, 44, 51, 94, 118, 131, 166, 186
Santa Barbara oil spill (1969), 35
See also Taxes: on oil companies

O'Keefe, Sean, 253
OPEC, 55
Outsiders, 5, 27, 44, 47, 73, 76, 131, 166, 219, 250. 252

Palin, Piper, 183, 189
Palin, Sarah, xvii–xviii, 3, 6, 9–11, 32, 48, 56, 64, 69, 72–75, 131, 200–201, 203–204, 209, 242–243, 254
adversaries of, 192–193
and Alaska constitution, 10, 154, 161, 170, 171, 185
approval ratings as governor, xix, 197, 213, 223
army of, 161, 171–172
and Bill Allen, 102–103
and Bridge to Nowhere, 224
children of, 11, 183, 189, 255
and constitutionally mandated services, 186
criticism of, 191, 192, 248
and Democrats, 189, 211, 220, 223, 248
emails of, 175, 245, 248, 260–261
enemies of, 245
ethics complaints against, 248, 255
flaws of, 219
and Frank Murkowski, 108, 109–110, 113, 119, 134–135, 141–142, 188, 240
inauguration as governor, 9–11, 15–16, 188
inner circle of, 190, 191, 192
and Joe Miller, 256, 257–258
and natural gas pipeline, 71, 186, 187, 196–197, 198–199, 212, 217, 261
and Oil and Gas Conservation Commission, 114, 116, 118–122, 240
and oil companies, 10, 213, 220, 222, 226
Palin truth squad, 221–222
parents of (*see* Heath, Chuck and Sally)
and Permanent Fund, 42
political action committee for, 245–246, 255
as pregnant, 211–212
and Randy Ruedrich, 115–116, 118, 119–120, 121, 259
resignation as governor, 251–252, 255
run for governor, 140–141, 159–161, 162, 167, 168–176, 180
run for lieutenant governor, 102, 103, 105, 106, 113, 172
run for mayor, 69, 72–75, 172
run for president, 241

Palin, Sarah (*continued*)
   run for vice president, 217, 219–223,
      224, 235, 240, 247
   Sarah Palin's Alaska (TV show), 254
   and special legislative sessions, 206, 207,
      212
   and state-owned gas pipeline, 71
   and Ted Stevens, 76–77, 241–242
   and Troopergate, 235–236 (*see also*
      Troopergate)
   vice presidential acceptance speech, 192
   and Walt Monegan, 215–216
   wardrobe of, 240
Palin, Todd, 6, 11, 69, 131, 160, 185, 214,
      215, 222, 254
Palmer, 63, 159, 182
Parker, Dave, 260
Parnell, Sean, 254, 261
Penney, Bob, 91
Perdew, Bev, 174–175
Perry, Kris, 190
Persons, Bob, 81, 82, 231, 249
Petroleum Club, 13, 212
Phillips Petroleum, 15, 52, 94
Point Hope, 36
Polar Pen investigation, 123, 127, 128, 143,
      145, 162, 181, 202, 224, 228
Police, 31, 67, 68, 123, 126, 186, 215, 260
Populism, 170
Porcaro, Mike, 169, 175
Potter, Louise, 67–68
Poverty, 49, 243
Powell, Colin, 227, 238
Prince William Sound, 25, 31, 57, 70, 83
Prisons, 100, 123, 127, 136, 149, 163, 224,
      249
Profits. *See under* Natural gas; Oil
Prosecutorial misconduct, 241, 249
Prostitution, 30–31, 124, 145, 225
Prudhoe Bay, 24, 30. *See also* Oil: Prudhoe
      Bay oil field
Public Policy Polling, 223

Racism, 27
Railroads, 104, 108
Rampart dam, 37
Ramras, Jay, 191–192
Rare earth metals, 262
Rasmuson, Elmer, 22, 23
Reagan, Ronald, 55, 61, 220

Real estate, 29, 55, 57, 90
Red Dog Saloon (Juneau), 34
Regulators/regulations, 48, 53, 55, 100,
      114, 115, 120
Reilly, Paul, 66
Religion, 61, 68, 72, 73, 112, 151, 170,
      198–199. *See also* Assembly of God
      church (Wasilla); Christian Right;
      Republican Party: Christian Republicans
Renkes, Gregg, 135
Republican Party, xiii, xvii, 4, 6, 19, 20, 22,
      24–25, 26, 32, 34, 35, 47, 48, 58, 59,
      61, 69, 72, 73, 99–100, 102, 109, 119,
      122, 134, 159, 162, 173, 185, 189,
      197, 203, 216, 221, 241
   Christian Republicans, 114, 115 (*see also*
      Christian Right)
   National Convention (1988), 62
   National Republican Senatorial
      Committee, 259
   picnic in 2006, 168, 171–172, 173–175,
      236
   Republican in name only (RINO), 220
   Republican National Committee, 240
Rezko, Tony, 234
Rickard, Thomas Arthur, 7
Roads/highways, 24, 28, 29, 40, 64, 79,
      105, 186, 208, 223
Roberds, Paula, 225–226, 249
Robertson, Pat, 61–62
Roderick, Jack, 22–23, 81
Romney, Mitt, 170
Roosevelt, Franklin, 20, 21, 63
Ross, Wayne Anthony, 173
Rove, Karl, 222
Rubini, Jon, 89–90
Ruedrich, Randy, 100, 115–116, 118,
      119–122, 134, 162, 172, 173, 174,
      240, 256, 257, 259
Russia, 26, 80, 127
Russian Orthodox Church, 61
Russian River, 167
Russo, Frank, 126–127
Rutherford, Marty, 137–138, 139–140,
      187, 188–189, 191, 192, 246
Rydell, Rick, 169

Safeway, 93
Salmon, 37, 90, 167
Samaritan's Purse, 247

Samuels, Ralph, 202
Sarah Palin's Alaska (TV show), 254
Saudi Arabia, 55
Seafood companies, 150
Search warrants. *See* FBI: search warrants
     served by (2006)
Seaton, Fred, 19
Seattle Times, 51
Second Amendment, 105
Sedwick, John, 207, 208
Senior citizens, 112, 115, 136, 174–175
Service, Robert, 13
Seward, 39
Seward, William H., 80
Seward Highway, 79
Seward's folly, 244
Seward's Success (housing development),
     37–38
Sex, 117, 123, 124–125, 126, 145, 151,
     181, 208, 225, 231–232
     sex drug rings, 123, 126
     sexual abuse, 199, 215, 226, 249
     See also, Allen, Bill: alleged sexual
          misconduct of; Gays
Sexism, 173
Shale gas, 251, 254
Shea, Wev, 173
Sheffield, Bill, 10, 254
Siltstone, 12
Skagway, 65
Smith, Rick, xiii, xiv, 145, 147–148, 149,
     154–156, 158, 159, 164, 201
Socialism, 8, 42, 43, 154, 161, 248
Special Olympics World Winter Games, 89,
     150, 240
Spending issues, xv, 9, 15, 40, 42, 43, 46,
     77, 81, 160
     federal spending in Alaska, xv, 75, 87, 89,
          92, 93, 129, 130, 131, 206, 224, 227,
          257
     military spending, 89, 90, 91
Sports, 105, 216
Stambaugh, Irl, 68, 73, 74, 77, 102
Stapleton, Meghan, 190
Steel prices, 188
Stein, John, 68–69, 72–73, 74, 77, 104
Stevens, Ben, xv, 87, 88, 89, 95, 109, 150,
     153, 162, 163, 164, 172, 201, 240
Stevens, Ted, xiv, xv, xx, 3, 9, 17–20, 22–23,
     24–25, 32, 48, 75–77, 102, 104, 108,

109, 123, 129, 130, 133, 145, 150,
     207, 223
     and AGIA, 254
     battle to clear name of, 248–250
     childhood, 17–18
     daughter of, 238
     death of, 250, 253–254, 257
     final speech on the Senate floor, 243–244
     friends/supporters of, 81
     indictment/conviction of/tossed
          convictions, 118, 181, 216, 241
     influence on Alaska's economy, 92
     and Native lands claim, 26–27
     run for reelection, 217, 224, 243
     /and rural Alaska, 86–87, 88
     "Ted's cabin" remodeling, 80, 81–82, 84–
          85, 125, 128, 143, 144, 182, 205–206,
          217, 227–228, 230, 254
     trial of (2008), 223–224, 226, 227–233,
          238–240, 241
     and Utah land deal, 91
     wives of, 19, 28, 32, 82, 84, 85, 229,
          238–239
Sturgulewski, Arliss, 69
Subsidies, 197, 198, 200, 211, 212, 259, 261
Sullivan, Brendan, 227, 229, 231
Sullivan, Emmet, 228, 232, 248, 249
Sundborg, George, 10
Sununu, John, 69
Suttles, Doug, 212

Talkeetna Mountains, 62
Talk radio, 169, 172, 173, 191
Tamarack, 11
Taxes, 72, 113, 115
     expert consultants concerning, 44, 157
     income tax, xvi, 41, 46, 55, 93, 95, 101,
          108, 131, 185
     locked-in tax rates, 136–137, 139, 142,
          153, 159, 198
     on natural gas, 142, 198
     on oil companies, xiii, xiv, 6, 40, 41–42,
          44–48, 52, 55–56, 58–59, 62, 70, 94,
          106, 108, 133, 134, 136, 139, 142,
          149, 151, 157, 162–164, 166, 167,
          175, 183, 196, 198, 203, 206–207,
          210, 220, 251
     sales tax, xvi, 41, 67, 68, 93, 131
     20/20 plan, 152, 158, 159
Tea Party, 9, 171, 255, 256, 260

Ted Stevens Anchorage International
  Airport, 92, 241, 242
Television, 56, 153, 169, 254. *See also* Media
Teller, Edward, 37
Temperatures, 7–8, 11, 29, 237. *See also*
  Alaska: winters in
Thermonuclear bombs, 36–37
Through the Yukon and Alaska (Rickard), 7
Thurmond, Strom, 258
Tillion, Clem, 86
Time zones, 67
Tongass National Forest, 104, 112
Toomey, Sheila, 168
Torricelli, Robert, 231, 248
Tourism, 91, 131
Trans-Alaska pipeline, 31, 36, 39, 41, 64,
  70–71, 101, 133, 137, 138, 187, 190,
  197, 251
  work camps, 29–30
Trans-Alaska Pipeline Authorization Act, 244
TransCanada Corporation, 212, 217
Transportation, 170
Troopergate, xix, 216, 220–221, 222, 233,
  234–236, 245
Tucker, Nick, 246–247
"Typhoon Teddy" (song), 93
Tyree, Bambi, 117, 118, 123–127, 142,
  143, 145, 181, 207–208, 224, 225,
  227, 249, 250
Tyree, Mark, 123, 125

Ulmer, Fran, 106–107, 109
Unemployment, 29, 55, 93, 130, 259
Unions, 30, 53
United States
  Atomic Energy Commission, 36
  Defense Department, 89
  Department of Interior, 19, 35, 95
  Homeland Security funds, 136
  household income in, 29
  House Transportation and Infrastructure
    Committee, 129
  Justice Department, xvi, 54, 201, 207,
    248, 249, 254 (*see also* FBI)
  Labor Department, 93
  Postal Service, 86
  Senate Appropriations Committee, xv, 75,
    80, 224
  Senate Energy and Natural Resources
    Committee, 104, 257

User fees, 112–113, 115
Usibelli, Emil, 19

Valdez, 25, 31, 39, 40, 169, 187
Values, xviii, 103, 185
Van Flein, Thomas, 234–235
VECO Corporation, xiii, 48, 52, 53,
  54–55, 57, 80, 82, 84, 85, 86, 91, 94,
  103, 106, 113, 128, 134, 143, 144,
  149, 150, 155, 158, 179, 183, 187,
  201, 202, 206, 209, 217, 227, 233,
  240
  and private prisons, 100, 123
  revenues/workforce of, 127
  up for sale, 142, 181, 224
Venezuela, 213, 248
Ventura, Jesse, 173
Vietnam War, 20, 35
Vogler, Joe, 69–70
Vogue, 211

Wages, xv, 31, 57, 89, 93, 108
Washington Post, 76
Wasilla, 29, 62–65, 183
  Valley Hospital in, 62
  See also Assembly of God church
    (Wasilla); Elections: Wasilla mayoral
    elections
Watergate, 29
Weekly Standard, 203, 204
Wells Fargo, 94
Weyhrauch, Bruce, 158, 201
Whales, 26, 35, 79, 83
Whittier, 100
Wilderness Society, 27
Williams, Rocky, 227–229, 232
Williams & Connolly law firm, 227
Wolves, 61, 62
  aerial hunting of, 34, 113
Wooten, Mike, 214–215, 221, 234
World War II, 18, 91

"You Are Alaska's Children" (constitutional
  resolution), 9
Young, Don, xv, 37, 84, 100, 108, 112, 129,
  130
Yukon River, 37

Ziff Energy Group, 213
Zoning rules, 67